Battle for the Wilderness

T0204350

WITHDRAWN

BATTLE
FOR THE
WILDERNESS

Revised Edition

Michael Frome

THE UNIVERSITY OF UTAH PRESS
Salt Lake City

University of Utah Press edition 1997

∞ Printed on acid-free paper

LIBRARY OF CONGRESS CATALOGING-IN-PUBLICATIONS DATA

Frome, Michael.
   Battle for the wilderness / Michael Frome. – Rev. ed.
      p.   cm.
   Includes bibiographical references (p.   ) and index.
   ISBN 0-87480-552-X (pbk. : alk. paper)
   1. Wilderness areas–United States. 2. Nature conservation–
United States. I. Title.
QH76.F76   1997
333.78'216'0973–dc21   97-30314

He labored with purpose:

> We are a great people because we have been successful in developing and using our marvelous natural resources; but, also, we Americans are the people we are largely because we have had the influence of the wilderness on our lives.
>
> –John P. Saylor, introducing the Wilderness Bill in the House of Representatives, July 12, 1956.

John Saylor died October 28, 1973 after twelve terms in Congress. He was my friend, but every American who enjoys and loves wild places lost a friend and champion. His monumental contribution endures, however. I dedicate this work to his memory.

Contents

Acknowledgments

First, I recall the cooperation and confidence of Paul H. Oehser and George Crosette, who as a committee representing the Wilderness Society invited me to write the original *Battle for the Wilderness*. I benefited from their continuing encouragement, with utter lack of interference. Now I lament that both have passed on. I am deeply grateful to Stewart M. Brandborg, who was then executive director of the Wilderness Society and who has remained my close friend and advisor; and also to Harry Crandell, Ernest Dickerman, and Clif Merritt, staff members of the old days, and to Ben Beach, Bill Reffalt, and Steve Whitney, present staff members of the society.

I appreciate the review of sections on biological science, ecology, and wildlife by Angela Evenden, Edward E. C. Clebsch, Barrie K. Gilbert, John W. Grandy, Hugh Iltis, Thomas E. Lacher, Eugene P. Odum, and David Wilcove. I was helped immeasurably by members of the committee (composed of Ben Davis, Dave Foreman, Joyce Kelly, Mary Kelly, Michael Kirkhorn, Connie Richardson, Liane Russell and John Tallmadge) who directed and approved my doctoral work on wilderness (completed through the Union Institute in 1993).

I am grateful for input and counsel from federal employees of past and present, including Roger Allin, Lennie Eubanks, Paul C. Fritz, David Klinger, Tom Kovalicky, Riley and Pat McClelland, Connie Myers, Jerry Stokes, John Twiss, Paul Weingart, and William A. Worf; and also to Mike Bader, Les Berenson, Brock Evans, James R. Fazio, Mitch Friedman, Charles H. Stoddard, Lynn Kinter, Bart Koehler, Greg Lais, George C. Nickas, Mark Peterson, Mack Prichard, Paul C. Pritchard, Kevin Proescholdt, Alfred Runte, and Dean Terry.

I am grateful to Jonathan Duncan, photographer and wilderness explorer, for his striking cover photograph; to Jeff Grathwohl, director of the University of Utah Press, and to all his good colleagues; and especially to Edward Lueders, the consulting reviewer who recommended publication.

Finally, thanks to my wife, June Eastvold, and the blessing of her prayers. Thanks to you all for believing in me and in this work.

Preface
Wilderness is Here to Stay
1997

It was a lovely bright day when I went to Alabama to help celebrate the dedication of the Sipsey Wilderness, a chain of deep gorges threaded with streams and waterfalls, where the southern tip of the Cumberland Plateau meets the coastal plain. I had been there before, out on the ground with members of the Alabama Conservancy, who felt strongly that the Sipsey should be recognized and protected under terms of the Wilderness Act of 1964. Now this was their day, and the Sipsey's. The congressman of the district, Tom Bevill, spoke cheerfully before the two hundred-plus celebrants. He was a conservative, scarcely known for any particular interest in the environment, but he was plainly proud of his people and pleased they had prevailed over the Forest Service, a powerful federal agency locked into a hard official position that there was no wilderness left east of the Rocky Mountains.

This was shortly after publication of *Battle for the Wilderness* in 1974. Since then till now considerable wilderness has been identified and protected in the East, mostly in the national forests, and the Forest Service has learned to accept it. The Alabama Conservancy and other citizen groups have had much to do with making this happen. How much? Enough to say that it would never have happened without them. The truth is the Wilderness Act opened the way to a new level of citizen involvement and activism, a grass roots conservation movement in which local people could be heard in behalf of wilderness areas they knew best.

I've been to a lot of wildernesses and have met with groups like the Alabama Conservancy in many parts of the United States, observing the work that individuals do, rising above themselves and above institutions. Looking back on these experiences, back to 1974, and to 1964, when the act was passed, and to 1954, when the idea for it was incubating, and looking to where we are now, and trying to look into the century ahead, I appreciate wilderness preservation anew as an idea that works, a manifestation of democracy, an expression through law of national ethics.

Ethical concern is the creative force in the battle for wilderness. I learned that in first preparing *Battle for the Wilderness*. It was published under the auspices of the Wilderness Society, which wanted a book that would explain wilderness and the Wilderness Act, not as a text but as a guide that anyone could understand. I was impressed with the ethical quality of people in the wilderness movement. Olaus Murie was already gone, but his widow, Margaret, "Mardy," and I became lasting friends. She had been with Olaus on his pioneering surveys and research in Alaska and elsewhere for the Biological Survey (later the Fish and Wildlife Service) until he left the government to be free of its restraints. And she had been with him on the epochal 1956 expedition that led to establishment of the Arctic National Wildlife Refuge, embracing the largest mountains of the Brooks Range and their foothills sloping north to the coastal plain and southward toward the Yukon River as a book of life the way God wrote it.

Olaus was a leader of the Wilderness Society from its incorporation in 1937 until his death in 1963. In addition to extensive technical and popular writing, he executed many exceptional paintings of animals as he found them in the wild, a legacy of art in nature. His strength, like the strength of Aldo Leopold, Howard Zahniser, and the others, derived from more than admiration of nature, but from the desire to save nature through personal involvement. Olaus and his younger brother, Adolph, were field biologists who wrote natural histories, but who also went far beyond the normal parameters. In the foreword to *A Naturalist in Alaska*, Adolph's best known book, Olaus described his brother's way of living out among wild animals, trying to think as they do, establishing an intimate relationship that reveals the motivations of creatures in all they do. Such intimate contact, he noted, leads to an understanding of nature desperately lacking in our time. He continued, "What is much needed today is more mutual respect among the exponents of science, philosophy, esthetics, and sociology. Although we are beginning to think in terms of human ecology, it is now time that we recognize all elements of the good life and give them the emphasis they deserve." The Muries, their training in science notwithstanding, conceived wilderness saved in federal preserves as a cultural achievement, in which values of the human heart and spirit take precedence. That remains a powerful message.

Now, all these years later, I realize the battle can never fully be concluded. Wilderness is unfinished business, still a pressing item on the agenda of society. For this reason, I am glad to prepare this new, expanded edition. The original remains intact, so the reader can see how things were and what we were thinking in that particular period of history. Some things are dated or have changed significantly and I will try to indicate them. But wilderness is still the chorus of thrushes and the thunder of waterfalls, an exercise in solitude, a learning laboratory, and the antidote to an overurbanized, supertechnological age. Lyndon Johnson still signed the Wilderness Act in the Rose Garden, and I am still deeply troubled about "Where the Battle Begins," still asking, "Is wilderness valid in the face of poverty, inequality, the social issues of man's relationship with man, his brother?" But, of course, I should have referred to man's relationship with woman his sister—just as the Wilderness Act itself should have done better than define wilderness as an area "untrammeled by man." On page 12 of this book I refer to "the experience of mankind," "the man who believes in wilderness," "man's rootstocks in nature," "man evolved from the apes," and "man's civilization." I know better now.

There is much to add: about new laws following the Wilderness Act; the performance of administrations, the management that federal agencies provide to wilderness, the lessons science has learned. The truth is we still know very little about wilderness—how it functions or the role it fills in society. An entire new series of questions demands attention. We need to explore the actual and potential values of wilderness, its ecology, economics, the effect of human impact, and mechanisms to protect small, relatively untouched parcels wherever they may be.

The battle for wilderness is unending, yet I feel hopeful and confident. The National Wilderness Preservation System has grown from its original 9.1 million acres in 53 areas in 13 states in 1964, to 103.5 million acres in 630 areas in 44 states as I write these lines. These range in size from six acres in the Pelican Island Wilderness in Florida to nine million acres of wilderness in the Wrangell-St. Elias Wilderness in Alaska. Although more than one-half of the total acres—57.4

million—is in Alaska, the ratio likely will change as the system continues to expand, considering the potential additions in 50 million roadless acres in the national forests; more than 50 million acres of roadless land administered by the Bureau of Land Management (not including roadless portions of its 75 million acres in Alaska, which have never been inventoried for wilderness); more than 40 million acres in the national parks; and more than 60 million acres under study in the national wildlife refuges.

The same is true of the companion Wild and Scenic Rivers System. Under the original 1968 Wild and Scenic Rivers Act (which defines wild rivers as "free of impoundments and generally inaccessible except by trail . . . with shorelines essentially primitive"), eight rivers were designated as components of the system, and 27 others were named for study by federal-state teams for possible later inclusion. By 1996, the system had grown to include more than 10,800 miles of 156 rivers or river segments, with further additions to come.

Those laws have worked. And there's much more underway, including:

• The citizen movement in the Northeast for a 3.2 million-acre Maine Woods National Park, with wolves restored to their wild Maine homeland, and in the Northwest for the Northern Rockies Ecosystem Protection Act (NREPA), first introduced in Congress in 1993, designating federal roadless areas in Montana, Idaho, Wyoming, eastern Oregon and eastern Washington as wilderness and establishing connecting corridors between major ecosystems to protect wildlife movements. Dr. John Craighead, noted authority on grizzly bears and a strong supporter, believes that "We need these large areas of near-pristine environment as reservoirs of undiscovered information, as ecological benchmarks, as keys to understanding both natural and man-made changes of the future, and as sustainable economic assets when these uses do not degrade or destroy other uses."

• In the same vein, conservation biology, the "mission science," combines scientific theory and wilderness advocacy, most notably through The Wildlands Project, founded in 1992 and based in Tucson, Arizona, envisioning an ecological wilderness network that begins with existing preserves, but enlarged, connected, and surrounded by buffers providing wild animals safe passage, as in the concept of "Yellowstone-to-Yukon" the wild heart of western North America.

• Designation of state wilderness systems in almost a dozen states, with others on the way. In upstate New York, the Adirondack Forest Preserve, the country's largest park outside of Alaska, three times the size of Yellowstone, includes one million acres designated as wilderness, with, I hope, more to come in the Adirondack Council's proposed 408,000-acre Bob Marshall Great Wilderness Area.

• Emergence and growth of the natural areas movement as a complement to wilderness, bringing together professional and volunteer researchers, managers, and naturalists in the acquisition and protection of all kinds of ecosystems and demonstrating their value as living laboratories and repositories of biodiversity.

• The growth in diverse programs designed to develop human potential, like Wilderness Inquiry, headquartered in Minneapolis, that take able and disabled persons into the wilderness together, sustaining an atmosphere of trust and cooperation, with respect for each person's dignity. I will always remember my own trip with Wilderness Inquiry in the Boundary Waters Canoe Wilderness in Minnesota as humbling and uplifting.

I cite these as evidence that wilderness preservation is here to stay and as harbingers of more in our tomorrows. Even during conservative national politics in the 1980s and 90s, with its hostility to the environment, the wilderness cause has progressed. I think of the unending assaults on the Arctic National Wildlife Refuge for whatever raw oil supplies it may hold. Yet Congress, notwithstanding all the pressures, has consistently protected the refuge. In fact, together with an adjacent Canadian national park, it constitutes an international wilderness sanctuary of dimensions and values scarcely matched anywhere on earth.

Even beyond our own country, preservation is a universal calling, a global need. In December 1994 I visited the Galapagos Islands, Darwin's laboratory of evolution, as part of an international group of scientists and conservationists. In briefings to the group, the executive director of the natural resources department of Ecuador, INEFAN, and the superintendent of Galapagos National Park both stressed their desire to satisfy demands for commercial development by the islands's growing population—that was *their* priority. Imagine my surprise, therefore, when we were met at Puerto Ayoro, the main settlement, by a delegation of thirty-plus persons, children included, which presented an altogether different message. Their mimeographed appeal includes the following passages:

> The Galapagos Islands have come of age. By this we mean that they have, like every other place on earth, including Antarctica, come, in the due course of time, under the hammer of man's restlessness and greed. . . . The observation of Chief Seattle that by destroying nature we will die of a great loneliness of spirit, haunts us, for we sense that by the destruction of nature we wound and disfigure our own minds.
>
> We ask for the victory of moral responsibility in the case of the Galapagos, a moral responsibility not compromised by motivation for personal gain and power. We ask that this unique archipelago, with its complexities of natural communities almost complete, be left in peace for all time, that we don't demand so much from the islands that we destroy their charm, magic and deep breathing of their inner souls. . . .
>
> We ask you to join forces with us to save our islands, as a last chance for mankind to show an ability to live in peace with nature. . . . The islands require the concerned involvement of people everywhere to find solutions that will never harm the natural function of the Galapagos ecosystems.

It isn't only the Galapagos that require the concerned involvement of people everywhere. The whole world has come under the hammer of restlessness and greed. For every step forward, society seems to take two (or more) steps backward. We set aside wilderness because everything else is going downhill, and then wilderness is endangered by abuses from without and within.

"Each year I see land that once was wilderness receive the blessings of what they call multiple use," wrote Ted Trueblood, my old colleague at *Field & Stream* who was celebrated for his stories about the Idaho back country. He was never an activist, but the time came early in the 1970s for Ted to speak in behalf of the River of No Return Wilderness. "First came the bulldozers, then the loggers and logging trucks. Then came the ORV riders, riding just to be riding, or perhaps trying to shoot a deer without the honest sweat that should be part of any hunt. Idaho has already lost some of its choicest wild country and even now the Forest Service proposes to open still more roadless areas to development. So we're not looking at how much more wilderness we're going to have, but how much less of it there will be."

I recognize that protecting wilderness by law no longer suffices to protect wilderness, that society needs transformation, a viewpoint of human concern, distress and love. But wilderness is the place to begin, a sanctuary that opens to the search for a moral world. "In wildness I sense the miracle of life," wrote Charles A. Lindbergh, "and beside it our scientific accomplishments fade to trivia."

Wilderness is a way of experiencing wholeness, the world within oneself, of respecting people, plants, animals, water, sunlight, clouds, of experiencing life with a spiritual ecological dimension, a way of finding everything sacred and connected.

WHEREVER THERE IS STILL WILDERNESS
CITIZENS HAVE FOUGHT FOR IT
AND THEIR STRUGGLE GOES ON

In 1994 the Wyoming Wilderness Coalition issued the impressive booklet *Wilderness at Risk—The Citizens' Wilderness Proposal for Wyoming BLM Lands*. In the foreword, J. David Love, a renowned geologist and Wyoming native, wrote that the official wilderness review by the Bureau of Land Management marked a very small step toward reversing the traditional negative approach toward the wilderness in its trust:

But many regard it as tainted by bureaucracy, politics, real-estate conflicts, nonrenewable resource economics and inadequate knowledge or appreciation by policymakers 2,000 miles away [in Washington, D.C.]. The Citizens' Wilderness Proposal for Wyoming BLM Lands, on the other hand, is a grassroots effort. It provides some of the common sense, long-term volunteer input and long-range vision we need—not just for our lifetimes but for generations to come.

That is the way it goes, in Wyoming and everywhere else. Wilderness has been saved, and wilderness history written, by citizen groups like the Wyoming Wilderness Coalition with their common sense, volunteer input, and ethical long-range vision unclouded by petty short-range politics. In the case of Wyoming, the BLM had come up with a meager plan that would allow one million acres of pristine roadless country to be transformed into powerline corridors, roads, military bombing ranges, and garbage dumps. Choice scenic, historic, and archaeological sites, geological study areas, and unusual plant communities would have been disrupted or destroyed.

The lands administered by BLM were not treated in the original edition of *Battle for the Wilderness;* the vast areas in the West administered by that agency, a branch of the Interior Department, were still excluded from wilderness review. Until 1976 they were considered public domain, subject to disposal in the pattern of the past. At best, they were uncontrolled and overgrazed for years; livestock associations blocked management at every turn, while millions of acres deteriorated and all values suffered. Then at last the Federal Land Policy and Management Act of 1976 (FLPMA) gave permanence to the BLM and a mandate to manage the lands in behalf of all the public.

Among its provisions, FLPMA opened the National Wilderness Preservation System to include BLM lands. It directed a review and inventory of roadless areas with wilderness characteristics within fifteen years (by 1991) to determine if they should be recommended for addition to the system. Study areas were to be managed to preserve wilderness characteristics, but existing uses such as mining, mineral leasing, and grazing were allowed to continue, subject to regulations. (Alas, it did not in any way amend the Mining Law of 1872 or impair the right of locators or claimants under that archaic, outmoded law.)

During its review of 175 million acres, the agency identified nearly 25 million acres in 795 different areas as suitable for consideration as wilderness. A major piece of legislation followed, the Arizona Desert Wilderness Act of 1990, designating 1,077,260 acres of public land wilderness in 38 new BLM areas and adding 12,710 acres to the existing Aravaipa Canyon Wilderness in southern Arizona (which had been the first area BLM recommended as wilderness to Congress). Above all, the act brought attention to the abundant wilderness treasures on the public lands: desert bighorn sheep, desert tortoise, raptors, mammals, reptiles, birds, giant saguaro cactus, and joshua trees.

Some BLM personnel worked diligently to fulfill their assigned responsibilities. Of all the people I've known in government, hardly any was more courageous or competent than Joyce Kelly, who directed BLM recreation, cultural, and wilderness programs in the early 1980s. She understood the value of citizen input. "If the Forest Service has the trees, the National Park Service the jewels, Bureau of Land Management certainly has some exquisite gems," she said in 1983. "We now have the public's attention and it's up to us to get people involved. All of our efforts will be worthless if the public does not understand, accept, and support what we do."

Citizens may not qualify as "resource professionals" in the accepted sense, but they care about the resources and that may count more. The experience of the Wyoming Wilderness Coalition, and of the Alabama Conservancy, which I cited earlier, have been duplicated many times over. Maybe it began seriously in the late 1960s and early 1970s when Stewart M. Brandborg, who had succeeded Howard Zahniser as executive director of the Wilderness Society on Zahniser's death in 1964, and his associates systematized grass roots wilderness activism. Brandborg, "Brandy," grew up in the Bitterroot Valley of western Montana, and spent many days and nights in the wild Selway-Bitterroot in company with foresters (his father was one), outfitters, biologists (he himself earned a graduate degree for a pioneering study of mountain goats), local rednecks, and fancy dudes. At the Wilderness Society he and his folks grasped a provision of the Wilderness Act that guarantees the citizen the right to be heard, to share decision-making with the federal agencies administering wilderness; it stipulates that prior to consideration by Congress, public hearings must be held in the vicinity of the lands in question with advance notice on each proposed new wilderness unit.

Harry Crandell, who worked for the Wilderness Society from 1970 to 1975, recalls,

The Society was in the forefront and led major wilderness and public land issues. We all worked together as a team, each helping the other, but often we had to work alone for long stretches simply because there were so many balls in the air at once. Successful conclusion of issues would have been highly unlikely absent citizen involvement and telephone "trees" manned by volunteers and staff and "alerts" prepared by staff.

The field representatives of the Society in those years, working under Clif Merritt, the field director, were missionaries who worked long hours for low pay without complaint to build and empower grass roots leaders. Some are still on the firing line more than twenty years later, though under other auspices: Dick Carter in Utah; Jim Eaton in California; Bart Koehler in Southeast Alaska, and Dave Foreman, who co-founded Earth First! and later The Wildlands Project. Brandborg left the Wilderness Society in 1976 and then things changed.

As I review history as I've lived through it, working for the environment—even working for wilderness—in a national organization has changed from a cause to a career, with more sophistication and less self-sacrifice. All have their roles and do good works, but national organizations such as the Sierra Club and Wilderness Society seem to be run by bright people who know their way around Washington better than around wilderness. Leaders seem to be chosen for efficiency in office management, political connections, and skills in hobnobbing with people who contribute or might be induced to contribute big bucks. They have their field representatives, but few started as volunteers and worked from the ground up.

It's different for an organization like the Friends of the Boundary Waters Wilderness, which was organized at a critical time in 1976 "to protect and preserve the wilderness character of the Boundary Waters Canoe Area Wilderness and the Quetico-Superior Ecosystem through public advocacy, ecosystem preservation, scientific understanding, user education, and enhanced public appreciation." The Boundary Waters Canoe Area, the BWCA, covering a substantial portion of Superior National Forest in northern Minnesota just below Quetico Provincial Park in Ontario, has been the field of one battle after another down through the years, starting virtually in 1921 when Arthur Carhart, the Forest Service planner, urged that it be set aside free of development.

Those endless battles led to the monumental campaign of the 1970s to establish a Boundary Waters unit of the wilderness system free of intrusive logging, mining, motor boating, and snowmobiling. One of the heroes of the campaign was Sigurd Olson, the celebrated author and conservationist, who was ridiculed and ostracized and hung in effigy by redneck neighbors at Ely, in the North Country, but who never wavered from the wilderness cause. I knew Sig Olson and greatly admired him as an author and activist, but I think he would defer in the Boundary Waters cause to Miron (Bud) Heinselman, forest ecologist, who retired early from the Forest Service to devote his energy to the Friends of the Boundary Waters Wilderness. Heinselman grew up in the country and knew it intimately. He was like Zahniser, with a rare combination of humility and intensity. After he died, Representative Bruce Vento, the Boundary Waters' champion in Congress, paid tribute to Heinselman in the *BWCA Wilderness News* (Spring/Summer 1993). "Bud inspired everyone," wrote Vento.

Of all the bills that Phil Burton [the subcommittee chairman] passed, and of all the work I've done on land-use issues, this bill holds the essence, the spirit of that special synergy between legislators, policy makers, and environmentalists. In those early morning hours we hugged, we cried, we laughed like children when finally, in 1978, some fifteen years ago, we passed the law that protected Bud and [his wife] Fran's BWCA Wilderness.

That was Heinselman, one of the heroes in the history of the wilderness movement. I feel fortunate that I was able to spend a day with him less than a year before he died. We visited at his cabin at Ely, where he was trying to finish his scholarly ecological study on the Boundary Waters. Then that evening we had supper with three other close friends of Sigurd Olson at Listening Point, Sig's cabin retreat at the edge of watery wilderness. We talked through dusk into dark, all of us, I think, feeling Sig's presence in the shadows. Bud, who shared with Sig the years of struggle, said, "I know Sig would be glad we're here talking about the wilderness he loved." Looking back on it, I feel doubly blessed, for the time with Olson and Heinselman.

Philip Burton, who ingeniously maneuvered the wilderness legislation to passage, served in Congress as a two-fisted fighting San Francisco liberal from 1964 until his death at fifty-six in 1983. He wrote an incredible record for wilderness during the three years from 1977 to 1980, when he served as chairman of the House subcommittee on national parks. Besides the Boundary Waters Canoe Area Wilderness Act, his 1978 omnibus bill —"the national parks bill of the century"— tripled the acreage of park wilderness, tripled the miles of national trails, and doubled the miles of wild and scenic rivers, and much, much more. The day after he died, the House of Representatives devoted almost three and a half hours to eulogies from colleagues of both parties and then, as a memorial tribute, passed the California Wilderness Act, Burton's legislation to preserve five million acres of wilderness.

Burton served as chairman of the national parks subcommittee in a golden era, a period when Morris K. Udall, of Arizona, was chairman of the full Interior Committee and John Seiberling, of Ohio, was chairman of a special subcommittee dealing with Alaska lands. The latter two were both heroes in their own right, instrumental in passage of the largest land preservation bill in American history. It didn't come easily. Alaska had won statehood in 1959, leading to disagreement and dispute among state and federal governments and native communities over the ownership of millions of acres. In 1978 President Carter boldly withdrew key areas from state selection and proclaimed others as national monuments. The effect was to save 113.5 million acres. It was done legally, but never had a president used the power of his office for such an extensive land withdrawal. Congress two years later defied corporate lobbying to validate Carter's action with the Alaska National Interest Lands Conservation Act (ANILCA). Carter signed it on December 2, 1980, calling it the environmental vote of the century.

But struggles are unending. At Boundary Waters in the late 1990s, Rep. James Oberstar, a Democrat, the congressman of the district, and Senator Rod Grams, a Republican, were pressing legislation to open the million-acre BWCA Wilderness to motorboats, trucks, and jeeps, and to create a locally-dominated citizens council for the BWCA (and another for nearby Voyageurs National Park) to dictate how these internationally significant treasures should be managed.

Wherever there is still wilderness, citizens have fought for it. And their struggle goes on. In *Battle for the Wilderness* I quoted Governor Nelson Rockefeller, of New York, declaring, "The Adirondacks are preserved forever." He had just signed legislation in 1973 governing land use in the country's largest park outside of Alaska, three times the size of Yellowstone, half public and half private, with a million acres of wilderness. But for the Adirondack Council, "dedicated to protecting and enhancing the natural and human communities of the Adirondack Park," life has been one red alert after another. "Hardly a week goes by without some new issue coming to our attention," wrote Timothy J. Burke, executive director of the Council, early in 1997. "Some issues, such as the over-zealous widening of a trail into the Forest Preserve, can be resolved with a couple of phone calls to appropriate state agencies, while other issues, such as the issuance of illegal temporary permits for private homes on state land, involve years of research and negotiations with state agencies and affected parties."

The Adirondack Council decided to cope with issues—that Governor Rockefeller did not foresee—by establishing its own Activist Network, whose members listen to public hearings, lobby, and respond to action alerts. "Council activists have used their skills and passion for the Park to influence policies for the better, time and time again," wrote Lisa M. Genier, the full-time activist coordinator. "We have had some terrific victories, but our work is never done."

The California Wilderness Coalition chose a similar approach. In February 1997 it reported that nearly one hundred new activists attended Adopt-a-Wilderness training programs, aimed at watching what the managers do, or fail to do, and that it worked hard through its activist network in dealing with "the salvage rider." That law, adopted by Congress in 1995, was probably the most anti-environmental legislation in decades. Supposedly intended for emergency salvage logging in public forests, it suspended environmental laws for eighteen months and denied the public all legal review. CWC generated thousands of letters, faxes, phone calls, and peaceful demonstrations that stopped many of the most destructive rider sales in the state, though other salvage-rider sales were completed, too often in roadless areas with wilderness potential.

Citizen groups all across the country fought to protect the roadless areas from the effects of the salvage rider. In *Battle for the Wilderness* I discussed an early phase of the struggle to save the roadless areas, the *de facto* wilderness. I wrote (page 163) that the roadless inventory, the Roadless Area Review and Evaluation, or RARE, showing the early wilderness system estimate of fifty to sixty million acres was low by far, and that the second stage of review, challenging citizen activism, was only beginning.

Indeed, when Jimmy Carter became president he tried to resolve the issue. In his environmental message to Congress, May 23, 1977 he called the Wilderness Act a landmark of American conservation policy and said the National Wilderness Preservation System "must be expanded promptly, before the most deserving of federal lands are opened to other uses and lost to wilderness forever." The Endangered American Wilderness Act was passed in 1978, adding sixteen choice undeveloped areas to the wilderness system, including Golden Trout in California, Lone Peak in Utah, Gospel Hump in Idaho, and the addition of French Pete Creek Valley to Three Sisters Wilderness in Oregon.

Then came another nationwide review, RARE II, designed to include analysis of social and economic impacts of various management alternatives. RARE II was conducted from 1977 to 1979. The inventory phase generated massive public involvement with replies from approximately 360,000 people and identified 1,920 areas covering

65.7 million acres with wilderness potential. The trouble was that the Forest Service recommended only fifteen million acres for wilderness (plus eleven million acres for further study) and declared that all other roadless lands would be "released" for other uses.

With each step of the way, the process became more complicated and more removed from concerned citizens. RARE II proved a device to sacrifice some of the choicest wilderness and wildlife areas of the West from protection and to open them to logging and other commodity uses. As a federal judge ruled early in 1980 in sustaining a legal challenge brought against RARE II in California, the Forest Service did not deal sufficiently with adverse impacts of opening roadless areas to development, did not seriously consider wilderness values, and did not give the public a fair chance to comment.

Congress answered the California challenge with a code of sufficiency and release: If an environmental impact statement for public land in a state or a section of a state was found "legally and factually sufficient," there would be no further review, or judicial review of the decision, thus releasing the land for nonwilderness uses. There were different kinds of release: "hard," permanently releasing roadless lands not designated as wilderness or wilderness study; "soft," allowing for reconsideration during revision of forest plans, interim management as wilderness or wilderness study; and "compromise," somewhere between the two.

Congress has passed many items of wilderness legislation since the Wilderness Act of 1964, more than 100 by 1987 alone. Some bills added to existing wilderness, others added areas to the system, provided for study areas, or changed names. Some laws strengthened the act and some weakened it. "State Acts" focused on particular states, containing sufficiency/release language for public lands within those states.

In one sense, the process showed citizens what they could do in behalf of special places not yet protected by law. But they also learned the wisdom in the statement of Ted Trueblood that I quoted earlier: "We're not looking at how much more wilderness we're going to have, but how much less of it there will be." The release language served industry that had lobbied for it, rather than serving wilderness. The state acts reduced the scope of involvement and attention, giving control over the legislation to congressional delegations from states richly endowed by nature but dominated politically by exploitive interests; so laws were passed with specific qualifications and allowances—for airplanes, helicopters, snowmobiles, and motorboats—at variance with the Wilderness Act and the principles of preservation.

Consequently citizen groups learned to organize, challenge, to stand on their own and to spread their message without dependence on national organizations. Even while writing these lines, I have at hand an alert from the Southern Utah Wilderness Alliance (SUWA) rallying its forces to protect the Grand Staircase-Escalante National Monument, which President Clinton created by proclamation in 1996, from proposed oil exploration by Conoco Inc. The "nationals" may join, but SUWA has built its own constituency responsive to its message that if Conoco has its way, the heart of the monument could be transformed into an industrial oil field and some of the 1.3 million acres of wilderness would be lost.

Challenges of the Forest Service's accelerated road building (and the legal right to challenge) have proven crucial to the survival of wildlife species dependent on wilderness—including grizzly bear, wolf, lynx, wolverine, and bull trout. Building roads, in fact, may be the most destructive of that agency's management practices. Roads built at public expense have degraded water quality, increased landslides, erosion, and siltation, ruined streams, and fragmented habitat for wide-ranging species.

But the Carter administration was at least willing to listen. One month into the Reagan administration in 1981, Interior Secretary James G. Watt announced that no federal land was sacred. He campaigned to open wilderness to oil and gas drilling and to lease the Arctic National Wildlife Refuge. BLM Director Robert Burford, working under Watt, issued a directive eliminating the overall plan for public participation (as required by prior BLM regulations) and proposed directing public participation to "maximize resource values." They had to be restrained by Congress. But Watt, Burford, John B. Crowell, a timber industry lawyer serving as Assistant Secretary of Agriculture, and the entire Reagan administration were bent on exposing public lands, including wilderness, to commercial development.

The very extremism of the administration stirred overwhelming public opposition. Watt caught on to this fact to the extent that he represented the Wilderness Protection Act of 1982, "the Watt Bill," as meant to assure that wilderness lands are "last to be exploited, if ever." It was a cynical hoax that would automatically open the wilderness system in the year 2000 and, in the meantime, allow the president to open any area to mineral development by making a finding of "urgent national need" and would release RARE II and BLM study areas at the discretion of the Secretaries of Interior and Agriculture. The Watt Bill went to oblivion, and in due course so did its author.

Reagan, Watt, and their Sagebrush Rebels had come to Washington with fire in their eyes and determination in their hearts to dismantle federal resource programs, with hard wacks at wilderness. But Bill Clinton certainly looked like he would do better, especially when he personally became involved and tried to resolve the issue of the spotted owl in the old-growth forests of the Northwest.

This came in June 1990, after the U.S. Fish and Wildlife Service, following considerable research, pressure, and politics, placed the northern spotted owl on the endangered species list. This led to the grim warning from the timber industry that sawmills would close, with a resultant terrible loss in jobs, and supporting testimony from the Forest Service that saving that little bird of the night would halt up to a third of its timber harvest in the Northwest. With federal judges ruling favorably on suits brought by environmental organizations and temporarily halting logging, the president flew to Portland in April 1993 to host a "forestry summit" with leaders of industry, labor, environment and science, plus members of his cabinet in hopes of breaking the stalemate.

Following the summit speeches and presentations, the president appointed a working group of scientists to produce a blueprint for the Northwest forests that would protect the old-growth and its creatures and cut timber for the mills. It was the old call for "balance" and "consensus" that always costs in wilderness lost. The team developed ten options. For the spotted owl and the natural forest Option 1 plainly was the best hope, but the team, and then Clinton, struck a balance and chose Option 9, allowing timber harvesting at a reduced level, although even within designated owl "reserves,"where the logging would also harm northern goshawk and marbled murrelet and reduce biological diversity.

Then came the Salvage Rider, attached to a massive 1995 budget-cutting bill. Clinton first vetoed and then later signed it—a matter of politics when something has to give to get something else in trade. The bill called for a period of salvage logging on national forests and BLM land, giving the agencies a virtual blank check to cut whatever they wanted in the name of salvage, exempting all the sales from requirements of environmental law and appeal. It would plainly allow logging in roadless areas and along wild and scenic rivers. The rider expired December 31, 1996. Before it ended, Secretary of Agriculture Dan Glickman directed changes in the program to increase public involvement in decision making and to prohibit the use of the rider in pristine inventoried roadless areas. But considerable damage was already done.

Citizen groups kept watchdogging roadless areas and wilderness. In 1995 the Northwest Ecosystem Alliance made headlines by submitting the high bid for a key timber sale on the Okanogan National Forest in eastern Washington. The agency ultimately denied the sale, but the point was made: "market value" deserves to be measured in more than timber, but also in wildlife, wilderness, watershed, and natural beauty. In New Mexico in 1996 the environmental group Gila Watch, with support from Wilderness Watch and the Rio Grande chapter of Trout Unlimited, won a suit ordering removal of 900 cattle illegally grazing—with the knowledge and consent of the Forest Service—in the Gila and Aldo Leopold Wilderness areas.

Other groups were doing the same, or trying to, in many different parts of the country, but I've wondered at times if there isn't some other way of dealing with the issues than beating chronic brush fires. I remember Dave Foreman once telling me how, while working as a lobbyist for The Wilderness Society in Washington, he grew disenchanted and quit:

I looked around at my colleagues in the environmental groups. They were turning into yuppies, concentrating on political maneuvering with compromise rather than demand. The environmental movement accepts the world view of the other side, then tries to reform and modify it a little bit. It doesn't challenge the basic insanity of the system or its world view.

In 1980 Foreman and a handful of friends started an uncompromising new movement, Earth First!, organizing demonstrations of civil disobedience, blockading logging trucks, climbing into trees and staying up there weeks at a time, and, taking a leaf from Edward Abbey's *Monkeywrench Gang*, spiking trees. In due time Foreman moved on to work on The Wildlands Project, a campaign for an ecological wilderness network, and to join the board of the Sierra Club.

I'm not sure whether Foreman changed the Club or the Club changed him, but Earth First! even without its founding guru, or any more tree-spiking, still crusades from the fringe for wilderness as though it really matters, challenging legalistic and political approaches

Earth Firsters care deeply about wilderness in a manner different from the established environmental community. They want direct action to affirm the rights of nature; they want their life-style to challenge a society bent on consumption and alienated from nature. With enthusiastic campaigns and demonstrations, Earth Firsters have brought public attention to threatened areas like the redwoods of northern California and the cove-mallard in the national forests of northern Idaho. With relish they throw darts at the moderate environmental community, as in this passage from an article in the Earth First! journal of February 1997:

> Gone is G. Jon Roush, the Wilderness Society chieftain who clearcut his hobby ranch in Montana. Peter A. A. Berle is now gone from Audubon, back to his job as a high-powered NY lawyer. Jay Hair drove off from his $250,000 per year job at the National Wildlife Federation and went to Seattle, where he surfaced as a PR flack for Plum Creek Timber Co., pushing their woeful owl-killing habitat Conservation Plan. . . .
>
> There's the strange case of William Cronon who, through Weyerhaueser's publishing arm, has authored numerous treatises maligning the entire concept of Wilderness. Astoundingly, Cronon now has been appointed to TWS's [The Wilderness Society] Board of Governors, joining timber CEO Walter Minnick, oil baroness Caroline Getty, Rockefeller heir Christopher Elliman, and assorted venture capitalists, Wall Street tycoons, wealthy ranchers and real estate developers.

Plainly irreverent, and Roush may possibly have logged without clearcutting, but the Earth First! slogan, after all, is "No compromise with Mother Earth," and history shows that Mother has been beaten enough. The William Cronon mentioned, a prominent history professor at the University of Wisconsin, was cited for a strange essay, "The Trouble with Wilderness," that he contributed to the book *Uncommon Ground: Toward Reinventing Nature* (Norton, 1995) in which he expressed the theme that "wilderness poses a threat to responsible environmentalism at the end of the 20th century." He might even be right, but it seems the wrong notion to come from someone connected with *the* Wilderness Society.

Citizen groups deal in a different set of realities. As a case in point, the Southeast Alaska Conservation Council (SEACC) has labored for years to protect the resources of the Tongass National Forest, usually uphill against the combined odds of government, industry, and politics. The Tongass, the country's largest national forest, covers seventeen million acres, cleft by bays, inlets, and rivers, all highly scenic, misty and moody. But following World War II, the Forest Service felt obligated to promote a large-scale timber industry. It initiated two huge fifty-year sales, centered at Ketchikan and Sitka, and tried for a third that would have cut enough timber to build a plank road from the Arctic Circle to the tip of South America, virtually all of it for shipment to Japan. That sale would have wiped out virtually everything growing on Admiralty Island, stronghold of a thousand brown bears and the greatest concentration of bald eagles in the world, but the Sierra Club and Karl Lane, a big game guide, brought suit and effectively blocked it.

With passage of the Alaska Lands Act in 1980, most of Admiralty was protected as wilderness, and so was most of Misty Fjords, in Alaska's southernmost corner, two million acres of rain forests, steep granite fjords, hidden glaciers, alpine meadows and snowfields. But the current Alaska congressional delegation has sought continually to undo this protection. In 1996, the two senators, Ted Stevens and Frank Murkowski, and the lone congressman, Don Young, all powerful committee chairmen, went after the Tongass with vengeance, to such an extent that some of their own Republican colleagues backed off and the president promised a veto on anything attacking the Tongass.

SEACC's victory was absolutely unforeseen: The big pulp mill in Ketchikan closed in March 1997, eight years before the fifty-year contract was due to expire (though two sawmills were allowed to continue for two years with timber already under contract). "Working with all kinds of allies, we were able to stop all the Alaska delegation assaults on the Tongass–a barrage of 15 hearings and 17 pieces of legislation," wrote Bart Koehler, executive director of SEACC. "As long as the Alaska delegation stays in power, we'll see renewed attacks, but we harbor the hope that the future will provide jobs for Southeast Alaskans and sustain a management course where we all respect the forest as a renewable and renewing resource."

The Forest Service got a message, too: twenty-two thousand

comments on its Tongass management plan, from every zip code in Southeast Alaska, and from all fifty states. The Tongass plan drew more comments than the reintroduction of wolves into Yellowstone and most called for less logging and more protection.

SCIENTISTS AND CITIZENS WORKING TOGETHER FOR DIVERSITY

When the Wilderness Act came before Congress, the idea of ecology was still new to many people, but scientists testified in behalf of the legislation, showing wilderness as the best place, perhaps the only place, where life can still function in wholeness and diversity. They said that all kinds of ecosystems furnish valuable living laboratories where science can discover wonders that ultimately prove of practical value to humankind.

Since then preservation of diversity has been identified as a major role of wilderness. A cadre of scientists has improved understanding of how ecosystems function and conservation biology, the "mission science," has emerged to combine theory and action, with advocacy in behalf of diversity in public decision-making.

Ecology itself goes back a long way, though not quite in the public purview. I recall that forest activists became more aware in the 1960s and 70s, during the controversy over clearcutting in the national forests, which F. Herbert Bormann of Yale and Gene E. Likens of Cornell addressed in their studies at the Hubbard Brook Experimental Forest in New Hampshire. Some of their peers in forest research were angry with them for their findings of depleted soil nutrients subsequent to clearcutting. However, in *Scientific American* of October 1970 Bormann and Likens wrote,

Failures in environmental management often result from such factors as failure to appreciate the complexity of nature, the assumption that it is possible to manage one part of nature and the belief that nature somehow will absorb all types of manipulation. Good management of the use of land—good from the viewpoint of society at large—requires that managerial practices be imposed only after careful analysis and evaluation of all the ramifications. A focus for this type of analysis and evaluation is the ecosystems concept.

Bormann and Likens stirred criticism and attack, but in terms of forest ecology the Hubbard Brook study opened a new dimension. Interviewed in the *Yale Alumni Magazine*, April 1982 ("The Knowledge Flows from Hubbard Brook," by D. Kimball Smith), Bormann said,

We have enlarged the perspective of what ecology takes into account. This project is an attempt to think wholly, and there really aren't a lot of them around. In the past, most biological ecologists focused only on the biological fraction of the system. They'd go and look only at forests, only at the populations that composed them. Our studies have more effectively linked the forest ecosystem to the larger biogeochemical cycles. It's important in our attempts to understand man's impact on the forest.

Many professionals learned ecology from the textbook *Fundamentals of Ecology* by Eugene P. Odum, of the University of Georgia. Odum has long stressed the need to preserve a substantial portion of the biosphere in a natural state, citing wilderness and other natural areas as life-support for humanity. Based largely on this principle, the newly defined conservation biology enables scientists to advance conservation of biotic diversity as a primary mission of society. Variety, or diversity, is offered as the key to the health of cohesive natural systems, in sharp contrast to deforestation, desertification, decimation of fisheries, and other designs for disaster.

Thus, William Alverson, Stephen Solheim, and Donald Waller, botanists of the University of Wisconsin and colleagues of Hugh Iltis, after extensive field inventories of the Chequamegon and Nicolet national forests in the late 1980s, entered a strong appeal against plans for Chequamegon National Forest that ignored principles of conservation biology. They showed that periodic logging and resultant fragmentation jeopardized certain plant and animal communities. They showed that the creation of "wildlife openings" by logging and roading benefited species adapted to forest edges and disturbed environments, mostly popular game species like white-tailed deer, but others, requiring forest interior habitats, inevitably are lost. They cited an example in the Great Lakes region where deer populations had increased many fold, while their overbrowsing interfered with the regeneration of plant species. Likewise, breeding populations of migratory songbirds had been sharply reduced due to increased predation and parasitism by birds and mammals favored in disturbed areas.

Botanists have identified a range of forest types (mature hemlock/hardwood and white cedar swamps) and individual species endangered by loss of interior and old-growth forests.

How many species do we need? How many do we know? In *Battle for the Wilderness*, I wrote that science knows very little about life, perhaps less about the simplest, most fundamental forms or about the interrelationship of all forms. Since then, Edward O. Wilson of Harvard in *The Diversity of Life* and other works has shown that we don't know the life-forms, not even to the nearest order of magnitude; but how can we know, asks Wilson, when about 2,000 additional plant species, newly discovered by scientists, are added to the total in an average year? We *do* know by name approximately 440,000 plant species ranging from the tallest trees to the humblest algae, plus about 47,000 species of animals with backbones, and probably more than 750,000 species of insects. But these provide merely a glimpse of the total diversity of life on earth.

I wrote that obscure plants and herbs undoubtedly hold future keys to health. The Pacific yew is a tree that was long considered a weed, worthy only of burning on slash piles. But researchers have found an extract from yew bark, taxol, effective in treating several kinds of cancerous tumors, including ovarian cancer, which kills thousands of women each year. Leaves of the rosy periwinkle, a native of Madagascar, contain alkaloids vincristine and vinblastine, both of which have brought advances in treatment of Hodgkin's disease, and vincristine alone in treatment for leukemia. Scientists dealing in pharmacology and medicinal plant research believe the most productive period lies ahead, that somewhere lies the one plant to cure AIDS or to ameliorate Alzheimer's Disease.

The same holds true for food. Humans have used the immense diversity of the Earth's plants and animals, mixing and matching genetic strains to create prize-winning domestic stock or crops resistant to pests. In the United States, crops of potato, tomato, melon, sugarcane, oats, wheat and Asian rice have been improved—and in some cases saved from destruction—through introduction of genes derived from wild or primitive species.

I referred in a note (at bottom of page 52) to ecosystem research under auspices of the U.S. Committee of the International Biological Program. Such ecosystem-level programs have expanded and evolved into a "landscape ecology" approach, with emphasis on interaction of different ecosystem types. The National Science Foundation's Long-Term Ecological Research (LTER) sites and Department of Energy's National Environmental Research Parks (NERPs) provide conservation biologists with baseline information on ecological processes, as well as access to representative habitats under more-or-less-controlled conditions suitable for long-term studies. The sites include deserts, humid salt marshes, arctic and alpine tundra and taiga, tall-grass prairie, deciduous and coniferous forests, and tropical rain forests. The National Oceanic and Atmospheric Administration provides additional long-term research access at National Estuarine Research Reserve sites.

Another significant advance has been the growth of the natural areas movement, which now links federal, state, and private agencies in protecting areas of various sizes as ecological reference sites for research and education and conserving biological diversity. Many of these areas safeguard rare and endangered species. The Bureau of Land Management alone has designated nearly 500 natural areas, including almost 100 in California, ranging in size from 40 acres to 180,000 acres.

The Forest Service, to its credit, has been a leading influence in the Research Natural Area (RNA) program since establishment in 1927 of the Santa Catalina Natural Area on the Coronado National Forest in Arizona. The National Forest Management Act of 1976 led to a regulation providing for establishment of new RNAs as part of planning through "identification of examples of important forest, shrubland, grassland, alpine, aquatic, and geologic types that have special or unique characteristics of scientific interest and importance." The Forest Service has now dedicated more than 400 RNAs nationally, with several hundred more in the works. Although relatively small, these areas protect ecosystem types that may not be represented in the National Wilderness Preservation System.

In addition to the federal government, many of the states, private organizations like the Nature Conservancy and the National Audubon Society, and colleges and universities maintain their own natural areas with substantial public support and participation. Florida's monumental Preservation 2000 Act of 1990 provides approximately $300 million per year for ten years for the acquisition of land and rivers, including areas in the Florida Natural Areas Inventory, a statewide data base of rare and endangered species and natural communities, operated for the state by The Nature Conservancy. In 1996 the Tennessee Natural Areas Program marked its 25th anniversary. Since the Natural Areas Preservation Act of 1971, Tennessee has protected more than 70,000 acres in 47 natural areas. The Roan Mountain Massif Natural Area covers 20,000 acres of federal, state, and private lands (Nature Conservancy) in the Southern highlands, one of the most significant sites in the southeastern United States.

The Natural Areas Association was organized in 1978, bringing together professional and volunteer researchers, managers, and naturalists. For example, Illinois natural areas, principally presettlement prairie and oak savanna, are being actively restored, almost entirely by volunteers. The Illinois Volunteer Network not only monitors plants, insects and vertebrates, but conducts hundreds of walks for the public and recruits new stewards. Yes, even in New York City, the Natural Resources Group of the Department of Parks & Recreation has developed urban natural areas management plans to protect rare serpentine barrens, oak-hickory forests, and wetlands. Hundreds of acres of endangered habitat have been protected from development for inclusion in the department's refuge system.

In 1990 I went to a conference on preservation of public lands in the state of Maryland. My first reaction was that there are no public lands in Maryland, for the moment confusing the term "public lands" with the public domain of the West. Yet at the conference I learned of the Maryland Wildlands Committee's campaign to work within state parks and forests for a Maryland Wildlands Preservation System, detailed as follows:

Our primary goal is to protect the natural diversity of Maryland ecosystems, including biological community, species, and genetic diversity. We still lack desirable representation of Maryland ecosystem diversity, e.g., boreal bog, limestone forest, tidal marsh are missing. We still urgently need to add a few large unfragmented areas of forest wherever they are least disturbed and most valuable ecologically.

The most heartening development has been the growing degree to which scientists and citizens find common ground to work together. Peter H. Raven, director of the Missouri Botanical Garden, discussing "The Politics of Preserving Biodiversity" in an address August 5, 1990, to the American Institute of Biological Sciences, cited destruction of old-growth forests of the Pacific Northwest:

This significant regional problem has been disguised as a battle between the undoubtedly hardworking people employed by the lumber industry in the Northwest and a romantic obsession on the part of environmentalists with the northern spotted owl. . . .

These ancient forests have been attacked in a frenzy of greedy exploitation, in which they are cut as rapidly as possible and sold as unprocessed logs to Japan to maximize short-term profits. The clearcutting practices ignore the health of the regional economy, which depends on the long-term sustainability of the forests.

Today, strong links need to be rebuilt between biologists and conservation groups, which depend directly on information developed by systematic biologists and stored in museums and similar institutions. . . . Political leaders are hungry for authentic expressions of opinion from informed people, and we need to take part in the political process at all levels to make that process work.

We must begin to give credit to our colleagues who do speak out, often making severe professional sacrifices in the course of doing so. We need to approach the media, the politicians, one another—anyone who will listen—and try to improve the sustainability of the world.

And now Dave Foreman, the activist personified, and scientific colleagues, Michael Soulé', Reed Noss, and others with the ambitious Wildlands Project have opened another chapter. Their mission statement declares,

We are called to our task by the failure of existing wilderness, parks, and wildlife refuges to adequately protect life in North America. While these areas preserve landscapes of spectacular scenery and areas ideally suited to non-mechanized forms of recreation, they are too small, too isolated, and represent too few types of ecosystems to perpetuate the biodiversity of the continent. Despite establishment of parks and other reserves from Canada to Central America, true wilderness and wilderness-dependent species are in precipitous decline.

They foresee systems of interlinked wilderness and other large nature reserves, surrounded by multiple-use buffers managed in an ecologically compatible manner. The immediate opportunities appear to be in the Greater Yellowstone Ecosystem, Northern Rockies Ecosystem, Yellowstone-to-Yukon, Sierra Nevada in California, and

Southern Appalachia, with six national forests surrounding Great Smoky Mountains National Park, but there will be others as the concept catches on. Making it happen through the political process is another story.

But science with ecological and social conscience certainly helps. "We must examine and manage resources holistically," as Dr. John Craighead insists in his advocacy of the Northern Rockies Ecosystem Protection Act (NREPA). "Thanks to satellite imagery, electronically digitized data, and the computer's power to analyze and integrate digitized information, scientists can map and quantify the vegetation of entire ecosystems, track animals throughout these ecosystems, determine habitat use and preference, and scientists can also superimpose on this biological base, via computer, data relating to man's use or abuse of the ecosystem-wide resource. None of this was possible a decade and a half ago."

Turning pages of the chapter "A Place for Wild Animals, Wild Plants," I note that a lot has become possible within one or two decades. "The wolves are gone," I wrote (page 69). But now the wolves have come home to Yellowstone, Selway-Bitterroot Wilderness, and Frank Church-River of No Return Wilderness, and I hope they will return to other places where they belong. Further on (page 73), there are a few lines that certainly influenced my own future:

Much of sport hunting has scant relevancy to primitive instincts or old traditions. It does little to instill a conservation conscience. Blasting polar bears from airplanes, hunting the Arabian oryx—or deer—from automobiles, trail bikes, or snowmobiles, tracking a quarry with walkie-talkie radios, killing for the sake of killing annihilate the hunt's essential character. There can't be much thrill to "the chase" when there is little chase.

Nothing wrong with that statement. I still think it's right and reasonable. But in 1974 I was conservation editor of *Field & Stream* magazine and the editor there, Jack Samson, found my few lines quoted in another book, *Man Kind?* by Cleveland Amory, the hunter's arch enemy. Samson didn't like it and fired me, with a pronouncement, "No one who is anti-hunting will remain on the masthead of *Field & Stream* as long as I am editor."

I think my statement actually was pro-hunting, suggesting a standard of ethics—but never mind. Now I question whether wilderness hunting is valid or an anachronism in modern America. Hunting and trapping, after all, grew up with rural traditions and family farming, mostly gone now. Theodore Roosevelt and George Bird Grinnell, big-game gurus of the Nineteenth Century, believed wilderness hunting was a sport for he-men, sound of body, firm of mind, self-reliant, and capable of self-help in a crunch. There aren't too many of those left either. Much of modern sport hunting tends to focus on the kill, even if it takes dogs and portable phones to track and kill mountain lions and bears. In contrast, the attitude that fosters and encourages wilderness protection is founded on principles of respect for life.

Wildlife management as practiced by state fish and game agencies differs from wildlife stewardship. Managers by the nature of their training at resource schools of land-grant colleges think narrowly of the use of wildlife as either "consumptive" or "nonconsumptive." Their emphasis is on game species—deer, elk, rabbits, waterfowl—ignoring hundreds, or thousands, of native plants and animals that comprise ecosystems. Their objective is to sustain or to increase the "take." Active management practices include habitat manipulation, artificial propagation, predator control, and providing watering devices and food plots, most of which require access to the back country through a network of roads.

State fish and game agencies want to hunt grizzly bears in Montana, bison at Yellowstone, and sandhill crane in Utah. They have introduced pheasant from Asia, brown trout from Europe, and mountain goats from Alaska and Canada hoping to sell more hunting and fishing permits. The Montana department in 1986 introduced mysis shrimp into Flathead Lake to feed young salmon. But the shrimp ate the plankton on which salmon depended, wiping out the salmon run. So the bald eagles depending on the salmon virtually disappeared.

Then there are the jet-set gunners, superpredators who roam the planet for super-kills. In 1990 George Schaller, the biologist, was on his third visit to Mongolia, helping to set up projects to conserve the snow leopard and brown bear, when he saw a bulletin issued by the Mongolian government describing the success of an Austrian hunter in bagging a snow leopard in the Gobi desert. The hunter had brought with him two dogs to run the leopard. The hunting license cost $16,000 but the press information bulletin said it was all worth it: "A marvelous skin and the excitement of chasing became excellent compensation for all the efforts and expenses." I'm glad that while at *Field & Stream* I never had to defend that sort of thing.

MANAGING WILDERNESS:
ASK HARD QUESTIONS, BE CONSERVATIVE

Max Peterson, then Chief of the Forest Service, struck at the heart of the issue. He was speaking at the First National Wilderness Management Workshop at Moscow, Idaho, in October 1983. "We have to ask very hard questions," he said, "and be quite conservative in allowing entries into wilderness which, one at a time, don't seem to bring much impact; but when I add those up over my short career of 35 years, I wonder where the wilderness will be 35 years from now if the door is opened to making those exceptions."

I've heard it said many ways but scarcely said better—one simple small exception may not hurt, but making exceptions gets to be a nasty, destructive habit. I'm sure that Chief Peterson meant every word in issuing a call that should be sounded continually as long as there is wilderness. But still, five years later, in July 1988, when a congressional subcommitteee conducted hearings on Forest Service management of wilderness, witnesses agreed the management in his own agency was weak and inadequate.

The subcommittee chairman, Representative Bruce Vento, of Minnesota, summed it up in a letter to Dale Robertson, Max Peterson's successor as chief. Vento wrote,

. . . planning, construction, maintenance, reconstruction and rehabilitation of wilderness trails and campsites were inadequate; wilderness meadows were overgrazed by ranchers and outfitters and the outfitters were privy to inappropriate "privatization" of land within wilderness on which they established quasi-permanent facilities; acid precipitation and air pollution were modifying wilderness ecosystems; litter and garbage, soil erosion, barren areas and polluted streams all were impacting and altering ecosystems; most professional managers had little wilderness knowledge, experience or interest, even while competent wilderness rangers had little opportunity in the ranks.

"The Forest Service no longer can afford to treat wilderness as a second class resource that merits little management," wrote Vento. "The evidence is overwhelming that the wilderness system is deteriorating under Forest Service stewardship and that poor management is a major reason why."

Vento delivered further criticism in speaking at the National Wilderness Conference held in Minneapolis on September 12, 1989. Now it was directed at all four federal agencies administering wilderness:

The wilderness revolution has changed the way the American people use and view their public lands and transformed land management patterns and priorities in the United States. Surprisingly, however, this wilderness revolution has not been mirrored within the agencies charged with the nomination and management of the wilderness areas that the revolution created. Although wilderness today is a major land allocation, it apparently remains a low agency priority and wilderness management clearly has not kept pace with wilderness designation.

He cited the report he ordered of an investigation by the General Accounting Office showing that even though Congress substantially increased funding for wilderness management, 60 percent never reached wilderness management programs. The Forest Service actually decreased funding, took the money, and used it elsewhere.

In November 1994, another National Wilderness Conference, this in Santa Fe, New Mexico, heard the directors of all four agencies pledge anew to raise wilderness management to a new level of priority. Chief Jack Ward Thomas (Dale Robertson's successor) announced major changes at the Forest Service. These would include a new wilderness director position in the Forest Service hierarchy, on equal standing with timber, wildlife, and range; upgrading in wilderness staffing, and setting up a single management unit for the Frank Church-River of No Return Wilderness, covering 2.4 million acres in central Idaho, the largest Forest Service wilderness unit outside Alaska in the wilderness system.

One year later, in 1995, the four directors issued a joint Interagency Wilderness Strategic Plan with a signed pledge to do better. The trouble presently is that of the four, Jack Ward Thomas retired from the Forest Service on a downbeat; Mollie Beattie of the Fish and Wildlife Service passed away; Roger Kennedy announced his intent to leave the National Park Service, and Mike Dombeck moved from the BLM to the Forest Service. Of more value to wilderness, in 1995 Stewart Udall and Orville Freeman, Secretaries of Interior and Agriculture when the Wilderness Act was signed in 1964, joined the board of Wilderness Watch, a feisty little outfit, a burr under the saddle of the agencies, with the goal of "keeping wilderness wild." Udall, in the Winter 1995 issue of _Wilderness Watcher_, wrote,

There are now wildernesses overrun by people unaware of minimum impact use; others in which wilderness quiet is shattered by commercial aircraft and military fighter jets on training missions, and others in which the political timidity of the stewards in charge has permitted abuses of these protected lands.

The Diamond Bar Allotment issue in New Mexico is a case in point. Here, the Forest Service plans to use bulldozers and dynamite to build huge stock tanks in a previously untouched wilderness, because the areas where cattle currently are allowed to graze have been overgrazed to the point of desertification. The fact that foresters could even propose doing this demonstrates clearly how far from the intent of the act some officials have strayed in 30 years. Even more disturbing, this project is underway deep within the Gila and Aldo Leopold Wildernesses, which Leopold himself proposed as a model for the nation.

In 1997, I don't see that much has changed, except the rhetoric associated with a new plan with the same promise to do better. Wilderness management still ranks low in the hierarchy. The wilderness office of the Forest Service is still a branch of the recreation division and wilderness is regarded as a phase of recreation. The Frank Church-River of No Return Wilderness is still managed by 12 ranger districts, 6 national forests, and 2 regions, while, on the other hand, the nearby Moose Creek Ranger District, a unit of the Nez Perce National Forest, the only all-wilderness district in the entire National Forest System, has been dissolved. The Arthur Carhart National Wilderness Training Center and Aldo Leopold Wilderness Research Institute were established with promise in 1993 in Montana to work with all four of the agencies, but their resources and status in the system to sustain their efforts are meager.

There are people in the agencies who individually care deeply about wilderness and have labored long and hard in its behalf. They do good work, but many are frustrated and unfulfilled. Their bosses and coworkers talk about wilderness protection only when they have to, and usually better than they practice it. Decisions about wilderness are made in offices by people alienated from the outdoors.

I've seen wilderness areas all over this country, maybe more than anybody, and found them in poor condition, mostly getting worse rather than better. In many cases degradation and dissipation of wilderness are scarcely recognized or acknowledged by those in charge. A few years ago I was invited to a National Park Service mid-level training program on "remote areas management"—the trainers in charge didn't even want to call it wilderness or face the real problems. Another time I joined a field workshop of wilderness managers of the Southwest Region of the Forest Service, conducted in the Pecos Wilderness of New Mexico. The group of twenty-five or thirty was too large for the fragile terrain. Some hadn't camped out in years, as evident in their mistreatment of the resources at hand. They busily occupied themselves with such techniques as building water bars across trails, strictly superficial to wilderness protection and enhancement, without any reference to ecosystem responsibilities.

Perhaps the trouble is in the word "management." Management differs from stewardship. Many of these personnel lack philosophy or feeling for wilderness, having been trained in traditions of agronomy, to manage and manipulate, to convert "resources" into commodities. They acquire the analytical type of thinking that gives power over nature but smothers the powerful in ignorance of themselves as part of nature. Wilderness to them is another commodity, okay in its place as long as it doesn't interfere with commercial resources that really count. They want to impose management on wilderness, too, screening out insects, lightning fires, and natural erosive forces, rather than identifying and defending them as valid parts of a dynamic primitive landscape.

The Forest Service likes to claim it invented wilderness, citing Carhart, Leopold and Marshall, the wilderness pioneers who worked in its ranks. But Carhart's pleas for preservation were unheeded and he left the agency in despair in 1923; Leopold was dispatched from the Southwest to an office position at the Forest Products Laboratory in Madison—then he quit too; Marshall died in 1938, after which much of his wilderness work was undone. Now, the Forest Service points to its corps of wilderness rangers, which does indeed include competent and committed people, mostly at the lower levels. When it comes to predator control in wilderness or clearcut logging to the wilderness boundary, however, the decisions are made by district rangers and forest supervisors, the "line officers," often with different frames of reference and different sympathies.

The National Park Service in my thinking is the most culpable, precisely because it is mandated to protect and preserve and has done precious little to implement the Wilderness Act. Ronald F. Lee, Special Assistant to the Director, in *Public Use of the National Park System, 1872–2000*, published in 1968, gave the clear historic reason:

Wilderness area designations reaffirm that wilderness has a definite, resolute and permanent home in the National Park System. That home should be generous and rooted in ecological concepts, but it cannot be so large that it tends to deprive important numbers of traveling American families of the opportunity to identify themselves at firsthand, by a personal visit, even by automobile, with the great examples of their own national heritage preserved for them in the National Park System. The Wilderness Act adds to the original and evolving functions of the National Park System but does not nullify or supersede what has gone before.

In *Battle for the Wilderness* I quoted Lee's boss, Director George B. Hartzog, Jr., making the same point at the 1967 Wilderness Conference of the Sierra Club (page 181). Resistance to the law was motivated not by desire to protect wilderness but to weaken it, so that parks would remain open to recreational and commercial development. Hartzog himself in dealing with the first national park wilderness proposal in the Great Smoky Mountains in 1966 pushed for a multi-million dollar transmountain road across the park, plus additional inner loops and massive campgrounds.

"It is amazing how many persons from all over the country supported wilderness designation," Ernest Dickerman, a leader in the citizen Save-the-Smokies crusade, wrote to me in retrospect thirty years later, "and opposed any new roads in the course of the campaign— which lasted six years from 1965 until 1971, when George Hartzog finally threw in the towel. Frankly, the Park Service, except perhaps during its earliest years, has commonly been out of touch with the owners of the national parks in its basic policies and practices. The Park Service, instead of working closely with the citizens knowledgeable about national parks and devoted to protecting their extraordinary natural values, has considered them as antagonists."

It was up to citizens to make the case for setting wilderness aside, and it remains for citizens to ask the "very hard questions" about appropriate use to which Chief Peterson referred in his Idaho remarks. The national organizations—Sierra Club, Wilderness Society, National Parks and Conservation Association—pay some attention to management, but not nearly enough. If they did there would be no need for the organization Wilderness Watch, with aims "to have every designated wilderness and wild and scenic river monitored and protected by an individual or group of private citizens; to educate and inspire Americans about the nature of wilderness and about minimum impact use; and to change and expand the attitudes toward wilderness of the federal agencies."

Wilderness Watch was born in 1989 largely out of the concern of William A. Worf, who had worked for the Forest Service for thirty-three years, most of them with intimate involvement in wilderness. In 1964, when the Wilderness Act was passed, he was supervisor of the Bridger (later Bridger-Teton) National Forest in Wyoming. Then he went to headquarters in Washington where he was in charge of the wilderness office and drafted management regulations that are still in effect. He spent his last twelve years in the agency in charge of recreation and wilderness at the Northern Region headquarters.

Worf was part of a little cadre of people, loyal to the agency but with wilderness fixed in their conscience in the tradition of Carhart, Leopold and Marshall. These have included the late John Herbert in the Intermountain Region; Paul Weingart, who after retiring from the Southwest Region continued his work in wilderness training programs in Africa; and Tom Kovalicky, a courageous forest supervisor in Idaho who resisted political pressure to place priority on timber and continued as a wilderness advocate following his retirement in 1992. I should also mention Jim Bradley, who developed a program of education for wilderness users in the Northwest until he went to Washington as a staff aide to Representative Bruce Vento in some of the best congressional work ever on wilderness. Bradley, unfortunately, died in 1996. There have been such people in the other agencies as well. I think of Harry Crandell, who was in charge of the wilderness program for the wildlife refuge system until he left to work for the Wilderness Society and later for a congressional committee, and of the late Bill Lester, preeminent as wilderness ranger at North Cascades National Park in Washington State. There are more like them, and there should be still more.

If there were, the Forest Service in 1996 wouldn't do such foolish things as issuing an environmental impact statement proposing 129 helicopter landing sites within wilderness on the Tongass National Forest to provide easy access for tourists, with the explanation that "It allows people with limited time or physical ability easy access to some extremely remote Wilderness settings. This makes it possible for a greater number of visitors to easily enjoy more remote wilderness locations." Wilderness Watch has sued or challenged those plans, as well as those for the watering reservoirs in the Aldo Leopold Wilderness and Gila Wilderness (to which Stewart Udall referred above), and permanent outfitter structures, caches, and corrals in the Frank Church-River of No Return Wilderness.

Those outfitter caches and camps turn up in a number of wilderness areas, tolerated by managers and sometimes even defended by environmental groups on the grounds that most outfitters support wilderness (and their support is needed), provide an economic return, and cause little impact on the land. True, some care about the wild country—that's why they are there—and take wilderness as it comes, without looking for handy little intrusions that make it easier and cheaper for them. But other outfitters see wilderness as a place to do business: They are commercial users, like loggers, grazers or miners. And like national park concessioners, they merchandise convenience and comfort, not wilderness challenge or wilderness ethics. One step leads to another—a septic system, a resort, a demand for private property rights in public wilderness—until the wildness has been tamed out of it.

That isn't right. Preserving the wilderness resource should be the overriding mission. The administrator's responsibility should not be to outfitters or tourists, but to wilderness, free of economics and commercial considerations. The common goal of the visitor and the administrator should be to insure that future generations will know and enjoy the same degree of solitude that past generations have known and the same sense that nature, rather than humankind, prevails.

Each of us, no matter how well prepared or intended, makes some impact on entering wilderness. It's encouraging that outdoor educational schools like Outward Bound and the National Outdoor Leadership School (NOLS) are proving that people are capable of practicing individual ethical responsibility to avoid doing irreparable harm. NOLS teaches bright young leaders-in-the-making minimum-impact use as a hands-on, practical approach; they, in turn, are demonstrating that principles of "Leave No Trace" and "Soft Paths" do work. Leave No Trace, LNT, has expanded considerably into an organization of its own, educating federal land managers and the public through training sessions, publications, videos, and electronic webs to leave little or no evidence of human use or abuse and to instill a land stewardship ethic. Considering that the fewer restrictions the better, and that most restrictions come after the damage is done, this is definitely positive and promising.

I don't want to keep anybody out, but I keep coming back to Max Peterson's admonition. It recalls the strong position taken by Newton B. Drury, an early director of the National Park Service. During World War II he resisted pressures to open the parks for military purposes. Consequently, little damage was done, none needlessly. Following the war, new demands arose to open the parks to mining, logging, grazing, and dams. Drury held firm, insisting,

If we are going to succeed in preserving the greatness of the national parks, they must be held inviolate. They represent the last stands of primitive America. If we are going to whittle away at them we should recognize, at the very beginning, that all such whittlings are cumulative and that the end result will be mediocrity.

I think it's a way of looking at nature that counts most. Informed people who understand and love wilderness, who love people and reach out to teach will find the way to stewardship that works. I offer the lines of John Ruskin for guidance. "Great art accepts Nature as she is," he wrote, "but directs the eyes and thoughts to what is most perfect in her; false art saves itself the trouble of direction by removing or altering whatever it thinks objectionable." Blizzard, cold, drought, earthquake, fire, flood, heat, hurricane, storm, volcano, and wind, which humans often find uncomfortable, are inevitable, and actually beneficial influences that shape and reshape the land into landscape and continually recast form and function of plants and animals.

Fire is a natural force in wilderness, but managers and scientists disagree about how to deal with it. Many Indian tribes considered fire a friend, just as primitive peoples in various parts of the world set fire to "green up the grass" and stimulate new growth. But as a consequence of wildfires devastating to commercial timber forests, American public policy for the past century has been designed to suppress all fires. Now some experts reason that in certain circumstances fires should be started as "prescribed burns" in wilderness to restore natural conditions. Maybe so, but Bill Worf warns that, "Where man chooses the 'appropriate conditions' where it will be ignited, fire ceases to be a natural force and becomes a manipulative tool. Conceptually scheduled is no different than herbicides, a chain saw or an anchor chain between two D-8s. In fact, these tools can be applied with a great deal more precision."

A cornerstone of the wilderness concept is to avoid deliberate action interfering with natural ecological process. True, we need to acknowledge that humans have interfered already through fire suppression, pollution, and the introduction of non-native plant species, "weeds." These actions have been unintentional. We ought also recognize differing views that may be valid. Worf warns that, in cases where deliberate action is believed to be desired and appropriate, it should not be initiated by managers "who believe they know what the people want or at least what is 'best for them.'" We can't all be experts, but at least people ought to know that fire has a long and valid history.

This became evident in connection with the great Yellowstone fires of 1988. Drought, dry woody fuels, high temperatures, and strong winds combined to create severe burning conditions. When lightning and careless humans set the tinderbox ablaze, there was no stopping the fires, nor the ensuing media coverage that emphasized flames and billowing smoke, largely ignoring deeper ecological questions. I revisited Yellowstone in June 1989 and found life after fire, a rebirth, the continuation of an historic life cycle. The "damage" was more extensive to the tourist trade than to the ecology of the park. The heaviest fires were in stands of aging lodgepole pine, waiting to be ignited to make way for new growth. Plants, insects, fish, and wildlife found new food sources.

"Too often, it appears, the definition of fire suppression and fire use objectives in wilderness have been abdicated to fire managers," declared John Mumma, the regional forester at a Wilderness/Parks Fire Conference at Bozeman, in late May 1989. "While fire managers must be involved, wilderness management objectives should dictate the nature of the fire use program and not vice versa." This makes sense, and I hope that management with public input will "ask very hard questions and be quite conservative" in behalf of wilderness.

A GROWING WORLD MOVEMENT

In June 1993, British Columbia established the new Tatshenshini-Alsek Wilderness Provincial Park, covering 2,367,218 acres, a vast area larger than Yellowstone. It connects with both Glacier Bay National Park in the United States and Canada's Kluane National Park, which, in turn, adjoins Wrangell-St. Elias National Park (in the U.S.) for a total of 24,278,386 acres. These parks now are administered cooperatively as a world wilderness reserve—the largest on earth—a complex of tundra, glaciers, and massive mountains, a stronghold of grizzly bears, wolves, caribou, and other wilderness-dependent species.

The momentum to save the wild places has grown steadily in the past thirty years, and so has the cooperation among countries, professionals, and citizen groups. The timing is none too soon. In Canada, for instance, the decision to safeguard the "Tat-Alsek" was made in response to a proposal for a huge open-pit copper mine, with likely serious effects on wildlife, fisheries, water quality, wilderness, and recreation. Such is the universal challenge.

"Wilderness" is a word the world is learning. It evokes different definitions and different approaches, but universally responds to a public desire to see nature prevail and see it protected. In *Highland Wilderness*, published in 1993 (Constable, London), Magnus Linklater, writes of the challenge of preserving the Scottish Highlands, "the last great unexploited lung of Europe." Based on his readings of Thoreau and Muir (who was born in Dunbar, in East Lothian), Linklater warns, "We cannot simply stand back and allow these wild places to be eroded, whether by commercial exploitation, by pollution, by uncontrolled tourism or by simple neglect. Conserving that 'heroic sense of beauty and subtlety in nature' has become a vital cause in an age where everywhere the environment is threatened."

The Scots until now have been slow to adopt meaningful conservation measures. Even when national parks were established in England and Wales during the 1950s, similar proposals for Scotland were blocked by large landholders with political clout. This has only spurred the nonprofit organization Trees for Life in its campaign to link some of the isolated forest remnants and thereby restore natural tree cover to a contiguous area of six hundred square miles in the northwest Highlands. This remote area, according to Alan Watson

Featherstone, executive director of Trees for Life, provides one of the best opportunities for re-creating a true wilderness in Britain—a daring and commendable concept.

In Africa, wilderness designation and nature conservation have been regarded as concepts of the white minority in a land mostly black, but a report in the *International Journal of Wilderness* (December 1996) shows this changing, with notable community-based projects, as evidenced at a June 1996 symposium in Namibia on wilderness designation and management. The nearly one hundred participants were mostly Namibian, but also included representatives of seven other countries. Though their emphasis was on wilderness in existing parks, they also considered inventorying potential additional areas in coordination with local communities.

South Africa has already set areas aside and built a wilderness movement, due largely to the efforts and influence of Ian Player. As a young ranger in the 1950s, patrolling game reserves in southern Africa, he became involved in conservation of the white rhinoceros. This led him to study the American wilderness concept. Player found inspiration in the American precedent and concluded that Africa, too, needed wilderness if its game reserves and parks were to survive. He and others developed the Wilderness Leadership School, dedicated to leading visitors on "foot trails" or walking excursions through wild areas of southern Africa. "I was convinced," he wrote in *The White Rhino Saga,* "that by getting visitors out on foot into the reserve we would make far more friends for conservation. Tourists in cars never properly understood or appreciated a game reserve."

That is one approach. Some nations, like New Zealand, have designated areas within their parks and preserves as "wilderness zones," reserving them for scientific research or for primitive recreation. The Nature Conservation Law of Japan classifies regions in their virgin state as wilderness, with all human activity prohibited except for academic research. One of the major challenges across the planet is to deal with indigenous peoples and their traditional cultures which they have developed from living in the wild, to see *them* as valuable to humanity as the environments they steward, without portfolio, and to save wilderness with their participation.

Such ideas were scarcely thought of when the Wilderness Act was passed, but they are thought of now. In the Amazon Basin, native peoples and environmental activists work together, as they sometimes do in North America, too. The organization Cultural Survival, headquartered at Cambridge, Massachusetts, continually brings the human dimension into the equation. "Preservation" to native peoples means perpetuation of living cultural conditions—beliefs, lifeways, languages, ceremonies—as well as places and properties associated with them. They want to be part of a modern world, while kindling and rekindling Earth-based tradition. It makes sense.

Recognition that ecology is as much a global issue as economics, communications, or human liberty has come slowly. But now the world sees that acid precipitation is carried by the winds, that oil spills cause grave damage to the common heritage of bird and marine life, and that ideas that work are meant to be shared. Considering that corporations have long reached across borders for raw materials, labor, and markets, it is fitting to strengthen the understanding of wilderness and to seek common action. The World Wilderness Congress has convened five times, with the sixth scheduled for Bangalore, India, in October 1998.

WINNING FRIENDSHIP AND UNDERSTANDING

Howard Zahniser and the other citizen leaders of thirty-plus years ago left a monumental legacy, and a dream to fulfill. I was privileged to know many of those pioneers who have gone to their reward, Zahnie, Harvey Broome, Charlie Callison, Art Carhart, William O. Douglas, Benton MacKaye, Olaus and Adolph Murie, Michael Nadel, Sigurd Olson, and Benton Stong, all imbued with principle and purpose. They and others I wish I'd known were patriots, demonstrating that wilderness preservation is Americanism, just as wilderness is America, the vestigial symbol of the original America as God made it. No, I haven't mention women here, but I've known them too, including Polly Dyer, Celia Hunter, Margaret Murie, and Liane Russell, all still alive, and Louisa Wilcox, younger than the rest, and one of the new generation of leaders.

Wilderness makes statesmen and stateswomen out of politicians. It enables them to fulfill their dreams and patriotic rhetoric, to show that wilderness documents human history and democratic government. President Theodore Roosevelt in 1903, after spending three days in Yosemite with John Muir, delivered a speech at Stanford University, demonstrating his deep interest in preserving both the giant sequoias of the Sierra Nevada and the coastal redwoods:

I feel most emphatically that we should not turn into shingles a tree which was old when the first Egyptian conqueror penetrated to the valley of the Euphrates, which it has taken so many thousands of years to build up, and which can be put to better use. That, you may say, is not looking at the matter from the practical standpoint. There is nothing more practical than the preservation of beauty, than the preservation of anything that appeals to the higher emotions of mankind.

Roosevelt's successor, William Howard Taft, in a special message to Congress in 1912 recommending the establishment of a new agency, the National Park Service, declared the legislation essential to the proper management of those wonderful manifestations of nature, "so startling and so beautiful that everyone recognizes the obligations of the government to preserve them for the edification and recreation of the people." In more recent times, Senator Clinton Anderson, of New Mexico, at the dedication of the Aldo Leopold Memorial north of Silver City in 1954, spoke of his friendship with the wilderness pioneer and how Leopold had made him a believer:

It was the true wilderness that attracted him—the places where he could go and be alone, the spots in the White Mountains of Arizona or in the forests of New Mexico where a man could lose himself in his surroundings and be dropped into complete comradeship with nature. I talked to Aldo Leopold many times about the development of a wilderness area. We now become trustees of his inheritance. Those of us who visit within the wilderness have an obligation to see that the work of one generation shall not be sacrificed by those that come after. We have an obligation to make sure that this area may remain untouched for generations and perhaps centuries to come.

Senator Richard Neuberger, of Oregon, was a man I much admired as a journalist who made it in politics and maintained his integrity. His finest hours, in my book, came as co-sponsor, with Senator Hubert Humphrey, of Minnesota, of the Wilderness Bill. At the first committee hearings in 1957, Neuberger spoke eloquently, tolling the bell at "the eleventh hour" for saving the nation's wilderness heritage. He told of the great forests of the Northwest. "If only such magnificent trees might endure forever," he said. "But are we letting commercialism and exploitation rob us of our chance for unfettered enjoyment under the blue heavens and the stars?" Then he added,

Public life often can be a sort of prison, so my visits to these beautiful places are rare. Yet it reassures me to know that they continue to exist—that, somewhere, the sparkling Lochsa foams toward the sea with the same lilting resonance over the same mossy rocks as when Captain Meriwether Lewis called it Kooskooskee, the river which flows fast and clear.

I know that millions of Americans feel likewise. They gain both security and comfort from the fact that a segment of the old original wilderness has been saved. The whole continent has not yet been tilled, paved, or settled. Some of these people may never see the real wilderness; their sentiments are purely vicarious. But they are aware of it nevertheless—just as Mount Everest and K-2 inspire pride among people in remote parts of India.

My friend, John P. Saylor, of Pennsylvania, who died in 1973 after almost a quarter century in Congress, was a principal sponsor of the Wilderness Act and a champion of wilderness throughout his career. He was a towering figure with indomitable will, and highly respected by his colleagues. I recall that he phoned me from his sickbed at Bethesda Naval Hospital asking that I help prepare a statement denouncing the killing of eagles in the West—that was his way. When he died, Joe Skubitz, an influential Republican from Kansas, took up the cudgel for one of Saylor's favorite campaigns: legislation to protect the vista of the Potomac from George Washington's home at Mount Vernon. "We must do this for John," Skubitz pledged and pleaded, though he himself was generally negative on environmental issues.

John Saylor left his mark alongside Theodore Roosevelt and Gifford Pinchot as Republicans who blazed conservation trails. Yet he was not "liberal" or "progressive," whatever those words may mean, in all things. He received the John Muir Medal from the Sierra Club, but also the distinguished service award from the ultraconservative Americans for Constitutional Action. He was never divisive or destructive, never impugned the motive nor questioned the loyalty of those who disagreed with him. He demonstrated that conservation advocacy belongs to no party and to no single point of view.

If I were to give advice to wilderness activists, I would say, "Believe in the system and see only potential allies." That was Zahniser's way, though it wasn't easy. In the long, arduous campaign for the Wilderness Act, he never let go of the dream and, despite all odds and opposition, never saw enemies.

Martin Luther King was that way, too, in his Principles of Nonviolence: Hang tough in what you believe, he said, but work to win friendship and understanding. Choose friendship instead of hate. Gather information, then use grace and humor to educate and transform and find the reconciliation that leads to universal justice.

Believe the universe is on the side of justice. Stay centered. Study history, learn from previous wilderness campaigns. Set an example for others of commitment and caring, free of vanity, concerned with purpose rather than perks. Those willing to sacrifice most never do it for salaries; yet crusades for social issues, whatever they may be, show how people—at times a very few—can and do bring needed change.

So always trade in hope, never in despair. Stick to issues without getting involved in personalities. Be patient, working for the long haul; no matter what happens, it's not the end of the world. Get outdoors in the wilderness and get some fun out of it, never too busy for laughter, love, sand pebbles, snowflakes, and sunbeams.

There's something else important to work on. In the Winter 1996 issue of *Race, Poverty & The Environment* (published under auspices of Earth Island Institute and California Rural Legal Assistance Foundation), Jacqueline Denise Ruffin wrote with deep feeling about "The Terrain of Exclusion." The exclusion didn't come from wilderness, but from the company with which she had gone to experience a backpack trip in wilderness conducted through the University of California Extension.

She had taken a quarter off from college to work and save money for the trip, but once underway she felt, "as the only person of color and as the only person from a lower-income background, no one really understood the relationship between social injustice and common notions of environmentalism." The longer the trip went on the worse things became. She felt alienated: "For all the incredible experience I had on that trip, some of them absolutely sacred, I still feel angered by the fact that we met with all sorts of government officials, but not a single representative from any of the tribes whose land we were living in for almost six weeks." When she returned to school in the fall, she found her environmental studies program even more alienating, frustrating, and disappointing.

I can understand. Higher education can be a frustrating terrain of exclusion, but I like to believe that wilderness breaks down artificial barriers between people bred to believe they are different from each other by reason of class, color, race, or gender. Jacqueline's article is a reminder of an elitism of a white middle/upper class movement that needs to be recognized and dealt with by activists.

We have allowed ourselves to be separated and compartmentalized—into rich and poor; young and old; men and women; physically and mentally able and differently able; over-schooled and under-schooled; black, white, red, yellow; Christian, Jew, Muslim, Buddhist, Hindu—finding in caste, class, and color the illusion of protection from others who are different. Aldo Leopold talked of the need of a land ethic, a code governing interactions with the environment. The same ethics ought to govern the behavior of people toward people. I like to think of the spiritual dimensions of the natural world that bring people together to recognize difference of appearance but unity of source.

Perhaps the best of all messages is that to heal the earth is to heal the soul. Such recognition empowers individuals to face the world with hope and heart. Perhaps Jacqueline will go again and find herself and others of color in the terrain of inclusion.

Working for wilderness makes for a great life. I can attest that it has been for me and has made me a better person. I remember listening to Sigurd Olson when he accepted the John Muir Award at the 1967 Sierra Club Wilderness Conference in San Francisco. He was a handsome, heroic figure, a teacher and outdoors guide who began his writing career at the age of fifty. In later years he was afflicted with a debilitating palsy tremble, but when he rose to speak he set aside the physical disability. He said,

The stakes are so high, the threat so desperate, we can no longer think of wilderness as being a minority need, a need of two percent of the population. I feel that wilderness is the concern of all Americans and all humanity, that if we do not save some wilderness mankind and his spirit will suffer, and life will not be so happy for future generations.

My only suggestion to this conference is to consider, as wilderness battlers, ways and means not for reaching each other—we are converted—but reaching the other 98 percent of the people. Make the wilderness so important, so understandable, so clearly seen as vital to human happiness that it cannot be relegated to an insubstantial minority. If it affects everyone—and I believe it does—then we must find out how to tell the world why it affects everyone. Only when we put wilderness on that broad base will we have a good chance of saving it.

His words seemed meant for me, like a mandate to go forth and spread the word, to continue the battle for wilderness. There is still plenty of work ahead. Whatever the future may hold, the wilderness ideal and wilderness cause free the spirit, displacing cynicism and despair with promise and hope.

Battle for the Wilderness

Prologue

A Navigational Perspective

Night faded slowly. Stars dipped into the dark horizon that lay ahead to the west. Behind the aircraft, to the east, the sun splashed a touch of brightness, like an alpenglow, on a new day. Presently the colors of heaven covered a spectrum from pale white through pink and soft blue to the lingering nocturnal black. As a people, we are conditioned from infancy to bathe in light and shun the dark, but one cannot be lonesome, as John Muir once said, when everything is wild and beautiful and busy and steeped with God.

If this be true in the world Muir knew best, of mountains, forests, meadows, and glaciers, how much more it applies to the seas. For there is a logical connection between all things in the immense connected body of salty water that covers more than two-thirds of the earth's surface, a grand pattern embracing all the storms and calms, the deeps and shallows, the animals, plants, and birds, and the humankind traveling the surface and the skies above and living on the shores of all the oceans.

Volcanoes and undersea earthquakes disturb the water to the farthest drop on the other side of the world. Each small particle in the entire ocean, even in the deepest part, feels the pull created by the sun and moon. So does each little particle on the land, but the water responds by moving in ebb and flow, joyous, unfettered and free, in the cyclic movements of the universe. Always the waters are in motion, beneath the birds, ships, and planes, keyed to the rolling and lifting of the waves.

In the navigator's compartment, located behind the copilot, I contemplated my own small role. It was early 1944, when planes were slower and navigation a painstaking personalized effort. I had been doing a lot of flying that year over distant watery wildernesses, including the Amazonian equatorial trough, where massive clouds rise to carry moisture outward to other portions of the world, and the high latitudes of Greenland, where glaciers break into icebergs that sail majestically southward to their doom. I had been exposed to weather in many moods. I had seen it display violence, even while providing a balancing effect, a regeneration, to the earth's atmosphere (as in the case of hurricanes that bring rain to the tropics and shift heat to warm the temperate zones).

I had landed at far-flung islands of the Pacific that had been pre-empted by Japanese and American military forces and had seen coral atoll life communities, patiently developed by natural processes over thousands of years, abruptly disrupted and obliterated. It was over the Pacific that my crewmates and I now flew onward through the fullness of the natural night. I had two lights to work with, one bright and one very small to illuminate only the desk itself whenever I was engaged in shooting the stars, while the rest of the cabin remained in darkness. During the long night I had stood in the astrodome to shoot celestial fixes, had plotted them on my chart, and calculated the wind vector and actual speed of the plane. I had watched and marveled at the thin pencil line representing our intended course as it became crossed with other lines that revealed our location on the face of the earth. I wondered at my perception of wilderness horizons of the universe through the artificial bubble of an octant and at my ability to transpose the infinite of celestial distances into the practical finite of the plotting table. This was possible because of celestial mechanics, one of the greatest achievements of the human intellect, the combined work of astronomers and mathematicians, of Kepler, Galileo, Laplace, Newton, and Simon Newcomb. Here, clearly, was a rendezvous of nature and technology, where one served the other without conflict.

But I learned the heavenly bodies are fundamental. The stars never lie. There is no substitute for the natural essence. I daresay each one of us somehow absorbs this lesson in the course of his life. Thor Heyerdahl did so when he took the *Kon-Tiki* across the South Pacific. People told him that old raft sailors had used hempen ropes only because they had nothing better. "Hemp might rotten or slacken," he was told. "To be absolutely safe, wire is the thing." But when he and his colleagues got out at sea and the raft was moving up and down, especially during the storms, all the pressure was taken by the ropes. In their creaking and groaning, chafing, and squeaking, the ropes furnished an underlying natural music to everything on board. Every morning the crew examined the ropes, tightening them. And the ropes held. Had Heyerdahl listened and lashed the logs with wire, in no time the movements of the logs would have cut the soft balsa wood to pieces.

As night wore on aboard our little plane and the canopy of the heavens changed, I felt navigation had brought me close to them, that I could sense the harmonious pattern of the universe, of time beyond time and space beyond space joined as one. The celestial navigator can expand the dimensions of his experience, can free himself of the containment of the moment, can become part of the continuum of history. This the ancients knew instinctively; being close to the source of existence, they felt the rhythms and cycles that bind the hours of human life with the centuries of time and with the stars and seas and all living things. Certainly, men have eternally sought their individual places in the universe, but most wander for the entire span of their existence, finding release only in their dreams. Can it be because they fail to follow the lead of the high stars to the sanctuary of creation, which we now recognize and define as wilderness?

We landed at Kwajalein, a small place, girdled by the sea and scarcely known in the world beyond. At dusk, after a day's rest, the pilot and I strolled along the beach. The western ocean breeze cooled the air of the Marshall Islands, although most of the palm trees had disappeared as victims of the war. Other Micronesian islands had been hit worse, suffering heavier bombing in World War II than any part of Europe or Asia. These atolls are the home of a peaceful people highly adapted to an oceanic environment. Their most serious disasters had been thrust upon them by technologically advanced nations. Presently we encountered a Marshall Islander fishing with a net. He was bronze-skinned, well built, wading in the surf. He smiled with friendly eyes, openly, and free of guile, then as we watched, cast gracefully several times until he caught a fish and brought it in patiently. The net has been unchanged for 3,000 years, since man began to tap the wealth of rivers, lakes, and seas, and this fellow was proving that it remains a valid tool. He might also have been saying to us with his honest smile: "Our wilderness waters are rich, unpolluted, with ample oxygen to support marine life. We have not undermined our resources. Therefore, have you come to teach or to learn?"

During those years of World War II we traveled in the shallow layers of space, finding guidance from stars and planets, with coordination provided by the almanacs and precomputed tables. Then equipment became more sophisticated, utilizing radar and navigational computers.

In 1973 I crossed the Atlantic Ocean aboard a Boeing 747 jumbo jet, the largest type of passenger plane yet built. For all its size I marveled at its gracefulness and comfort. During the course of the journey I visited the flight deck. The speed of the plane was more than 600 knots, three times faster than the speed of the transport planes I had known thirty years before. There was no navigator. The pilot and his crew demonstrated the computer in action. By pressing the proper buttons they received instantaneous reports on the wind vector and actual speed in flight and advice on the correct heading to follow. It impressed me as an extremely efficient system, geared to the accelerated speed of the age. But these men had been trained in the operation of mechanical instruments, rather than in astronomy or celestial dynamics. They were insulated from the universe.

Man's flight to the moon now represents the high point of technological progress. Nevertheless, I think of voyages to outer space in comparison to those of the early Pacific circumnavigators across thousands of miles of unknown waters and uncharted currents in wooden vessels made by their own hands, without compass or chronometer. Was their wilderness crossing any less monumental or daring than going to the moon? The astronauts looked down on a canopy, a layer of smog enveloping the world, created by emissions from the smokestacks of all the factories on earth and from the exhaust of all the cars, buses, and trucks. And with each trip the canopy grew thicker and wider. The primitives saw only a clean world and clear skies, and so they left them.

The whole world has been altered immensely by the discoveries of science and the practical applications of technology. Whatever problems the generator devises the computer is expected to resolve or vice versa. The work done by scientists such as Max Planck, Wilhelm Roentgen, and Albert Einstein has led this century of men to believe the ultimate units of our world are not rocks, caves, bears, and the like, as man had thought before, but quanta, atoms, atomic nuclei, electrons, and electromagnetic radiation. Yet even at this critical point in time a lesson appears to be imminent: We have always been governed, and continue to be governed, by the natural laws that controlled the lives of primitive peoples and that still control the lives of wild animals and plants. We are learning of the earth as a planet richly endowed with life, so complex we shall never understand it fully or run out of problems worthy of study. It's a new kind of science, a sense of being. It reveals the need to replenish air and water, to maintain the soil nutrient cycles basic to food production, and to recognize that, despite the ingenuity of automation and electronics, when the generator fails, man must revert to the day-and-night cycle.

We have been hurtling through space at breakneck speed but without a navigational perspective. Was man destined to zoom like a skyrocket into a wild, glorious, and brief existence? High population and expanding technology are contributing to the rapid depletion of nonrenewable resources, such as petroleum, coal, and the fossil fuels, and are rendering renewable resources, such as soil and forests, nonrenewable. The second law of thermodynamics, the saddest law of the universe, states that eventually the earth will die. It proves that wherever free energy is converted into work or heat a certain amount is irretrievably lost, no matter how perfect the conversion system. Man can perpetuate his species within the sad confines of this law for several million years. Or he can squander his irreplaceable energy reserves, as we have been doing, and shorten the survival time to a few hundred years, possibly less.

The new awareness—a recognition that a generation or nation or a whole society of nations cannot be the owners of the globe but only its trustees in behalf of succeeding generations—may still save us. This is the navigational imperative for the journey through time and the universe. We can't all reach outward to touch the moon, at least not yet, but we can reach inward to touch and appreciate and to protect the wonders of our own earth.

Part I

WILDERNESS VALUES

Chapter One

What Is Wilderness?

Wilderness has been defined by law as a specific type of untrammeled place, "where man is a visitor who does not remain." It sounds simple on the face of it. The law, however, serves only as a starting point for determining—or discovering—what wilderness really is, what it does, and whom it serves.

A football field is endowed with clearer dimensions. The playing portion is 100 yards long and 30 yards wide. The goal posts at both ends are precisely the same height and width. A basketball court also is fixed by prescribed measurements. It is rectangular, with identical raised baskets at each end, and is always played with a round inflated ball approximately thirty inches in circumference. Golf courses vary in size and shape, but the goal is consistently demonstrable: to hit the small white ball into a succession of holes, usually nine or eighteen, in the lowest number of strokes.

Wilderness is controlled by no such rules or evident objectives. It is more than a place, but equally an idea, a principle, a state of mind, even a dream. While the state of wilderness exists in the mind, it does so only to the degree it exists somewhere on the ground. It becomes worthy of description as wilderness because of its character, not because of any particular purpose it serves. Once it retains that character, however, it serves many purposes.

The principles of wilderness are based on the completeness of all life, rather than on the dominion of man alone. The principles are not new or restricted to science but extend to the artistic, ethical, spiritual, or religious, as well. They are predicated on the unified concept of land, community, and universe and relate the experience of mankind to a universe that is alive and not dead. The man who believes in wilderness doesn't lose sight of concrete objects but sees them in the totality of the world, which is loved for its own sake.

Some think of wilderness as being essentially a large area, ranging from 5,000 acres upward to a million acres or more, where one can get away from all evidence of civilization for a few hours or, even better, for days or weeks, without crossing trails with another soul. The large areas are desirable, but wilderness embraces a sample of the primitive in any degree. It may be as small as one's backyard or a clump of wild plants and grass that provide a feel for the original landscape. Even the sight, sound, or smell of a miniwilderness furnishes a tranquilizing and enriching interval, a subconscious reminder of man's rootstocks in nature.

Others insist that wilderness must be restricted by standards of purity to utterly primeval lands looking exactly as they did before man evolved from the apes. In this age of fallout there are no places left on the earth free of human disturbance, not even at the polar icecaps, but this need not be the basic criterion. Wilderness is where man's sounds, chemicals, and other by-products of civilized life are not dominant. It can be any area where nature prevails or might prevail given the passage of time. It can be any place, of any size, so long as active ecological succession, structural diversity, and naturalness are permitted.

Wilderness is a part of man's civilization. It is a civilizing force. Wilderness gives America the quality of spaciousness, the touch of frontier and far horizons that are rooted in the national conscience. It provides new generations a link with the adventure and history of old generations, something firm to hold on to while plunging through the onrushing uncertainties of time. Wilderness preserves in living form the tableaus memorialized by artists and poets, so that just as their works are part of the cultural heritage, so the sources remain to serve new artists and poets.

Wilderness is the antidote to an overurbanized, supertechnological age. Man has proved himself resilient, capable of adapting to smoky skies, polluted streams, crowded and noisy cities, but his adaptive potential is not unlimited. Little wonder that we are filling hospitals, mental institutions, clinics, prisons, and cemeteries with the fruit of terrible divorcement from a native environment. Modern man, after all, retains inherent biological characteristics of his ancestors, just as the long-domesticated dog retains characteristics of his wild forebear, the wolf. The human foot hasn't changed much since the paths men trod were grassy slopes, woodland trails, and spongy bog hummocks. The same set of genes governs emotional development, drives, and needs as when he was a Paleolithic hunter or Neolithic farmer. Wilderness furnishes diversity and stimulating experiences of the natural world for society to draw upon now that the material world has been seriously depleted of its resources.

Wilderness is a recreational resource affording the enjoyment of hardy outdoor sports—canoeing, hiking, climbing, riding, hunting, and fishing. It combines the thrills of jeopardy and beauty, an adventure into the physically unknown that has always constituted a major factor in the happiness of curious souls. The wilderness hunter, learning the habits of animals and meeting the prey on its own ground, appreciates the stillness, physical exercise, woodlore, the pride in roughing it, the kill that comes hard, rather than easy. The fisherman, rather than being concerned with the catch itself, focuses on the challenge; even when fish are few and scattered, he finds rewards in the setting and in his feeling of harmony with the flows of weather, wind, and water.

Wilderness is the chorus of thrushes, the thunder of waterfalls, the mist rising from a mountain meadow at twilight, the ancient voices riding the breezes of night enveloping the dark air. It is the chance to wade in marshes where, as Thoreau wrote, the bittern and meadow hen lurk, to hear the whistling of the snipe, to smell the whispering sedge where only some wilder and more solitary fowl builds her nest. It is the intimate contemplation of Darwin's tangled bank, heavily clothed with plants of many kinds, with birds singing in the bushes, with various insects flitting about, and with worms crawling through the damp earth, and the reflection that these elaborately constructed forms, so different from each other and dependent upon each other in so complex a manner, have all been produced by natural laws acting around us.

Wilderness is an oak forest furnishing acorns, leaves, twigs, bark, flowers, and buds to support bears, squirrels, white-footed mice, wood rats, wild turkeys, titmice, nuthatches, crows, doves, and owls. It is a mosaic, in which the reality of death needs no apology, where natural death advances through history as the nourishing helpmate of birth and blossom. Within the mosaic the observer finds beauty in the fallen tree feeding organisms of decomposition, such as fungi, bacteria, and myriad forms of animal life, and serving as the seedbed and nursery for new trees and flowering plants.

Wilderness is found in every type of terrain where a life community is found—forest, prairie, desert, tundra, rock and ice, marsh, in underground caverns, at the edge of the sea, and beneath that watery surface—with each community demonstrating its distinctive lessons in adaptation and function.

Wilderness is wherever it may stimulate curiosity over the natural cycle, even in an undeveloped fragment of a great city where one may watch the grace of a fluttering butterfly, the red and black of a milkweed beetle, or the shimmering back of a slow-moving slug.

Wilderness is an exercise in solitude, in which the individual achieves freedom from his own problems, but it also provides the opportunity for companionship with others, sharing joys and hardships, learning the meaning of comradeship, humility, and open dialogue among men and women. It builds partnerships through revelations of common origin and common destiny.

Wilderness is a humanitarian resource, the basis of a more healthy social structure, a banner of hope to the ghetto dweller deprived of human dignity and boxed in by crowds, noise, litter, and concrete. How can human life be valued highly in a society shaped by destruction, despoliation, degradation, and exploitation of man by man? Wilderness is the alternative to waste and dissent that characterize modern society. It restores belief in the environment, each other, and ourselves.

Wilderness is a spiritual sanctuary that opens to the search for a moral world. Even today religious leaders of the American Indians spend weeks on a high mountain or in the woods in contemplation of wilderness mythology so their feet may walk in the tracks of the Mountain Spirit. Leaders in many religions have sought a similar sanctuary. On one occasion Jesus Christ spent forty days in the wilderness, where he had been led by the Holy Spirit. On another, he and three disciples undertook to visit a high mountain, probably Mount Hermon, on the northern boundary of Palestine. It was a deliberately planned experience in the expectation of rising above hazards and finding unlimited good. They sought no short cuts and doubtless would have spurned any offer of one. They felt they had found their reward when Jesus was transfigured.*

Wilderness is a place for men, but not for men alone. A river is accorded its right to exist because it is a river, rather than for any utilitarian service. The American tradition has sought only the transformation of resources; wilderness recalls a fundamental and older tradition of relationship with resources themselves. This generation could clean up the Columbia River or the Hudson River. But without understanding the true role of the river, as a living symbol of all the life it sustains and nourishes, and our responsibility to it, we would merely be balancing the cost benefits of using the river one way against the cost benefits of using it another.

Wilderness is for the bald eagle, condor, and ivory-billed woodpecker, for birds that nest in the tops of old trees or in the rotted holes in tree trunks and that need dead or dying logs to house the grubs and other insects they feed on. Wilderness is the sanctuary of grizzly bears, mountain lions, bighorn sheep, elk, and wolves that need large areas set aside from civilization.

Wilderness is a learning laboratory, a classroom in biology, botany, and natural wonders, with examples and lessons on the

---

* The Bible mentions wilderness nearly 300 times and in many cases considered wilderness to be vast and uninhabited. Its earliest appearance in the Old Testament is the mention of the Sinai Peninsula, where Moses led the wandering Israelites for forty years. However, the Psalms, Job, Isaiah, and the lyrical passages in the discourses of Moses show remarkable empathy with nature.

the relationship of living things to their environment. It answers the needs of the sciences for undisturbed and recovering areas in which to conduct base-line studies concerning human influences on the earth and to determine the best ways of managing resources.

Wilderness is one of the incomparable freedoms, like freedom from want, war, and racial prejudice and the freedom to cultivate one's own thoughts in one's own way. Wilderness brings stability, a sense of permanence, to a shaky, unstable world.

Chapter Two

An American Happening

The Rose Garden of the White House was a fitting natural setting for President Lyndon B. Johnson to sign the Wilderness Act on September 3, 1964. On that day the United States became the first country in the long record of civilization to proclaim through law a recognition of wilderness in its way of life, as part of its culture and its legacy to the future.

The struggle had been long. Fruition came after eight years of discussion and debate by the U.S. Senate and House of Representatives and after eighteen separate public hearings conducted by congressional committees in Washington and other cities. The bill had been written and rewritten time and again, it had been passed in the Senate, then bottled up in the House. It had been aggressively fought by the timber industry and by the oil, grazing, and mining industries, all insisting that resources are meant to be "used," rather than merely admired. Two of the federal agencies principally involved, the National Park Service and Forest Service, had opposed the Act, too, when it was initially introduced. The public may own the land, but administrators prefer to exercise their own prerogatives without submitting their expertise to challenge or sharing their decision-making on either technical or policy questions.

The Act was passed, nevertheless, establishing both a definition of wilderness in law and a National Wilderness Preservation System in fact. The very effort surrounding passage may make the law more impressive as a statement of national philosophy than as a formula or compendium of rules and regulations, for it plainly evoked the feeling of countless individuals throughout the country—and likely throughout the world—who would speak for wilderness if given the chance and would say that natural islands within our expanding civilization are essential to the spirit of man.

The idea of protecting wilderness is not new in itself. In Europe kings and princes for centuries held the forests as a source of game for sport and food. Henry David Thoreau commented that sometimes they even destroyed villages to create or extend the natural domain. But those preserves were for the nobility alone. In America wilderness is protected as a common birthright.

"Why should not we, who have renounced the king's authority, have our national preserves," demanded Thoreau, "where no villages need be destroyed, in which the bear and the panther may still exist, and not be 'civilized off the face of the earth'— our own forests not to hold the king's game merely, but for inspiration and our own true recreation?" [1]

Thoreau foresaw man's need to reach out from the clatter of the mechanized age for a touch of the natural. He proposed that each community sustain a primitive forest of 500 or 1,000 acres. "Let us keep the New World *new*," he proposed, "and preserve all the advantages of living in the country." [2]

At the dawn of European settlement America was endowed with wilderness. As John Muir described it, the whole continent was a garden that seemed to be favored above all other wild parks and gardens of the globe. It was wilderness that dazzled the Europeans of culture and science when they thought about America. Seven Indian chieftains created a furor when they went to England in 1730, with painted faces and feathers in their hair, to present the king four scalps and five eagle tails and to pose for a portrait by William Hogarth. Peter Kalm, a pupil of Linnaeus, was among a number of botanists dispatched to collect flora from the New World and report on it. He found plants the like of which he had never seen before. "When I saw a tree, I was forced to stop and ask those who accompanied me how it was called," he wrote in his *Travels in North America*. "I was seized with terror at the thought of ranging so many new and unknown parts of natural history." *

As the New World became settled, open squares, greens, and "commons" were set aside for community purposes. In 1836 William Cullen Bryant began promoting the idea of a city park on a tremendous scale for New York. With the support of two noted landscape architects, Andrew Jackson Downing and Frederick Law Olmsted, Central Park ultimately was established in 1857. During the mid-1800s the groves of sequoia trees in California catapulted to world attention as a result of the stripping of one of the giant trees in the Calaveras Grove. At the behest of prominent Americans, Congress withdrew Yosemite Valley, in the heart of the big-tree country, from the public domain, generally open to settlement and private acquisition, and gave it to California as a state park, thus seeking to safeguard the big trees from commercial timber exploitation. President Abraham Lincoln signed the Yosemite Grant in 1864, the same year as the Emancipation Proclamation.

Then came the epochal establishment of Yellowstone National Park in 1872. Within five years after the end of the Civil War vast areas of the Middle West and Pacific West had been colonized. Pioneers were exploring unknown country, bringing with them the morals, values, and institutions of an older society, and thus devouring land for both settlement and exploitation. Yet on the raw, fast-developing frontier the concept of a national park was born. The bill to establish Yellowstone succeeded after one of the most formidable, public-interest lobbying campaigns in history—the same kind that swept through the Wilderness Act almost a century later. President Ulysses S. Grant signed the Act into law on March 1, 1872, thus placing a large parcel of the public domain under protection of the federal

* Linnaeus gave his student's name to the American mountain laurels, known as the *Kalmias*. Another important botanical explorer was the Frenchman André Michaux, who, with his son, spent ten years collecting specimens from Hudson Bay to Florida. In 1794 Michaux scaled the summit of Grandfather Mountain in North Carolina and believed he had scaled the highest peak in North America. In exultation he serenaded the skies with "La Marseillaise" and then proclaimed "Long live America and the French Republic. Long live liberty!"

government to be "reserved and withdrawn from settlement, occupancy or sale." It was a revolutionary idea, the beginning of a systematic effort to preserve natural treasures.

As recently as 1901 John Muir, champion of Yosemite and pioneer of the modern preservation movement, commented, with a measure of satisfaction, "When, like a merchant taking a list of his goods, we take stock of our wilderness, we are glad to see how much of even the most destructible kind is still unspoiled." [3] In the ensuing years, however, industrial growth far outpaced preservation. The greater the development of natural resources, the greater the public welfare—such was the prevalent view. The smokestack succeeded the pioneer's axe as a national symbol. If there were constantly more people to be supplied, it was presumed that bigger markets and more capital would follow, and so would research and development and endless new mechanical marvels. Allowing a resource to remain as it had been for millions of years was considered antisocial.

As a consequence many valuable resources were disastrously depleted. Wilderness became a prime victim. In 1926 the Forest Service made a survey of roadless units. Based on a minimum of 230,400 acres to each, it found seventy-four such units totaling 55 million acres.

The greatest depletion has come since then.

By the early 1960s Americans were startled to find how little of even the most indestructible kind of wilderness was still unspoiled. A survey conducted in 1961 by the University of California Wildland Research Center as an independent review commissioned by the Outdoor Recreation Resources Review Commission, a Presidential agency, showed that the larger areas had become scarce, so the sum of 100,000 acres was now predetermined as the minimum size for a wilderness to be considered. That acreage was believed to convey an adequately strong impression of undisturbed vastness and to provide an opportunity for maintaining relatively undisturbed biological conditions and ecological interaction. Smaller areas were recognized as "quasi-wilderness" but were not included in the study.

Where the largest roadless unit of 1926 covered 7 million acres, in 1961 it was about 2 million acres. The number of units

230,400 acres or larger in size had dropped from seventy-four to nineteen, and the total area from 55 million acres to 17 million acres. The report found sixty-four separate areas in national parks and national forests with over 100,000 acres each, containing a total of 28 million acres—about 1 per cent of the land area of the continental United States. If all the reserved quasi-wilderness areas down to 5,000 acres had been included, the total would have risen to 2 per cent, a far cry from the encouraging stock taken by Muir.

The report further determined that 19 million acres in fifty tracts were in reserved administrative areas, such as national parks and designated wilderness of the national forests. But only six of them were located in the eastern half of the country, while fully 90 per cent of the acreage was in the least populated regions of the West.

The protected wilderness existed more by accident than design. Most of its commercial resources, composed of lands by-passed in the rush of settlement and exploitation from east to west, were too poor to utilize or too costly to develop. About one-fourth of all acreage in reserved wilderness was composed of mountain peaks, desert, sand dunes, lava flows, and rock slides; about one-third was covered with brush or with scrubby and other nonproductive forests; another third was productive timberland, while a small percentage was meadow, grassland, or water surface. The timberlands contained 8 million acres of productive wood sources—only about 2 per cent of the nation's total, or a sufficient volume to supply national needs for two years.

The Wilderness Act came none too soon, serving as an emergency expression of self-restraint. But what has happened since passage of the Act in 1964? The expansion of civilization has continued in intensity across the continent. Golden Gate in San Francisco, Central Park in New York, Overton Park in Memphis, and a thousand other last touches of urban open spaces and wilderness are being filled, or threatened, with academies of science, galleries of art, skating rinks, solid waste disposal, and freeways. Many overdeveloped, congested suburbs were uninhabited wilderness or farmland only a few years ago; unoccupied lands are being devoured, month by month, day by day, without plan or restraint. The orange groves have virtually disappeared in Southern California, and the golden glow of poppies on the hillsides above them. The beaches of the East Coast are subdivided from mid-Maine to the Florida Peninsula, and around Florida's entire periphery, except for the Everglades, only two or three small fragments remain undeveloped by private interests. So it goes everywhere.

The fate of the Indiana Dunes typifies the scene. As a wildland at the edge of Chicago, it became the center of pioneer study in ecology. It was a beauty spot with an immense diversity of flora, from prickly-pear cactus to white pine, where city florists once plucked 100,000 orchids at a time. Part of it has been made into a national lakeshore administered by the National Park Service, but the park is barely a shadow of its deserved size and twenty years too late. Steel mills have been allowed to be built in the middle of it and may still destroy it.

In California the once majestic redwood empire has been invaded by freeways, while trees are being cut at the rate of about 10,000 acres per year. Of the original national heritage of 2 million acres in virgin redwood, less than one century ago, only 75,000 acres are preserved, and less than 190,000 acres of old, first-growth redwood remain in private hands. A small national park has been established, but intensive logging around its edges threatens the park with erosion that would seriously scar the choicest section.

Crowds are everywhere in America, at airports, hotels, and libraries, at playgrounds and parks. There isn't room for people who want to live on the beach or to get to it. The cost of access to beach, stream, lakefront, and mountain slope is rising; so the common man is shut out of common pleasures.

Crowds are overpowering the wilderness, too. High-country trails and campsites are congested and beaten down. According to government forecasts, the volume of outdoor recreation will rise 300 per cent by the year 2000, but the volume of wilderness use by 1,000 per cent. For every camper who now pitches a tent at Great Smoky, there will be ten in less than thirty years; for every sandwich wrapper that settles into the swamps at Everglades and every bottle that blights the roadside at Rocky Mountain there will be ten, and for every foot that tramples the soil beneath the redwoods, ten. And use has been rising at a sharper rate than projected.

Where will all these hikers, campers, canoeists, hunters, and fishermen go? The wilderness resource is contracting rather than expanding. At the time the Act was passed, the seven largest reserved wilderness units in the continental United States, excluding Alaska, each covered nearly a million acres or more in size. These were

1. A combination of national park and national forest in the Sierra Nevada of California
2. Yellowstone–Grand Teton–South Absaroka locality in Wyoming, also a combination of national park and national forest
3. Wind River Range in Wyoming, combining national forest and Indian reservation
4. Idaho Primitive Area
5. Selway-Bitterroot Wilderness, in Idaho and Montana
6. Bob Marshall Wilderness in Montana
7. Everglades National Park in Florida

Today every one of these is threatened.

The case of the Everglades is probably the best known. For years the U.S. Army Corps of Engineers concentrated on turning marshes above the park into farmland and real estate through a series of dikes and canals that effectively deprived the Everglades of its fresh-water supply. During drought years the park was so parched that thousands of birds did not nest and disappeared. Mammals vanished, too, alligators died, and the dry saw grass burned furiously for weeks on end. Then came the beginnings of a superjet airport, where the biggest runways were to be six miles long, promising disaster for the park, until a nationwide protest brought construction to a halt. Even at its best, Everglades is threatened by the exploding metropolis around it. The other areas, no matter how firm their boundaries, are also in danger of losing their essential wilderness aspects with the intensive development of surrounding lands.

To have been absorbed for even a day or two in peacefulness and naturalness is to become painfully aware of the endangered quality of wilderness with each sign of advancing human impact. There are plenty of reasons for gloom and pessimism in modern society. The broad-scale destruction of the natural environment is one of them. "Today is the first time in man's history that he is able to truly enjoy life, free from cold, hunger and disease," according to Dr. Albert Szent-Györgi, the Hungarian-born Nobel laureate and discoverer of more than one of biology's secrets. "It is the first time that he is able to satisfy all his basic needs. Conversely it is also the first time in his history that man has the capability of exterminating himself in one blow or making his tragically shrinking, lovely little globe uninhabitable by pollution or overpopulation. One would expect that any idiot could make a wise choice between these two alternatives. . . . Yet man seems bent on choosing the latter." [4]

Perhaps he is right. Perhaps in the threatening conditions of the present world, overindustrialized Americans are motivated by a subconscious death wish. Perhaps the continued destruction of our remaining wilderness is a symptom of society's basic incompatibility with earth's environment. A people desiring self-destruction can hardly muster the steadfast purpose to restore and conserve natural resources, let alone their own spiritual values.

Still, I wonder.

One day I heard a more optimistic viewpoint. It was in the middle of Manhattan at the peak of the evening rush hour. I stepped into a taxicab and directed the driver to La Guardia Airport. At first he refused to go. The traffic, he said, was too heavy.

"I'm desperate to catch a plane, and I'll give you an extra dollar," I pleaded.

"Never mind," he relented with a laugh. "I'll never get rich in this business anyway. But isn't it a scream that I should turn down a fare to Kennedy Airport just one minute ago and now find myself heading for La Guardia?"

He was middle-aged and wore one of those old fashioned caps favored by taxi drivers. While traffic barely crawled, he told me he had been driving for thirty years. It was a warm day in May, still rather pleasant before the advent of summer, when oppressive humidity settles over New York and the city seems to strangle under its own sweat. We passed a jogger in athletic shorts doing his stint on Third Avenue, obviously determined to shape his personal environment. This led the driver to recount some of his contacts with nature and his interest in it.

First he recalled the time a police officer jumped into his cab and shouted, "Follow that llama!" "Follow that—that what?" the cabbie shouted back in complete astonishment. Apparently one of those woolly-haired South American ruminants had escaped from the Central Park Zoo and was wandering through the streets of west Manhattan. The driver was as confused as the animal, but his and another taxi, from the opposite direction, blocked the llama's path until a pair of zoo keepers could capture it.

"I watch all those programs about animals and faraway places," he said, shifting gears abruptly to television. "Wild Kingdom, Disneyland, Bold Venture—you name it. Wherever they go, I go right with them.

"Did you happen to see the one about the two Florida bobcats? There was this good bobcat and the bad one. And then . . . and then . . ." In the midst of crawling traffic he was transported into another setting, relating his odyssey to the finest detail of his memory so that we journeyed together through the Everglades wilderness. Then he switched to an adventure of fishing for white marlin in distant Central American waters, where the fisherman was forced to play his catch for two or three hours on the line before bringing it in, and from there to breathtaking vistas of Jacques-Yves Cousteau diving for giant frogs.

We turned to the subject of national parks. I asked him if he had traveled much or seen any of the parks.

"No, but I've read about Yellowstone. Whenever I think of Yellowstone, I think of the geysers spouting right out of the ground. I've never been farther from New York than up to Connecticut on Long Island Sound, but I like to read about all those places. Sometimes I go fishing in the sound with my brother-in-law. One time last summer we caught nothing all day. Then another time, I thought I had a real big one on the hook. I fought it hard. You know what I came up with? Seaweed!"

He was a good-humored fellow, who made the most of our trip to the airport. "I never expect to see any of those places," he concluded, "but I sure enjoy pictures about them. I love them all."

The cab driver didn't discuss any philosophical or ecological questions. I doubt that he had heard of the Wilderness Act. Still, the responsive instinct was plain. In the same sense concerned citizens in Seattle have expressed their anguish over the plight of alligators in the Deep South, New Yorkers over the endangered wolves in Minnesota. The controversies and battles over the Alaska pipeline, the North Cascades in Washington state, the Four Corners in the Southwest, the northern plains of Montana and the Dakotas, the Miami jetport, the Cross-Florida Barge Canal, the Joyce Kilmer Memorial Forest in North Carolina, the Sunfish Pond in the Kittatiny Range in New Jersey, the Storm King on the Hudson River in New York, and a thousand other struggles of varied dimensions and consequences demonstrate that people care and are willing to stand and declare themselves.

The very ability to establish a National Wilderness Preservation System represents an antidote to pessimism, a stimulus for hope. As long as the beauty and grandeur of primitive scenery are preserved, so must they have a powerful influence in shaping the character of people, enabling each to observe and respond in his own way. After all, the national (or local) wilderness does not merely hold the king's game but signifies an American birthright and bond.

Chapter Three

The Cultural Heritage in Wilderness

The close examination and contemplation of a rock prove to be a revealing exercise. The object has shape, form, composition, purpose, history, and beauty. It may be inanimate, but the rock is far from being inorganic. The primary source of all minerals is rock. Through complex relationships the mineral makeup of rock influences the chemical qualities of water. It influences the top layer of soil and eventually the mineral composition of plants and of animals feeding on those plants.

A study of rock demonstrates the validity of Thoreau's idea that the earth is not a mere fragment of dead history, stratum upon stratum like the leaves of a book, to be analyzed by geologists and antiquaries chiefly. The earth is living poetry, like the leaves of a tree, which precede flower and fruit—not a fossil earth, but a living earth. As such, the earth represents our greatest heritage, the primary source of culture and art.

The artist in nature conveys the impressions of his personal vital force, but he is not the creator of the landscape. The artist does not invent the place; through his own eyes, intuitions, and skills, he serves as the interpreter of an earthly scene or mood, whether of sunlight over a hilltop, hints of clouds, or the fissures in rock. All kinds of creative persons are forever seeking out the primeval as cultural resources to draw upon. As Emerson wrote, literature, poetry, and science all are homage of man to the unfathomed secrets of nature.

Art colonies are located in settings that provide access to the natural; so are writers' schools and retreats. An author may or may not draw upon the environment, but it benefits him as both stimulant and tranquilizer.

Cities on the site of vanished forests, by contrast, erect stone palaces to house operatic, symphonic, dramatic, and dance companies and christen them as cultural centers. One can find modern and progressive paintings in banks, corporate headquarters, and government buildings, with the effect that they become somewhat like museum pieces. Museums, art galleries, and theaters are indeed the manifestations of culture; they function as collection and display centers of man's work. But are they in some sense like the zoo that preserves a few specimens of wild game after the wild habitat has been obliterated?

The art in modern society is produced by special people designated as artists: it is peripheral to the goals of society itself. In primitive society, whether of past or present, art is a form of expression central to the lives of people. Reaching back to the earliest cultural traditions in America—long before the dawn of European settlement—the wandering hunters crossed the dry land passage of Beringia from Asia, advancing during extensive periods of time down the dry central plain of Alaska, south along the slopes of the raw young Rockies. Their movements were intimately related to the Pleistocene climatic swings: vast natural pulsations driving life south with icy winds, then drawing it north as cold and dampness were replaced by warmth and drought. Somewhere in the course of their migrations early rituals developed, including fasting to reflect the time of starvation and want in winter when game was scarce and the future problematical, dances, lustrations, new-fire-making, new moon feasts. Primitive art that ties the generations together was born.

The elements of life art as it evolved were language, song, dance, ceremonials, craftsmanship, ascetic discipline, fighting, and the chase. Human personality and the web of life were tended with passion and reverence that simply have neither recognition nor base of understanding in the established American epic. It is ironic that society has disregarded the literary and artistic potentials in these traditions. American culture has embraced the qualities of Greco-Roman mythology and literature, as well as those of Northern Europe, and has recognized the achievements of peoples of the Orient, yet has consistently failed to realize that American Indians have a major contribution to make in this sphere.*

The native American races developed distinctive arts and crafts from the materials of their regions. In Alaska the people created a panoply of arts out of wood, feathers, minerals, shells, and ivory and, in the case of the Tlingit, were so richly endowed in wilderness resources, they felt compelled to give away their treasures at potlatch feasts. Aboriginal Californians wove baskets of reed, yucca, and grass equaled in beauty only by those of the Peruvians and Polynesians and yet devised so tightly they would hold water. The Plains Indians inscribed their shields and recorded history on buffalo hides. They utilized nearly every part of the buffalo, whether for clothing, teepees, rawhide, or vessels, plaiting the hair of the animal into rope and the sinew into thread, carving the horns into spoons and the skull into a ceremonial altar. In the Southwest the Hopi carved effigies of the rainmakers out of cottonwood root and made pottery by rolling native clay into coils, which they painted freehand with yucca leaves. For at least three centuries a large proportion of ceremonial pipes used by the Plains Indians (to symbolize peace and war, end quarrels, strengthen alliances, seal treaties, and show peaceful intent when meeting strangers) was produced at the

---

* Mythology and folklore of people all over the world actually have much in common. Myth themes that inspired paintings and sculpture of ancient Greece, Rome, and the civilizations of Eastern Asia are also found among North American cultures. Anthropologists have found in North American mythology counterparts of a Greek Zeus, a tormented Orpheus, a Prometheus bound, an anthropomorphic sun, a sex-obsessed siren, and a phenomenally strong Hercules. There are stories of supernatural spirits helping deities with monumental tasks, of great heroes and heroines, and of miraculous stories of traveling to the Land of the Dead and the Sky World, where wonderful adventures take place. Tales relate the relationship between mortals and gods, animals, and birds.

sacred quarries near present-day Pipestone, Minnesota. John Wesley Powell considered it the most important single location in aboriginal geography and lore.

From the beginning the white advance broke down the native culture. Traders provided guns and knives to repel invaders, clothing and farm implements to make life easier. The introduction of European materials transformed the Indians in many ways. "I can slay more deer," thought the brave. "No need to make an arrowhead of flint." During the eighteenth century stone tools vanished and flint chipping fell to a lost art. Since furs were the commodity the Europeans sought most and were the unit of exchange, hunting was carried to an excess. In a massive slaughter of wildlife, the Indians began to deplete their hunting grounds, for, as William Bartram lamented, "The white people have dazzled their senses with foreign superfluities."

The price the red man had to pay for new appliances was high, and there was no end to the payments. First came disease, wiping out whole nations; then followed settlers and wars and treaties, which the Indians honored, but the white man never did, except to suit his own convenience; and, finally, expulsion and degradation. In 1624 Captain John Smith reported approximately 5,000 Indians dwelling within sixty miles of Jamestown. Within six decades, wrote Thomas Jefferson in his *Notes on the State of Virginia,* the tribes were reduced to one-third their number; he called it a "melancholy sequel." [1]

The American earth was becoming not simply a place to live on but a commodity with a price tag to be bought and sold like an agricultural product or a manufactured item. Wilderness destruction was profitable and prestigious, with speculation practiced by some of the very best people. George Washington, among others, was highly regarded for his land promotions throughout the Virginia colony. Even the humble pioneers were concerned with subduing wilderness, reducing it "to possession"; many wanted a place to settle where they could make a better livelihood than before and through material gains sustain their sense of social justice and human dignity. Yet there were woodsmen, Indians, voyagers, and mountain men who fought the advance of civilization, aware that it spelled the end of their free ways of life; they had no choice but to move and follow the frontiers. Daniel Boone, as an example, served for a while as an agent of the Transylvania Company in a shady Kentucky land scheme, plainly an "advance man," but he left in disgust for other parts because his heart was in the forest and with the game.

To such people America's glory was in the unpolluted river and lake, nature's labyrinth of fallen logs, the swamp whose creation preceded man by far, the spread of the prairie unbroken for a thousand miles. When men and women were alone in the field and forest, they were touched with a sense of wonder, a feel of mystery whipping the grass, playing in the trees, blowing the clouds into a multitude of shapes, shadows, and endlessly changing colors.

For three-quarters of a century John Bartram and his son William pursued this mystery while they influenced the shaping of the national culture. They were the first of many writers and artists whose driving impulse was not to "carve a garden from the wilds" and who did not follow the notion that the earth was programmed especially for the use of man.

Born in 1699 on a farm outside Philadelphia, John Bartram was the plainest of men, a plowman, self-taught. He became fascinated with the miracles of plants in the field and wondered how many he had plowed under, how many blossoms he had destroyed, without ever understanding their structures and proper uses. He learned botany, then Latin so he could read the works of Linnaeus, who was then devising his new simplified system for classification of plants and animals. John planted his fields with every seed he could lay his hands on, first collecting in the surrounding neighborhood, then traveling in an ever-widening arc: in 1736 into the mountains of Pennsylvania, tracing the Schuylkill River to its source, then expeditions to upper New York State and Canada, the headwaters of the James River in Virginia, and beyond the white man's frontier in the Ohio River Valley. Sometimes he brought William to sketch plants while he collected; always he returned with saddlebags filled with plants and seeds. Through the media of fifty distinguished and wealthy patrons abroad (who considered it a mark of distinction to propagate trees, shrubs, and flowers from the colonies) John Bartram was responsible for the first appearance of at least 150 new plants from the New World wilderness in the gardens of England. In one year alone he shipped across the ocean several species of aster, gentian, ginseng, sweet fern, magnolia, witch-hazel, spruce, hemlock, and sugar maple.

John was a leading intellectual figure of his day. His friend Benjamin Franklin gave him a Franklin stove, by which they sat on wintry evenings in Bartram's stone house, with mugs of cider drawn from the mill in the garden. Writers, artists, and scientists, particularly those who came to explore America, frequented the place, for here they found a microcosm, a foretaste of the wilderness beyond the mountains, and a master of wilderness to instruct them.

His recognition reached its high point in 1765, when John was appointed American Botanist to the King and sent to the Deep South, including the subtropical Florida forest, "the very palace of Madame Flora," as William, who went along, called it. On this trip they discovered the mysterious flowering shrub *Franklinia alatamaha,* or the "lost Franklin tree," larger and more fragrant than its cousin, *Gordonia lascanthus,* and which exists today only because William later plucked the seeds and propagated it at Bartram's Gardens. The last instance of this plant found growing wild was recorded in 1803, though it has been searched for carefully and repeatedly.

William had but one ambition: to hunt plants and to paint and draw the natural world. After failing in a variety of undertakings, he left commerce behind forever and began his classic four-year probe of the southern wilderness that resulted in a major American work of literature, natural history, philosophy, and adventure, *The Travels of William Bartram.*

In the spirit of the pantheist, Bartram envisioned birds like people and people like birds. The Seminole in their native habitat were seen as contented and undisturbed, blithe and free as the winged creatures, active, tuneful, vociferous. Bartram observed the catbird as a talented buffoon and mimic, even to the point of imitating the distress of young chickens. Like a precursor of the modern ecologist, he described the interdependence of natural creatures: the spider preying on a bumble bee, which had lit to feed on the leaf of a plant; a coachwhip snake wreathing itself around the body of a grounded hawk; the battle between crayfish and goldfish; the swarming assembly of alligators feeding upon a vast solid bank of fish. To Bartram every living thing had personality, purpose, and beauty. He taught friendship even toward the rattlesnake, who is "never known to strike until he is first assaulted or fears himself in danger, and then always gives the earliest warning by the rattles at the extremity of his tail."

Bartram's work was shunted aside in the "empire of liberty," and a second edition of his *Travels* would not appear for a century and a quarter. In Europe, however, the book's reception was enthusiastic; within a decade eight or nine editions appeared in several languages. Coleridge adapted the "Alligator Hole" at Salt Springs in Florida for his scene in *Kubla Khan* where Alph, the sacred river, runs through measureless caverns down to a sunless sea. To Wordsworth, Bartram's encounter with fiery azalea of the southern mountains—"incredible profusions on the hillsides that suddenly opening to view from dark shades, we are alarmed with the apprehension of the hills being set on fire"— became the basis of his description in "Ruth"

> Of flowers that with one scarlet gleam
> Cover a hundred leagues and seem
> To set the hills on fire.

Although Bartram avoided involvement, preferring the sanctuary of the gardens left by his father, men beat a path to his door and sought him out through correspondence. The artist he influenced most directly was Alexander Wilson, who came to him as a melancholy poet and schoolteacher with an undying love of birds and literature. Bartram cheered the impoverished Scottish-born Wilson and took him into the gray stone house. He taught Wilson to observe, study, and paint, setting him on the road to becoming "father of American ornithology." Wilson undertook a 2-month walk across high mountains and dangerous rivers to Niagara that became the basis of his heroic epic poem, "The Foresters, Description of a Pedestrian Tour to the Fall of the Niagara in the Autumn of 1804," in which he told of sky-encircled lakes, lone hermit streams, and enormous cataracts.

Then Wilson walked across Pennsylvania and embarked in a skiff down the Ohio, visiting Indians and writing biographies of birds in the woods, often in the presence of the subjects he was describing. "I smile to think," he wrote his old master, "that, while others are immersed in deep schemes of speculation and aggrandizement, I am entranced in contemplation over the plumage of a lark, or gazing like a despairing lover on the lineaments of an owl."

In Kentucky Wilson met John James Audubon, then a young merchant and part-time painter. In their own time Wilson was far better known than Audubon, and each has partisan followers to our day. But Audubon's work represents an unequaled record, full of the vibrance of life, of the variety of wildlife in unspoiled America. For thirty years he labored prodigiously in chronicling wild America, impelled by a foreboding that it would soon be gone.

Audubon haunted the frontiers, in time from Labrador to the Dry Tortugas and as far west as the upper reaches of the Missouri to the Yellowstone. When he first went to Kentucky he kept a store in Louisville, selling shotguns and calicos, taking to the woods at four or five in the morning, following buffalo trails and Indian pathways, hunting and "barking off" squirrels with Daniel Boone. Later he tried his hand at running a sawmill and gristmill at Henderson, where he found the banks of the Ohio River aflutter with egrets, herons, bitterns, and warblers that excited his interest in perfecting his artistic techniques. Then he went to Louisiana, where he paddled through bayous teeming with herons and terns, pushing his pirogue through long grasses and securing the handsome, gigantic turkey cock immortalized on Plate 1 of *Birds of America*. Audubon traveled with all manner of people—hunter, trapper, Indian, whaler, sailor, farmer, and fisherman—combining in his paintings of birds and mammals elements of science, fine art, and folkcraft, with backgrounds of flowing festoons of vines and foliage and trees that assure the viewer that he is looking at the real thing and not museum pieces. Audubon was happiest in the woods, and his whole mind, he once said, was filled with passion for objects of nature.

On the way west, wilderness sustained the folk heroes who became part of the national culture: Daniel Boone, a rough Indian fighter but no Indian hater, who dressed as they did, in deerskin moccasins and breechclout; Davy Crockett, Simon Kenton, and Mike Fink; Jim Bridger, raw-boned, gray-eyed "Old Gabe," who discovered many of the landmarks between the Rockies and Sierras and for years was disbelieved with his tall tales of spouting geysers in the Yellowstone country; and Kit Carson, who learned to make fringed gun covers, buckskin shirts, and leggings, who rode his charger, Apache, without a saddle, and never slept under a roof for seventeen years. Likewise, wilderness sustained the artists who were like reporters of an age and a place in history, including George Catlin, Carl Bodmer, Albert Bierstadt, Thomas Moran, and Albert Jacob Miller. The last was the first painter of the upper Rocky Mountains and the only one to catch the mountain trappers at the summit of their pride; he painted them from almost every angle—setting traps in stream beds, pitching a lonely camp, hunting buffalo, dancing around a campfire, struggling in the quicksand, meeting the Indians in summer rendezvous on the Green River at the foot of the mighty Wind River Range. Wilderness evoked the finest expression of the American poets, too. As William Cullen Bryant wrote in "To Cole, the Painter, Departing for Europe":

> Lone lakes—savannas where the bison roves—
>   Rocks rich with summer garlands—solemn streams—
>   Skies, where the desert eagle wheels and screams—
> Spring bloom and autumn blaze of boundless groves.

By the early nineteenth century the wild aspect of the country began to take on national and spiritual meaning. Bryant in poetry, Thomas Cole in painting, and James Fenimore Cooper in the new form of expression, the American novel, led the way in making Americans aware of their surroundings.

Cole, while still in his teens, had started as a traveling portrait painter. His sitters were poor frontier families who often paid in goods because money was scarce. Through intimate experience he became aware of the values of wilderness, which he subsequently expressed through his pictures of the Hudson River Valley, the Catskill region, and the woods, mountains, and lakes of New England. Success never dampened his viewpoint. It was the wild virgin character of America, as distinct from the more civilized appearance of the Old World, that Cole praised in his "Essay on American Scenery," published in 1835. He and other painters of the Hudson River school took pride in the American heritage. As Asher Durand, his student and noted member of this school, exhorted nineteenth-century artists: "Go first to Nature!" Cole not only utilized the artistic resource, but through his writings he grieved at the way man was invading the New World and tried to alert contemporaries to the importance of respect and restraint.

Cooper likewise held no brief for exploitation and expressed an uncanny perception of the shape of things to come. His classic stories of Natty Bumpo, the Deerslayer, were laid in the natural environment bordering his boyhood home at Cooperstown, in upstate New York, during the frontier days. "This is grand!—'tis solemn! 'tis an education of itself to look upon!" exulted Natty on viewing Lake Otsego, the "Glimmerglass," where a man could stand on the shore and hear the song of the panther from the encircling forest. Cooper's novels bear new meaning in our time, for he warned with power and clarity against "wasty ways" (of burning timber and brush after clearing a tract of land) and that the appearance of infinite resources was sheer illusion. This idea is woven into the fabric of his fiction. In *The Pioneers,* for instance, Cooper described how the entire fictional village of Templeton turned out to slaughter an enormous flock of migrating passenger pigeons, utilizing every conceivable weapon, including a cannon relic of the French and Indian War, until thousands of dead birds covered the ground. The fish of Lake Otsego, the deer in the forest, and passenger pigeons would all disappear, he warned, if man continued to destroy them without restraint.

In this same era George Catlin gave up his career as a Philadelphia lawyer in 1830 to become an artist, drawing knowledge and inspiration from unspoiled nature and the Indians who lived on the land. When he rode the first steamer up the Missouri into the Mandan country of the Dakotas in 1832, prairie dogs chirped from the tops of their mounds and buffalos ran in fright. Catlin observed a large number of Indians camped near Fort Pierre, slaughtering buffalo to trade for whiskey, and realized the extinction of both Indian and buffalo was imminent "before the deadly axe and desolating hands of cultivating man." With the advance of time it became the same everywhere in the West: In exchange for knives, beads, gunpowder, hatchets, cloth, snuff, and rum, Indians disposed of their pelts of mink, beaver, and otter. In the Sioux country the military first crushed the Sun Dance with armed force. Then the missionaries influenced the Indian Service to impose regulations against all "pagan" ceremonies. They cracked down on the Navajo sings in the desert of the Southwest, on the vigils in the Pueblo kivas, and on keepers of the visions in the Mojave. Preachers and teachers induced the Tlingit and Haida of Alaska to destroy art works, which they denounced as pagan idols, rather than recognizing them as decorative records in the life of clan and tribe.

Catlin, however, was enthralled by the gorgeous colors, grace, and manliness of the native people. They, in turn, loved him as the great medicine man who would spend hours arranging their war dress and war paint and then create living beings with a brush. He painted the Sioux of the Northern Plains, Comanche of the Southern Plains, the Kickapoo, Chippewa, and remnants of the Six Nations in northern New York; he did heroic portraits of Osceola, the Seminole leader, and four others imprisoned with him at Fort Moultrie, South Carolina, and of Keokuk, chief of the Sac and Fox. Catlin lectured in London and at the Louvre in Paris, while real savages performed around him. The quality of his art has been criticized at times, but he was an accurate, intelligent observer, who furnished invaluable records of the Indians.

He went further by proposing that large sections of the Plains be preserved "in their pristine beauty and wilderness, in a magnificent park, where the world could see, for ages to come, the native Indian in his classic attire, galloping his wild horses amid the fleeting herds of elk and buffalo." Catlin evidently was the first to propose the national park idea, though his concept was broader than that of the parks we know today. He wrote:

What a beautiful and thrilling specimen for America to preserve and hold up to view of her refined citizens and the world, in future ages! A *nation's Park,* containing man and beast, in all the wild and freshness of their nature's beauty! . . .

Such of Nature's works are always worthy of our preservation and protection; the further we become separated (and the face of the country) from the pristine and wilderness beauty, the more pleasure does the mind of enlightened man feel in recurring to those scenes, when he can have them preserved for his eyes and mind to dwell upon.[2]

Catlin and other nineteenth-century artists ventured into wilderness to record its grandeur after the frontier had been pushed west. Albert Bierstadt, the first major landscape painter to go west, joined a military expedition to the Rocky Mountains in 1859, sketching and painting everywhere, assembling composites for his massive interpretive scenes. Such artists often traveled under primitive conditions and exposed themselves to dangers. The nature they chose to paint was rugged, remote in time and space from the normal worlds they had known. The paintings of Thomas Moran, the highly talented Philadelphian who served on the 1871 expedition of Dr. Ferdinand V. Hayden, helped promote the establishment in the following year of Yellowstone National Park. Another member of this expedition was William Henry Jackson, the pioneer photographer, who during his lifetime traversed the western mountains and plains by foot, horseback, wagon train, stagecoach, and rail, operating and improvising under trying conditions while assembling 30,000 negatives—priceless records of a land hardly better known than the surface of the moon.

Following the Civil War the West was opened to cattle kings, railroad moguls, mining nabobs, and lumber barons. The man who could get his hands on the largest slice of land was the most respected of all citizens. Affluence, influence, and wealth were confused with virtue. The chaotic grazing upheaval known as the "beef bonanza" was so intense that scars left on the land in a single generation may never be erased. Nevertheless, exploitation was defended in the name of progress.

Into this arena entered Major John Wesley Powell, who recorded some of the wildest classic adventures in history and then proceeded to evoke a balanced concept of land, water, vegetation, and man as a basis of public policy.* He was a prolific and brilliant writer, dealing principally with scientific matters, but he also could appeal to a popular readership and even tried his hand at verse.

Despite the loss of one arm in the battle of Shiloh, Powell, in 1869, set out with eight companions on the first of his two scientific expeditions down the Green and Colorado rivers into Arizona; this was the only region the trappers had missed. The expedition members saw wild country that few, if any, white men had seen before: treacherous canyons, a lonely land of isolated settlements, Indian shepherds, and hardy wild animals. Mishaps, near starvation, and the desertion of three men who climbed out of the canyons only to be slain by Indians, limited the scientific work, but Powell studied the canyon walls stratum by stratum and accumulated a wealth of data. The accounts of his hair-raising experiences appeared in *First Through the Grand Canyon, Explorations of the Colorado River,* and *Canyons of the Colorado.*

During this same period Mark Twain reached into the wilderness for his materials as frontier storyteller and folk writer. In writing of the Mississippi he conjured the mysterious river world,

* Powell, like Catlin, realized that he dwelled at a crossroads in time. As director of the Bureau of American Ethnology from 1879 to his death in 1902, he and his trained investigators charted movements of all the Indian tribes from the arrival of the Europeans, classified all known tribes, both surviving and long vanished, and recorded arts, industries, music, drama, and culture in all its forms. The published annual reports are highly prized by collectors. Powell's protegé, James D. Mooney, alone unlocked the secret storehouse of Cherokee prayers, sacred songs, and formulas and revealed the shamans to be like the Celtic druids of old. Powell was primarily a scientist (he also served as director of the United States Geological Survey), and he understood the Indians well, recognizing that many conflicts could have been avoided were it not for the white man's ignorance and lust for profit.

brimming with freshness and life, with the earthy smell of wild strawberries and the muffled sound of drumming grouse. In *Roughing It,* Twain recalled the buffalo hunt, coyotes, jack-rabbits, and lizards, the beauties of Lake Tahoe in its pristine state, as well as emigrants, desperadoes, and pony-express riders. His friend Bret Harte celebrated the virgin forest of the Sierras, fragrant with resinous pine and hemlock and the giant sequoias that outtopped the towers of Ilium and were older than Homer—this was "Bret Harte country."

Unfortunately, Twain, Harte, and Joaquin Miller, the "poet of the Sierra," were all swept up with gold fever in the wild Sierra; it was the same disease that destroyed the Cherokee in Georgia and surrounding states and the Sioux in the Dakotas and that left doomed ghost towns in its wake. Twain later called the Gold Rush "the watershed dividing an age of high morality and lofty impulses from an age of money lust, hardness and cynicism." Throughout his life Henry David Thoreau regarded digging for gold a disgrace to mankind. So did Herman Melville; the words of Babbalanja in *Mardi* expressed his feeling: "Deep, Yoomy, deep, true treasure lies; deeper than all Mardi's gold, rooted to Mardi's axis. But unlike gold, it lurks in every soil, all Mardi over . . . gold is the only poverty; of all the glittering ills the direst . . . but man will still mine for it; and, mining, dig his doom."

Many meanings have been attributed to Melville's work, especially to his masterpiece, *Moby Dick*. In the conflict between Ahab and the great white whale, the qualities of power, beauty, and mystery in nature are embodied in the whale, while Ahab's vengeance against the sea exemplifies the immorality of the quest to ravage and exploit, the inevitable destruction of the man who dares penetrate meanings of the universe. As Melville wrote, "the moot point is, whether Leviathan can endure so wide a chase, and so remorseless a havoc; whether he must not at last be exterminated from the waters, and the last whale, like the last man, smoke his last pipe, and then himself evaporate in the final puff."

Melville and Walt Whitman both exalted nature and the humble of humanity. The former glorified the whaler's calling.

Whitman sang of workmen, all kinds of workmen. He urged America to open its arms to all—the despised Chinese, Irish, and Italians, the pauper and criminal—and wanted the word "foreigner" stricken from the public press. In his editorial writing days on the *Brooklyn Eagle,* he criticized dollar worship, supported public baths for the poor, help for the unemployed, candor on sex, and friendship between the races.

"Whitman liked to read the great poets in the open air within the sound of the sea," wrote Van Wyck Brooks, "and at Coney Island, in mild seasons, on the long bare unfrequented beach, he raced up and down the sand, after a swim, declaiming Homer and Shakespeare to the surf and the gulls. He first read the *Iliad* thoroughly in a sheltered hollow of the rocks, in the full presence of nature, under the sun, with the far-spreading landscape and vistas and the sea rolling in." [3]

The shore, where the water married the land, symbolized for Whitman the blending of the real and ideal, and he remembered once that he must write a book expressing what he called "this liquid mystic theme." The poetic form that he gradually evolved was "oceanic," as he sometimes said, with verses that recalled the waves, rising and falling, now and then wild with storm, scarcely two alike in length or measure.

When he was in Washington during the Civil War, Whitman lingered along the Potomac, under the stars, delighting in the silences, the exhilarating air, the "nimbus floods" of the moon that left traces in his poems. In "Song of the Redwood-Tree," he foresaw a new society proportioned to nature:

> Fresh come, to a new world indeed yet long prepared,
> I see the genius of the modern, child of the real and ideal
> Clearing the ground for broad humanity, the true America,
>   heir of the past so grand.

But times were changing. The Civil War brought in the machine age. The power of money grew with railroad-opened markets in the West. Poverty rose, too; in 1879 Whitman was shocked at the sight of two good-looking men plodding along and spying for rags and bones. The western railroads, built with subsidies and fantastic land grants—the Northern Pacific alone received more land than Pennsylvania, Rhode Island, New Jersey, and the District of Columbia combined—dispatched agents to hunt for immigrants and made fortunes on the sweat of Chinese and Irish labor gangs. Such was the pattern of life "for broad humanity." Yet at the same time that exploitation of man and nature was intensifying, new forces in the American culture arose to their defense.

Ralph Waldo Emerson, like Whitman, was an optimist, be-lieving that evil is not a law but a sickness, that man essentially is good, that man's soul is capable of transcending the physical and material to reach the universal truths, that wilderness is the sanctuary of universal truths. "At the gates of the forest, the surprised man of the world is forced to leave his city estimates of great and small, wise and foolish," he wrote in his essay on "Nature." "The knapsack of custom falls off his back with the first step he makes into these precincts. Here we find nature to be the circumstance which dwarfs every other circumstance, and judges like a god all men that come to her." [4]

And again, in the spirit of Bartram, he expressed reverence for creation and belief in a mystical union with God through nature: "To the poet, to the philosopher, to the saint, all things are friendly and sacred, all days holy, all men divine," he continued. "For the eye is fastened on the life and slights the circumstance. Every chemical substance, every animal in its growth, teaches the unity of cause, the variety of appearance."

Emerson spearheaded a philosophy, while his friend Thoreau devoted himself to living as he wanted, rather than conforming in any of the socially accepted ways. Thoreau's outlook was positive and loving of all people. "I do not propose to write an ode to dejection," he declared, "but to brag as lustily as a chanticleer in the morning, standing on his roost, if only to wake my neighbors up." In a brief essay on *Walden,* E. B. White calls it the best youth's companion yet written by an American, "for it carries with it a solemn warning against the loss of one's valuables, it advances a good argument for traveling light and trying new adventures, it rings with the power of positive adoration, it contains religious feeling without religious images, and it steadfastly refuses to record bad news." [5]

Thoreau kept his life simple, flexible, and immediate, wary of possessions that might soon possess the possessor, observing, thinking, and doing for himself. For the most part the citizens of Concord, where he dwelled (and died unrecognized), were simply baffled by his propensity to spend an hour in the rain, lost in introspection over the sight of wild ducks on a pond, yet counting it a waste of time to engage in practical exercises. Nevertheless, Thoreau was probably the most intelligently industrious man at his calling. His view was plain: "If a man walks in the woods for love of them half of each day, he is in danger of being regarded as a loafer, but if he spends his whole day as a speculator, shearing off those woods and making the earth bald before her time, he is esteemed as an industrious and enterprising citizen." [6] As he insisted, "This curious world which we inhabit is more wonderful than it is convenient; more beautiful than it is useful; it is more to be admired and enjoyed than used."[7]

Thoreau was sensitive to rights of man as well as nature, a nonviolent civil disobedient when need be. His excursion in a jail cell was based on his hatred of slavery and refusal to pay taxes to support the Mexican War, an expansionist scheme to acquire territory for the slave states. This led to the essay "On the Duty of Civil Disobedience," an outpouring of conscience explaining why he felt compelled to stand up against the state's immorality, whatever the cost.

Even from his early vantage point, Thoreau saw unchecked profiteering set on a collision course that ultimately would devour all wild nature on the continent—perhaps on the entire globe—and warned that some wilderness must be preserved. He had no quarrel with civilization but defined wilderness as a necessary component. If it were not recognized as such, man would destroy himself in destroying nature. "In wildness is the preservation of the world"—this quotation has become the fitting motto of the Wilderness Society. He warned against having "every part of man cultivated," for to subject everything in man to rational and conscious control would be to warp, diminish, and barbarize him. So, too, the reduction of all nature to use for profit in due course would end in the dehumanization of man.

Thoreau published only two books during his lifetime, *A Week on the Concord and Merrimack Rivers* and *Walden,* but his collected works, including his journal, or daybook, run to twenty volumes, a mine of wilderness discoveries and observations. He had neither dream nor hope nor design that *Walden* would ever be recognized for what it is, a classic in the true sense of the word, a work of elevated prose that has no date, that speaks simply, directly, and inspiringly of matters momentous to the individual who would love life in a soul-satisfying manner. Anyone approaching Thoreau with a degree of natural feeling will never again view nature as a thing wholly apart from oneself. There is humor in his style and Yankee thrift, as he consistently demonstrates personal integrity and clarity of purpose. Saddened at the extermination of the cougar, panther, lynx, wolverine, bear, beaver, and turkey, for example, he writes on March 23, 1856:

I seek acquaintance with Nature,—to know her moods and manners. Primitive Nature is the most interesting to me. I take infinite pains to know all the phenomena, . . . for instance, thinking that I have here the entire poem, and then, to my chagrin, I hear that it is but an imperfect copy that I possess and have read, that my ancestors have torn out many of the first leaves and grandest passages, and mutilated it in many places. I should not like to think that some demigod has come before me and picked out some of the best of the stars. I wish to know an entire heaven and an entire earth.[8]

Thoreau's significance and influence have never been fully felt until now. He is as valid a guide and companion to the north country as the day his words for "The Maine Woods" were written. Though the surroundings are changed, many landmarks are not. His hopefulness is spread across the pages with expressions like "What a place to live, what a place to die and be buried in! There certainly men would live forever, and laugh at death and the grave." [9]

His three trips to Maine were largely in search of the red man in his native habitat; almost every page of his essay, "The Allegash and East Branch," includes reference to his Indian guide, Joe Polis, and his intimate mastery of woodcraft. In fact, Thoreau collected notes over the years on aboriginal history and culture for a projected major literary work that unfortunately never was written, but he stated his purpose thus: "They paddled over these waters, they wandered in these woods, and they had their fancies connected with sea and forest, which (should) concern us quite as much as the fables of the Orientals do."

In the West Charles M. Russell was stating the same thesis on canvas. In 1879, three years after the Custer massacre at Little Big Horn, Russell arrived as a fifteen-year-old tenderfoot at the gold camp called Last Chance Gulch, the present Helena. In another two years the last great Indian buffalo hunt was held, marking the beginning of the end of the West he adored.

As a cowpuncher Russell was on the range when tens of thousands of cattle perished in the winter blizzard of 1887, in the era of syndicates with financial roots in the East and Europe. He was also a hunter, trapper, and squawman, who lived for a time with the Blood Indians. Once he started cultivating his talent, however, nothing could stop him from recording the West with virtuosity in pen and ink, oil, water color, and bronze sculpture in a style that is romantic, earthy, breezy, bountiful, and genuine. He was so prolific and unrestrained that he once painted the circular glasswork in a saloon at Great Falls. More than 3,500 of his works are cataloged. His paintings have brought up to $150,000. Yet the more Russell saw trails plowed under, barbed wire strung, cities arise, and the Indians pushed back and beaten down, the more he yearned for a time before his own, when only the lodges of his "red brothers" marked the presence of man. His heart was in the simplicity of wilderness no less that John Muir's or Henry Thoreau's. His greatest works include buffalo hunt scenes showing the dead of winter and the dust of summer and Indian personalities in all their dignity, paintings bearing such titles as "Before the White Man Came," "When Great Herds Came to Drink," and "When the Land was God's." Once Russell astounded an admiring group at Great Falls, called the Forward Looking Citizens, with an outburst of revulsion at the sham of a profiteering society. "I have been called a pioneer," he exclaimed. "In my book a pioneer is a man who comes to a virgin country, traps off all the fur, kills off all the wild meat, cuts down all the trees, grazes off all the grass, plows the roots up and strings ten million miles of wire. A 'pioneer' destroys things and calls it civilization. I wish to God that this country was just like it was when I first saw it and that none of you folks were here at all." [10]

Russell expressed perplexity and distress at the destruction of wilderness. Thoreau struck out in its defense but functioned essentially alone. John Muir, however, inspired a movement and an organization in a period of rising concern. He was a long-bearded, long-legged uncommon champion of nature and of his fellow man, who wrote, "There is a love of wild nature in everybody, an ancient mother-love showing itself whether recognized or no, and however covered by cares and duties." [11]

Muir was born in Scotland in 1838, where as a schoolboy he read the works of Audubon and Alexander Wilson and dreamed of exploring America. When he was eleven, his dream came true; his family brought him to a homestead on the Wisconsin frontier, and he grew up studying birds mating, building their nests, and feeding their young and the habits of dragonflies, wild bees, butterflies, and wasps. He met Indians, too, and was moved by their forest wisdom. Though he enrolled for a time at the University of Wisconsin, Muir departed without a degree for the "University of the Wilderness," which stretched along his thousand-mile walk across the Southeast and in which he slept in the bedroom of the open night and gathered rare varieties of plants and shells and observed pelicans and herons. This was only a prelude to his western adventures. In 1877 Muir went prowling about the San Gabriel Mountains, compelled to creep for miles through chaparral thickets, his sole companions bears, wolves, foxes, and wildcats. For all the solitary travels of his lifetime, Muir probably never experienced loneliness or fear. "Oh, I am not afraid of anyone robbing me," he once told a muscular, brawny youth who barred his way through the woods, "for I don't carry anything worth stealing." This didn't satisfy the wilderness holdup man, who asked if Muir carried shooting irons. He had none but threw his hand back to his pistol pocket, marched up close, and whispered daringly, "I allow people to find out if I am armed or not." He proceeded in peace. Though he traveled over a wide range of the West, including Alaska and across the Bering Sea to Siberia, Muir's special kingdom was Yosemite, where he lived for six years among the ice-borne peaks and immense domes, forming and proving his theory of glacial erosion, which he expounded in Horace Greeley's *New York Tribune*. Muir was in great demand as a writer, for he lived more outdoors than indoors and described the mountain landscape in terms of science and poetry: "Vapor from the sea; rain, snow and ice on the summits; glaciers and rivers—these form a wheel that grinds the mountains thin and sharp, sculptures deeply the flanks, and furrows them into ridge and canyon, and crushes the rock into soils on which the forests and meadows and fruitful vine and tree and grain are growing." [12]

When he climbed a tree in the midst of a swirling California windstorm, Muir saw how the winds caressed the branches, bending them in lusty exercise, stimulating their growth, plucking off a leaf or limb, as required—now whispering and cooing like a sleeping child, now roaring like the ocean, the winds blessed by the forests, the forests by the winds, with ineffable beauty and harmony as the sure result. "We all travel the milky way together, trees and men; but it never occurred to me until this storm-day, while swinging in the wind, that trees are travelers, in the ordinary sense. They make many journeys, not extensive ones, it is true; but our own little journeys, away and back again, are only little more than tree wavings—many of them not so much." [13]

Another time, in 1896, while he was at the Grand Canyon with Gifford Pinchot (when both were members of the National Forest Commission), Muir felt that a tarantula they encountered had as much right to be there as he had and wouldn't let Pinchot kill it. He was impressed by the intelligence and courage of animals, as evidenced in his story about Stikeen, the small black dog that followed him through one perilous Alaska journey after another, showing loyalty, constancy, and prowess.

In collaboration with his friend and editor at *Century Magazine,* Robert Underwood Johnson, Muir inspired the creation of Yosemite National Park in 1890. In 1892 he proceeded to promote the whole park concept through a new group, the Sierra Club, of which he remained president till his death in 1914. The founders originally had in mind exploring and safeguarding the mountains of the Pacific Coast, but the group has since grown into a leading force in the protection of wild areas throughout the nation and the world. Muir himself fought resource exploitation, whether by grazing, logging, water development, or tourism. Still, he knew the national parks were not designed to keep people out but to make the wonders accessible; they were the "people's playgrounds." He objected to roads but not to use.

With the advance of the twentieth century, Aldo Leopold brought the philosophy expressed by Thoreau and Muir in the American epic full cycle, to that of Bartram and the Indians. He went further, to the ancient Eastern cultures, coining the expressions "land ethic" and "ecological conscience," based on the responsibility of man to the rest of life on earth. Leopold began as a trained forester, a graduate of Yale in 1908. The following year he joined the Forest Service in the Southwest and became absorbed in wildlife problems, which led logically into the study of wilderness. He later became associate director of the Forest Products Laboratory at Madison, Wisconsin; from 1933 to his death in 1948 he was a professor at the University of Wisconsin, holding the first chair in game management anywhere in the country. During this period he produced *A Sand County Almanac,* which has become the classic statement in behalf of a life style that protects the environment. In this and other works he combined the logic of the scientist with an articulate, concise literary style.

Like Thoreau, Leopold had no quarrel with civilization per se but warned that, "While the reduction of the wilderness has been a good thing, its extermination would be a very bad one."

For wilderness is a fundamental constituent of the national culture, an indigenous part of Americanism, bearing qualities that set it apart as a contribution to civilization.

Modern artists and writers have continued to draw from nature, though expressing more of their inner feelings and thoughts rather than recording outside objects and experiences. Georgia O'Keeffe's paintings of windblown sand, weathered rock, and cloudless desert sky express her personal vision in its barest essence. John Marin's windswept coasts, woods, and mountains are interpreted as he alone could have done them. Rockwell Kent's spare northern coastal scenes may be more representational, but they are plainly subjective expressions. So are the amazing studies of rocks and tidepools at Point Lobos, as photographed by Edward Weston—which shows how far photography has come since Jackson's time.

Among poets, no one reading Robinson Jeffers can escape the feel of the wild Pacific or the power of the Big Sur coastal landscape at the continent's end. Little wonder that his celebrated line, "Not Man Apart," became in time the title of a book about wilderness published by one conservation organization and then the title of a periodical issued by another.[14]

Robert Frost, writing about the ways of an idle crow or the downy flakes of snow, likewise expressed reverence for the values of nature in a rational social life, as part of the continuum that binds together the galaxies and the feeble lights of man. Ernest Hemingway also gave homage to nature; he saw most works of man as abominations and found solace in primitive rites, while sounding the ominous overture to our disenchantment with the present. More recently, James Dickey's novel *Deliverance* followed the travail of modern urbanized man in trying to reclaim, for a little while, the earlier ways.

The overpowering contemporary sense of alienation and bitterness has turned large segments of literature to cracked laughter and pornography and painting to pop art and anti-illusionism. Yet, artists and writers are still responding to and creating from the natural landscape.

When the Sierra Club launched its publication program with *This Is the American Earth,* by Nancy Newhall and Ansel

Adams, and *In Wildness Is the Preservation of the World,* with selections by Thoreau and photographs by Eliot Porter, it opened vistas that filled the imagination and spurred the artistic instinct. As Ansel Adams, a master in translating wilderness values into pictorial art, wrote: "Here are worlds of experience beyond the world of aggressive man, beyond history, beyond science. The moods and qualities of nature and the relations of great art are equally difficult to define; we can grasp them only in the depths of our perceptive spirit." [15] The Sierra Club books are part of a rich cultural movement of involvement, in which Rachel Carson, Sigurd Olson, William O. Douglas, Wallace Stegner, Loren Eiseley, Joseph Wood Krutch, Paul Brooks, and others have interpreted the role of the wilderness in a modern world.

Chapter Four

A Scientific Resource

George Washington Carver, the scientist, found that a weed was something good, even by practical human standards. Others simply hadn't been smart enough to discover its usefulness. They contented themselves with rejecting the weed—that is, any plant without apparent purpose—as harmful and damaging, an infringement of the evil in nature upon the good, or beneficial. As a chemist and botanist Carver knew better. During his long career he developed sound ideas of feeding wild acorn and lowly cowpea to livestock, using peanuts and wild plums in recipes, and of improving the fertility of the soil organically. He discovered more than 300 uses for *Arachis hypogaea,* the peanut. At the time of his death in 1943 Carver was working on revolutionary research using peanut oil as a medium for polio vaccine.

He wasn't the first, or last, to adapt the unwanted in the plant world. Long before his time the potato was thought of as useless and the tomato as poisonous. The goat nut of the California Mojave Desert until a few years ago was discarded as so much "brush" (a variety of weed) until it was discovered the seed contains a liquid with very high melting point, ideally suited to uses in heavy machinery hardening oils and in smokeless candles. Even now plants shunned as weeds actually yield edible and palatable fruits, nuts, leaves, stems, roots, and seeds.

Science still knows very little about life, perhaps less about the simplest, most fundamental forms or about the interrelationship of all forms. The plant kingdom embraces at least 350,000 botanical species, ranging in diversity from towering oaks to humble fungi. Grasses, trees, vines, shrubs, herbs, and legumes of infinite variety cover the land. The exact number of species is not known since about 2,000 new plants are added to the total in an average year. The potential has been barely explored; in fact, only 4 per cent have been analyzed so far. Virtually nothing is known of the active constituents of seeds.

The same holds true of insects. They play a valuable role on many fronts. The fruit fly, besides decomposing wastes and carcasses, serves as an experimental animal for the study of population cycles, nervous function, and heredity. Other insects have been utilized in basic studies of animal behavior, nutrition, metabolism, and in cancer research. Insects are part of the "new frontier" of natural products chemistry. They require little in the way of laboratory space and food and are immensely diverse. Many insects that Americans destroy indiscriminately are regarded in more frugal countries to be good food. Not all insects are dirty either; nearly all are cleaner than the residue of insect killers that agricultural producers spread on vegetables.

As in the case of plants, micro-organisms associated with insects are being discovered at a high rate. Giving them names may not be as important as understanding their biology and ecology. Whether plant or animal, millions of living species offer an unending variety of form and function, of unsolved evolutionary, biological, and chemical mystery, and rewarding beauty. Life science is at last coming of age, transcending the study of individual animals or plants to focus on the broadest spectrum, ranging from cells, tissues, and organs up to the response of organisms to their environment, the long-term economic values of biochemical diversity, and the application of wilderness as an environmental barometer.*

* Dr. Robert Jenkins, of the Nature Conservancy, has commented on what he calls the "revolution in research practices." One result has been the integrated interdisciplinary team approach, exemplified by the Analysis of Ecosystems Program of the U.S. National Committee for the International Biological Program. Analyses of biomes, or life zones, are focusing on major

The extensive use of wilderness as a scientific resource has barely begun. Little has been learned about it as compared with the total output of science. Yet thirty years ago Aldo Leopold declared the need to maintain wilderness as "a base datum of normality," a laboratory for the study of land health. As natural scientists generally recognize today, undisturbed ecosystems, or wilderness, are virtually imperative as research areas for making sound decisions in many phases of resource management. Knowledge of original habitats has already revealed practical lessons in where best to grow crops, where to graze sheep, where to grow forests (and of what types of trees), and which lands will naturally produce crops the longest.

Science for the most part, like society itself, has been pre-occupied till now with the immediacy of a man-centered world. Research is required to furnish results, demonstrable gains, profitable payoffs, in a hurry. It measures grass in terms of protein production, trees as cellulose, and a granite cliff as building blocks. Modern science has produced herbicides and pesticides, atomic power, and biological warfare and is now working on the brave new world of a completely controlled environment. Under pressure to produce results, science has considered everything except long-range effects on society, whether from poisons in the soil, automobile exhaust fumes in the air, or the by-products of the atomic cycle spread through time and space.

Wilderness by its very existence has contributed tangible, practical results, too—in furnishing sources of new foods and indispensable medicinal products, including many of the miracle drugs. The use of natural materials for healing is an old custom. The plant world, in particular, has been the "little black bag" for the witch doctor as well as the family doctor on Elm Street.

---

ecosystem processes whereby energy and materials are obtained, utilized, exchanged, cycled, and lost. Measurements include biomass, productivity, diversity, community structure, population numbers, and changes in all of these with time or location. These programs, according to Jenkins, are the most ambitious attempt ever made to understand ecosystems. Many discussions were published in reports of the U.S. Committee of the International Biological Program (1968–71).

As recently as the early 1900s, before the Synthetic Era, fully 80 per cent of all medicines came from natural sources. Humanity believed that a cure existed in the plants of field and forest for every ill. As Kipling wrote: "Anything green that grew out of the mold/Was an excellent herb to our fathers of old."

The Indian pharmacopeia included roots, stems, leaves, herbs, and barks (as well as animal dung and occasionally human urine for urea content), a number of which have found their places in the white man's formulary and dispensatory, though not necessarily for the same purposes as the Indians used them. As early as 1946 Dr. Ivor Griffith, of the Philadelphia College of Pharmacy and Science, foresaw "a great botanical renaissance, heralding a new day in preventive and curative medicine." This has come to pass. Medical research went back to nature because the test tube had failed to cope with man's greatest killers and cripplers: cancer, cardiovascular disease, and mental illness. At least 125 plants of the wild Appalachian forests alone are in demand, including witch-hazel, digitalis, sweet flag, wintergreen, *Lobelia inflata* (Indian tobacco), wild cherry bark, may apple bark and roots, wild ginger, and catnip. Many of the new miracle drugs, including penicillin, streptomycin, aureomycin, and other biotics are the improbable products of lowly fungi.*

Despite the widespread notion that modern drugs are developed essentially as a result of synthesis in the chemist's mysterious array of test tubes, an analysis of more than 1.05 billion prescriptions dispensed in the United States during 1967 revealed that the main ingredients in about 50 per cent were derived from nature. The prescriptions obtained from higher plants alone have a market value in a year of close to $1 billion.

In years of research cancer technicians have not had as much success with chemicals invented by man as they now report

* The U.S. Forest Service maintains a research project (in cooperation with the University of Kentucky, Auburn University, and the University of Mississippi) in Berea, Kentucky, to study propagation and growth of medicinal plants. These studies are part of the Forest Service program of development of the total forest resource. Propagation, both in the forest and in artificial culture, is a major problem; many plants are difficult, some virtually impossible, to propagate.

having with plant extracts. They have not found a chemical agent that will completely inhibit the growth of, or destroy, tumor tissue without causing undue disturbance in nontumor tissue. But in plants, because of great variety in chemistry (as well as in form), chemists are finding more compounds than they can ever hope to synthesize. And in recent years evidence has shown that many insects—butterflies and beetles, in particular— have a great potential for yielding new anticancer compounds. Clams have also been found to contain an anticancer compound (except for those taken from polluted waters).

According to Dr. Nestor Bohonos and Dr. Henry D. Piersma of Lederle Laboratories, natural products have played an important role in the last twenty-five years in increasing the life expectancy in the United States from 59.7 to almost 70 years. Some drugs formerly cultured from plants are now manufactured synthetically, but many of the most valuable have such complex chemical structures they may never be duplicated in a test tube. One advantage of plant compounds over the synthetic: the former are all biodegradable—that is, they disappear a short time after being used. Man-made drugs and chemicals often lack that quality. Some persist for centuries, because they are constructed so that no natural key can unlock their formula and degrade their ingredients.

Obscure plants and animals undoubtedly hold future keys to health. Wherever nature prevails, in North America and around the world, the search for new and better drugs has intensified.

More than twenty years ago Dr. Paul R. Burkholder discovered chloramphenicol, the most effective drug against typhoid fever, psittacosis, and Rocky Mountain spotted fever, in a Venezuelan soil mold. Some of his more recent antibacterial finds have come from sponges collected from as far away as Australia's Great Barrier Reef and Palau in the Caroline Islands. Other investigators have observed that the intestines of Antarctic penguins apparently are free from micro-organisms—a sterility due to the antibiotic activity of an alga eaten by the crustaceans that form a major part of the diet of penguins. Antibiotic substances, in fact, are widespread in marine life, having been detected in bacteria, algae, phytoplankton, sponges, mollusks, corals, and many other types of organisms.

Who can tell what comes next, or where in the world it will come from? Important materials are derived from the thyroid gland of sheep, urine of pregnant mares, pancreas of the ox, pituitary glands of the hippopotamus, the posterior salivary glands of the octopus. In 1971 researchers at the Gulf South Institute, New Iberia, Louisiana, and at the U.S. Public Health Service Hospital in nearby Carville, reported that armadillos might be ideal test animals for leprosy research. No animal species shares man's susceptibility to leprosy. Until then no artificially infected animal had lived long enough for the slow-developing disease to reach the later, progressive stages in which it can be fully studied—none except armadillos. Gulf South researchers had found that an armadillo infected with leprosy bacillus had survived well into leprosy's progressive phase, stirring hopes of raising a laboratory colony.

A plant or animal that may now seem entirely useless as food or for any other purpose may have the power to prevent serious human illness, but there is no way to forecast and no way to isolate the valuable and beneficial from their environments. The very existence of toxins obtained from the liver of abalone appears to depend on the presence of plant life that, directly or indirectly, serves as food for this invertebrate. Tinkering with the system may not (or may) be wrong, provided that all the parts are saved. The lowly earthworm, amoeba, moth, and spider contribute not only to man's health, but to knowledge of how and why we live on earth.

Economics and specific objectives are probably the least valid scientific arguments for saving plants and animals and entire ecosystems. Millions of living species influence each other beyond our comprehension. Until now, however, the production system has favored species considered commercially valuable and has strived to curtail or eliminate their competitors. For example, entomology research has largely been directed at finding ways to put the insects down in order to develop short-term higher yields of one-crop farming or one-crop forestry. Monocultural systems are prevalent by deliberate design. On the other hand, earth history reveals animals, including man, and plants working together through patient, evolutionary channels over a period of 2 billion years, since life began. The algae of the sea and the humblest land plants convert the energy of the sun into organic chemicals, the first link in the food chain. Animals derive their nutrients either by eating plants or by eating animals that have eaten plants. The present `atmosphere owes most of its oxygen and carbon dioxide to biological actions proceeding without interruption since the beginning. The oxygen we breathe is a waste product of plants, while the carbon dioxide that plants use is a waste product from animal bodies.

An acre of healthy soil is densely populated with millions of insects and tiny animals—earthworms, ants, termites, sowbugs, bacteria, fungi, diligent architects and engineers that sift air and water and return valuable nutrients to build the soil in support of higher life forms. A very great number of tiny organisms at the base of the pyramid of life support a slightly smaller number of still larger ones, and so forth up to the mammals, and man. But without the creatures at the base, the whole pyramid may come tumbling down. Or, as Aldo Leopold put it, the economic parts of the biotic clock cannot long function without the non-economic parts.

Preserving natural areas has shown how millions of living creatures struggle for water, sunlight, soil nourishment, and space. Some grow because others die, decay, and decompose. Others benefit through cooperation or partnership, such as that between the fungus and alga in a lichen, or the tree and fungi in which the fungi's vegetative portion becomes associated with the tree roots. In the case of the Indian pipe, a ghostly white plant appearing throughout moist woodlands of Appalachia, its roots have no actual contact with the soil, but it derives food, minerals, and water from fungi attached to them. Decay organisms, mainly bacteria and fungi, reduce the dead bodies of animals and plants to simple chemicals. These are then used again and again in the cycle of life—a chain of living to inert to living.

Insects and other animals aid plants by carrying pollen. Wherever insects are abundant, other insects come to eat them. About 1,000 different species of insects feed on alfalfa plants or live among them, but even plants that are less appealing attract at least 250 species. Among this latter group, about 100 are likely to be plant feeders, while others eat dead organic matter, fungi, or other organic materials not necessary to the life of the plant. In this finely composed cosmos, a large proportion are parasites or predators that attack the phytophagous, or plant-eating, insects and are responsible for destroying a large percentage of their populations. An abundance of insects means an abundance of birds, for the young of insect-eating bird species often hatch at the very time when insects are reaching their maximum numbers for the year.

Diversity and variety appear to be the cornerstones of survival. The more ways there are of consuming, or being consumed, the more favorable the chances to avoid high fluctuations in the birth and death of species. Unlike our "tree farms," which generally specialize in single species, a tropical wilderness rain forest embraces as many as 400 different tree species per square mile, but with only 3 or 4 trees of any one kind. It appears to be very stable, and if one species dies out the web of life is not disrupted.

Monocultural farming is doubtless the prime example of interference with the systems on which the carrying capacity of the planet is dependent, ignoring the details of natural integration. The modern computer-oriented big-scale industrial farm operator benefits from all sorts of scientific research that explains how to force production yields from his land but does not explain the problems that arise from taking out enormous quantities of organic matter while returning only chemical fertilizer. His cornfield has but one species, with none of the checks and balances to accommodate dry years or the invasion of strangers. The same is true of the tree farm devoted to accelerated yields of pine only. As with any land use that simplifies the ecosystem, farm-lot forest management favors the irruption of pests and disease. Infection is rapid and direct from tree to tree; if one species is destroyed there is nothing left.

Despite the extensive land abuse, or perhaps because of it,

scientists and educators since World War II have become increasingly interested in natural areas of all sizes, where diversity prevails, for scientific research. In the face of pollution, cultivation, and population buildup, they need access to plant and animal communities, geologic and soil features, and bodies of water relatively free of the influence of man. Despite all scientific advances, wilderness has still not been simulated in the indoors laboratory. Only an ecosystem without interference can demonstrate a system of conversion cycles and energy flow along the chain of life. "Without such a demonstration, no teacher, no matter how good, can ever transmit to the student the knowledge he needs in order to properly evaluate the effects of human activities on our surroundings or ever to know nature," according to Dr. Hugh Iltis, of the University of Wisconsin.[1] "To understand the soil of a plowed field, he needs first of all to understand the intact, unplowed soil." As a teaching and research resource, California's diversity has made it especially valuable. For years University of California classes have taken to the field for training in geology, paleontology, botany, zoology, geography, public health, and fine arts.* By 1968 the first *Directory of Research Natural Areas on Federal Lands* was published. It included more than 300 units of "base line" to be used in revealing whether and how technology harms the biosphere, not just whether it feeds or clothes human beings. Studies of many kinds are under way. Government agencies for some time have been utilizing natural areas in order to develop data on soil and vegetative productivity and on water flows. In the Boundary Waters Canoe Area of Minnesota, a unit of the Superior National Forest, plant ecologists have been pursuing the origin, maintenance, and restoration of plant communities, including an assessment of man's influence on the

---

* However, according to Dr. Mildred Mathias, chairman of the coordinating committee for the University System of Land and Water Reserves, in recent years it has become increasingly difficult to conduct field teaching and research. In an interview in *Pacific Discovery* (May–June 1972), she reported that long-known and well-used sites have disappeared under pressures of urbanization and growing populations. "We now find ourselves going farther and farther afield and classes that need field studies must be arranged where we can have extended trips of two or more days."

landscape. At Cape Hatteras National Seashore, on the Outer Banks of North Carolina, investigations have been conducted into the ecological effects of storm-driven waves on the ocean-bordering sand and plant community. Aquatic ecosystems represent a new area of emphasis. The Environmental Protection Agency, Army Corps of Engineers, and Department of the Interior all support base-line reasearch in the coastal zone. The National Oceanic and Atmospheric Administration operates a program called Marine Monitoring and Prediction, while the Smithsonian Institution has one called Ocean Acre, involving repeated sampling in specific spots at sea.

In its broadest uses, the study of natural areas in comparison with others already influenced by man will likely reveal the effect of environmental meddling. "If it can be shown that biotic diversity does indeed enhance stability in the ecosystem, or is the result of it, then we would have an important guide for conservation practice," as Dr. Eugene P. Odum, Director of the Institute of Ecology at the University of Georgia, declares.

Preservation of hedgerows, woodlots, noneconomic species, noneutrophicated water and other biotic variety in man's landscape could then be justified on scientific as well as esthetic grounds, even though such preservation often must result in some reduction in the production of food or other immediate consumer needs. In other words, is variety only the spice of life, or is it a necessity for the long life of the total ecosystem comprising man and nature? [2]

All kinds of ecosystems furnish valuable living laboratories. Marshes, for example, offer scenes 300 million years old, the same environment that produced the first vertebrates to walk on land. They depict nature's age-old method of flood control: storing supplies in ground-water reservoirs, then gradually feeding them out through springs, seeps, and open outlets. Salt marshes demonstrate a link in the ecology of the entire ocean. They act as nursery or feeding grounds for the bulk of fin fish and shellfish; even ocean species depend on them through their food chains. The desert is a classroom in the frugality of water. Conservation and wise use of water are essential to life, yet the desert ecosystem is abundant with plants and animals that have

adapted themselves to endure where water is scarce and un-
dependable.

The native prairie represents an extremely dynamic life community, with hundreds of herbs and grasses, thousands of insects, and many other plants and animals. Taller plants protect
the lower ones from the heat of the sun; lesser grasses reduce
water loss from the soil by mulching it with their prostrate
forms. Rodents help to build the soil, while their numbers are
kept in check by snakes, coyotes, owls, and hawks. Yet in all of
Illinois—the "prairie state"—pitifully little of deep-soil prairie
remains. Like most of America, the balance has been given
over to the production system in which everything must have its
economic quantification and be made useful, whether by grazing
more cattle, planting more corn, or filling in the swamps.

All wilderness areas, no matter how small or imperfect,
have values to land science, whether real or potential.* The
stability and completeness of life make wilderness an indispensable source of study. To solve which specific riddles? Who
can tell—and why try? Conservation does not only mean "wise
use" but preservation when no immediate uses are apparent.
Future scientists will appreciate the chance to identify a few
uses on their own.

---

* Dr. Russell F. Hansen, writing in the Cleveland Museum of History's
Explorer (March–April 1963), cites the example of Rock Island, a limestone
outcrop once found in the bend of the Ohio River near Louisville, Kentucky.
It was the home of a number of plants so sensitive to competition, shading,
grazing, and microclimatic factors that they were scarcely known at the
river's banks. Two species from this unusual flora have never been recorded
at any other location: one, a species of the scurf pea, *Psoralea*, an economically unimportant group in the legume family, the other a goldenrod. Alas,
the "unimportant" *Psoralea* and the humble goldenrod can only be known
superficially by inspecting a few herbarium sheets, for Rock Island was
blasted out of existence to make the Ohio River more navigable. Who can
tell what was lost? When Edison searched for new sources of rubber, he
found that *Solidadgo gattingeri*, a goldenrod, was the best, most quickly
grown natural latex available. What of the Rock Island goldenrod? Could
it have been a source of choice latex? Did it or the *Psoralea* contain some
prized miracle drug? We will never know, because every living representative
of these species has been destroyed.

Chapter Five

A Place for Wild Animals, Wild Plants

Wilderness is for men, but not for men alone, and in some cases, or in some places, should not be for men at all. Wilderness is also for grizzly bears, wolves, wolverines, and mountain lions, for seals, sea lions, and walrus and all the native species that symbolize the finest national values but that, alas, too frequently are slipping into oblivion.

National parks without their wildlife are not national parks but imitations of the real thing, more like amusement parks designed to satisfy the curiosity of mankind in padded comfort. Each wild species, whether animal or plant, large or small, possesses implicit scientific interest and therefore broad human interest. Yellowstone is more than the visual photographic spectaculars of Old Faithful and the paint pots; it's the grizzlies and the whole life system and the unfenced danger of a pioneer earthscape.

In addition to such areas designed for fitting use and enjoyment of people, perhaps there should be other great reserves for animals, insects, and plants to remind us of the genius of all God's creatures. People like to get away from too many people, but the animal—when he craves solitude, where can he go? There needs to be a recognition by man that, whether he takes a pack on his back or not, whether he ever sees or walks in the wilds, he is a little closer to eternity because somewhere a small part of earth's life has been granted its rights to be.

The right to be. Ernest Thompson Seton discussed this point in his classic work, *Wild Animals I Have Known*. Since animals are creatures with wants and feelings, he wrote, differing in degree only from our own, they surely have their rights. Taken one step further, to see they are given their rights is the obligation of human beings, the dominant species.

One could build a defense case in behalf of other creatures on thoroughly practical, man-centered terms. The abundance and variety of wildlife are basic measurements of environmental health, a barometer of biological change (and even an index of man's culture). The survival of the human species is inescapably linked with the survival of all other forms of life. A force that pollutes the habitat of any living thing pollutes the habitat of all living things. As more and more species disappear, man is apt to be affected, for each time one link is broken in the chain of life, every other form is disrupted and may become endangered as a result. In an increasingly dehumanized world, wildlife is an assurance that nature's life machine still functions.

But for whose benefit? The material survival of man is a valid point but not necessarily the most compelling. Man is the most highly evolved being, the only animal capable of massive environmental changes. The fact of superiority and power imposes special responsibilities as well as rights, a demand for compassion and stewardship. In any event, humans exist and enjoy the world only by virtue of conditions created long before the arrival of man and maintained through the millennia by all other forms of life. The earth's crust is a living organism, and all life is an extension of ourselves. Therefore, wilderness becomes important as the last home ground of countless species that would otherwise be doomed.

The human race perches atop the pyramid of life in such splendid isolation that it considers all things of earth manageable to its own advantage, without reference to interdependence with life forms on the pyramid beneath it. What is natural belongs, whether it be considered beautiful or ugly, useful or not useful. Each organism has a distinct function in its own right that serves to maintain the living system. Nevertheless, the idea prevails widely, even among those professionally trained and engaged in wildlife activities and sciences, that lower animals gain validity only when managed for the use and benefit of man.

Aldo Leopold defined game management on the opening page of his textbook on the subject as "the art of making land produce sustained annual crops of wild game for recreational use." Leopold advanced, fortunately, to a much broader ecological concept, though many others in his field became posssessed with the idea of manipulating food and cover in order to produce favored animals called "game." Such is the basis of game management as widely practiced today. It may sound reasonable; however, it does not consider human life in the context of nature but rather as being above and removed from it, as though man's hope lies solely on his technical skills and the synthetics produced by them. "The worst disservice we could perform to any form of wildlife would be to abandon the principle of sound management," as Thomas L. Kimball, executive director of the National Wildlife Federation, has declared. "Because man has so complicated and disrupted the animal habitat, there is little semblance in the balance of nature." [1]

Joseph Wood Krutch addressed himself to the same question, but from a contrasting viewpoint, expressing a philosophy that needs to be taught in technical resource management courses.

"The wisest, the most enlightened, the most long-seeing exploitation of resources is not enough," he wrote,

for the simple reason that the whole concept of exploitation for man's use alone is false and so limited that in the end it will defeat itself. The earth will have been plundered and laid waste, no matter how scientifically and far-seeingly the plundering and waste has been accomplished. Something is fatally lacking in the concept of conservation and the thing lacking is the feeling for, or the love of, the natural work of which man is a part. It is the failure to realize that this is not only one world, but one earth. Mankind is not only an island in respect to other men, but also an island in respect to nature as a whole. He must come to some kind of terms with it.

But without the glad appreciation of our relationship to nature, without the idea of living with nature, not merely upon nature, we must end sooner or later living—or I think more properly dying—in a world where man has paid the penalty for doing what he cannot do successfully; namely, think only of himself.[2]

Leopold, expressed the same philosophy. In *A Sand County Almanac* he delineated the difference in the outlook of two types of foresters. (This idea applies to game biologists as well.) His Group A of foresters is quite content to grow trees like cabbages, with cellulose as the basic forest commodity. It feels no inhibition against violence; its ideology is agronomic. Group B, however, sees forestry as fundamentally different from agronomy because it employs natural species and manages a natural environment rather than creating an artificial one. It worries on biotic as well as economic grounds. It worries about a whole series of secondary forest functions: wildlife, recreation, watersheds, and wilderness areas. It is Group B that feels the stirrings of an ecological conscience.

Some scientists, and others as well, have suggested that not all species need saving, because extinction has been a regular part of the evolutionary order of nature for millennia, a continual test of the fittest to survive. The dinosaur, saber-toothed tiger, four-toed horse, mastodon, and mammoth once held important places in the American life community but are known now only through fossils found in the earth's crust. Great numbers of species became extinct long before man's appearance. Even then, some species were rare, others common, still others abundant. Animals and plants have developed through natural selection, with special qualities that enable each to survive, fit for specific niches in the environment. With appreciable change— as in the earth's climate, or resulting from glacial flows and ebbs, flooding by ancient seas, or competition with other species —each animal has had to adapt or perish. When this happens through natural processes, new species evolve to succeed the old. Diversity is not diminished or lost. The animal never acts to destroy other forms except toward the end of sustaining its own life. The influences of man operate quite differently.

Along with the growth of civilization during the past 2,000 years, several hundred species of wildlife have been destroyed, purposely or inadvertently through the activities of man. With the age of industry and machinery the process of extinction has accelerated with prodigious power. Thousands of species, including hundreds of the higher vertebrates, are in danger or declining throughout the world. The expansion of cities, construction of highways and electric power dams, the use of poisonous chemicals in agriculture and industry, dumping of heavy metals in water, harvesting and conversion of forests, the increase in leisure activities that sends millions of people into wildlife territory, with or without guns—all those impose heavy pressures.

The principal focus of concern thus far has been on large mammals and birds, yet in the last 200 years mankind has wiped out an estimated 10,000 species of insects and snails. Many, many land snail species are on the verge of extinction. There is scant reference to them in the lists of endangered species, and they are hardly ever included in natural resource inventories, though insects and snails are indispensable in the cycle of life. Many plants are totally dependent on insects for pollination and continuation of their species. Some weeds and other plants would get out of hand and crowd out the less rugged ones, were it not for leaf-eating insects. Insects in old logs directly and indirectly cause their decay, returning tree to soil. Aquatic forms of certain types of insects comprise a large share of the food for trout and other fresh-water fish—because they are "useful," they are among the few actually protected by law.

Plants as well as animals have undergone serious change and elimination since European man began to spread across the continent. All kinds of plant communities have vanished through the civilizing process: taming the prairie, cutting the forest, draining the swamp, building of second-home subdivisions in high mountains of the East, and grazing sheep in high mountains of the West. Even the desert ecosystem is now an endangered species.

It's not only the grizzly, polar bear, wolf, sea turtle, whale, eagle, and falcon that are threatened. It's all of the greater and lesser creatures. At the same time that man has accelerated the pace of extinction, he has reduced the opportunities for adaptation and evolution of new forms. People are worried and responding to the challenge of endangered species because they're frightened, or because they're finally listening to what ecologists have been trying to tell them for years.

Many species were decimated in the nineteenth century. Following the Civil War, the cowman, sheepman, buffalo hunter, bounty hunter, and trader in skins, the agents and advance guard of society, marched across the continent. Anmials were exterminated through loss of food source and slaughtered by the millions. The buffalo, which had numbered 60 million or more in great herds, almost vanished from the face of America. In 1878 they were everywhere in the West. Ten years later there were no more than 500; a government expedition could hardly find enough to make the mounted group in the Smithsonian. The pronghorn, which had been nearly as numerous, almost met the same fate. Remnants of bighorn sheep and elk were displaced from the valleys and lower hills to their final refuges in the mountains. Kit fox, red fox, skunk, hawk, eagle, magpie— these and others perished by the tens of thousands.

Yet it became convenient to label the wolf as "the beast of waste and desolation." Wolves, beautifully adapted and intelligent animals, had at first been friendly, trusting of man. Once deprived of their natural sources of food, they were forced to prey on horses, cows, and sheep in farmyards and ranch corrals. But this was not the only cause of their undoing. After the beaver had been thoroughly trapped out, men on the frontier had turned to the wolfskin trade, spreading strychnine in meat baits across the forest and plains. In one winter two men working alone caused the death of 3,000 wolves, killing a great many animals that came to feed on the poisoned meat. Then followed the bounty hunters, an ingenious breed, who would sell the same scalps over and over, even while substituting scalps of dogs for wolves, and avoiding, when possible, killing female wolves in order to protect their future in business.

The ultimate war against wolves was waged in behalf of the livestock industry. In the 1870s and 1880s promoters and speculators went into Texas where they bought long-horned cattle and moved them into the new open ranges farther north. Cows poured north up the high Plains into virgin unstocked lands; the cattle empires swept over the West. They found valuable grasses on the Plains, so they slaughtered the buffalo (while the government disposed of the buffalo-hunting Indian) and replaced them with cows. Because grass was abundant, cattle were not fed during the winter, the owners preferring to risk the loss of their stock instead. During the winter of 1886–87, thousands of cattle perished of starvation on the northern Plains—losses were about 60 per cent. In 1893 the southwestern cattlemen underwent the same sort of experience. There were many other losses, through disease and at the hands of rustlers—far more damage to cattle than from all the wolves combined.

On top of the cows came the sheep in vast flocks of tens of thousands, rising higher in the path of melting snows to find edible weeds on steep cliffsides, their innumerable hooves breaking and trampling seedlings into the ground. They grazed the ancient established ranges of wild sheep, depriving the original animals of their food sources and inflicting decimating diseases on them. By night fires were built to keep away predatory animals and show the advance of rival herds. But fires were seldom extinguished and added one more source of devastation to the habitat.

Still the wolves and other predators were blamed. The paradox was that of all the land the livestock kingdom grazed and fought over, it actually owned less than 1 per cent. The remainder was national domain. Yet the government assigned men to destroy the "varmints" for the stockmen. These agents lured wolves into steel traps by devising sprays of attractive scents. They would stake a tame wolf to draw a wild one. As the wolves grew instinctively wary of one technique, another was devised. "Clientism" in government is now a common term; in the field of biological sciences, the special services of predator control to the livestock industry were among the first —and by all odds the worst. From their beginning until this day such programs, even though rendered and defended by professional biologists, have consistently disregarded and denied man's role as an interdependent part of nature. Ranchers destroyed mountain lions in order to protect cattle. They convinced the federal government to control the coyotes, and after that "succeeded," the gophers got out of control. Still the poisoning and trapping continue, disruptive and futile. As recently as 1939 wolves were still found in the high wilderness areas of national forests in the Pacific Northwest, but they were considered an interference to the sheepmen. So sodium fluoracetate was devised, a tasteless, odorless, colorless poison deadly to all members of the canine family. The wolves are gone, and other elements of the life community are gone with them.

By the mid 1880s the bison had been swept from the Plains; the grizzly bear and bighorn sheep were nearly gone south of Canada; the elk, which originally had ranged east of the Appalachians, were pushed back into a few pockets in the western mountains. The handsome little California wapiti, or dwarf elk, that had roamed the central and coastal valleys of California in herds of untold thousands, was virtually wiped out by ranchers eager to eliminate competition for their livestock and by market hunters supplying meat to stampeding miners of the Gold Rush. A few animals hid in the bulrushes, or tules, of the Miller and Lux cattle kingdom and came to be known thereafter as the tule elk. Market hunting, for birds as well as larger mammals, was rampant. The market hunters (also known as "butchers," "hide hunters," and "game hogs") preyed on the flocks of passenger pigeons, invading the breeding roosts of unbelievable density, with unrestrained assaults during the breeding and nesting seasons. The numbers of passenger pigeon once were so great that trees collapsed under the weight of perching birds; but the last one anywhere was seen in 1914.*

When they finished off the buffalo and passenger pigeon, the market hunters turned to other game. Improvements in transportation permitted invasion of the last western strongholds of mule deer, elk, and mountain sheep. Trainloads of ducks, geese, crane, plovers, and prairie chickens arrived weekly at processing

* Contrary to misconception, however, the passenger pigeon was critically affected not by man's slaughter alone. Another contributing factor to its demise was destruction of its habitat in the great eastern deciduous forests. Nesting and roosting sites were obliterated in the course of agricultural clearing and timber harvesting.

centers in Kansas City and Chicago, thus involving meat packers and rail shippers, as well as restaurant and hotel men, in legitimizing the market hunters. In the breeding grounds of migratory waterfowl in the North, the hunters were ruthlessly disrupting nesting activity and killing paired birds. In the nesting rookeries of the southern swamps, they were slaughtering hundreds of thousands of nesting egrets, herons, ibises, and other wading birds for fine feathers to adorn women's hats, leaving millions of parentless nestlings to perish.

The grizzly bear has almost gone the way of the passenger pigeon. Even now its fate is uncertain. Once about 1.5 million of these giants ruled a domain extending from the Mississippi to the Pacific. Now there are less than a thousand in the United States south of Alaska, possibly no more than 800. The intelligent, powerful grizzly walks with dignity and lordliness of carriage—it embodies the spirit of the wilderness frontier. Reports suggest that during the early stages of contact in the nineteenth century grizzlies were not hostile, so long as men exercised caution and restraint. The celebrated beaver trappers were deadly enemies of the grizzly, however. They led the way, overcoming its size with rifle and trap, and within seventy-five years of their first encounter with the covered-wagon pioneers, the great carnivores of the American West, monarchs since the Ice Age, were virtually wiped off the map.

Finally the public awakened. Early citizen conservation organizations joined with sportsmen's groups to press for a national policy prohibiting the killing of game for profit. This came with passage of the Lacey Act of 1900. The elimination of unrestricted hunting, however, was still inadequate; there was also a need for reservations in the face of destruction and reduction of habitats. The first great public wilderness, Yellowstone National Park, had been established in 1872, but the wildlife values had been only incidental—the original question there had been whether public or private ownership should govern a spectacular scenic resource. Nevertheless, after 1885, the last significant herd of bison in the United States had found refuge in the park. Yellowstone held the largest elk herds in the country, while beaver were still common on many of its streams and brooks. Outside its boundaries, these species had been nearly exterminated or greatly reduced in numbers.*

The demonstrated value of Yellowstone led to the establishment of forest reservations. They were intended to protect wildlife along with watershed and timber resources. "The preservation of forests and game go hand in hand," wrote Theodore Roosevelt in 1893. "He who works for either works for both." Thus, when he became President he set aside by executive order 132 million acres of the public domain as forest reserves (later to be renamed national forests).

Then in 1903 Roosevelt established the Pelican Island National Wildlife Refuge in Florida as a sanctuary for sea birds threatened by plume hunters. It was the first of its kind in America, but as one reviews the history of the network of wildlife refuges, wherever they may be, many of them came into being to protect wilderness species from extinction by the onrush of man-centered civilization. This holds true in the remotest corners of the continent, even the archipelago of the Aleutian Islands, between the North Pacific and the Bering Sea, where the Russians, then the French and Americans, decimated the population of sea otter, or "sea beaver," a marine mammal bearing the world's most valuable fur.

From a small group of 200 sea otters that had somehow survived, biologists have since repopulated other ancestral islands across churning Aleutian pathways and farther south as well. Here as elsewhere, wilderness refuges have played a key role in every successful wildlife restoration in our history, with conflicting interests and activities of man restricted or excluded altogether.

National wildlife refuges now cover about 30 million acres,

* Early regulations in Yellowstone permitted hunting for "recreation" and "for food," enabling poachers and market hunters to roam the plateaus and canyons at will while they slaughtered elk and buffalo. Sportsmen had had little to do with establishment of the national park, but the Boone and Crockett Club, an organization of big game hunters founded by Theodore Roosevelt, recognized it as a haven for endangered species of western wildlife. The Boone and Crockett crusade to end poaching and market hunting culminated in passage of the Act of 1894 "for the protection of Yellowstone National Park." It set the precedent in preservation for national parks everywhere.

but about 20 million of these are concentrated in a few large areas of Alaska, and most of the others are designed and managed to serve migratory birds en route. These hardly seem adequate in the face of continuing environmental deterioration around them, and when additional species are endangered, including the manatee, black-footed ferret, tule elk, wolf, grizzly, prairie chicken, peregrine falcon, bald eagle, and condor.

For years hunters have been led to exult in the resurgence of popular species through a variety of management programs, some more ecologically valid than others. Game departments have instituted licensing, bag limits, enforcement by game wardens, trapping and transplanting, habitat manipulation, and elimination of predators. Managers count populations and study habitat in order to calculate how many animals should be killed in order to keep things in balance within a given range. The hunter's money, paid through licenses and equipment taxes, has replenished game in short supply and underwritten wildlife research. In 1910 there were only 50,000 elk, by 1970 there were 250,000. In 1925 there were only between 13,000 and 26,000 pronghorns and no hunting, by 1970 there were at least 500,000 with 100,000 killed annually. The wild turkey was brought back from a population of less than 100,000 in 1952 to 500,000 in 1970.

Yet the focus has been on the "production" of game species to be "harvested." Such figures tend to give the impression of "deer" and "game" as synonymous, failing to mention that when one species moves in there is apt to be a mass exodus of many others. Each species, after all, is a lesson in how to live that can never be learned after it is gone. It isn't enough to know there are millions of deer, elk, wild turkey, pronghorn, pheasant, bobwhite quail and mourning dove "that can thrive in an environment molded by human beings," as some of the game biologists like to put it, for the idea of preserving wildlife gains legitimacy when it applies to man's relationship with his whole environment and not to isolated parts of it.

Despite the statistics, attempts to reverse the continuing decline of wildlife abundance have produced local success at most, so that hunters generally have to compete for game over shrinking areas. (Or, as Leopold wrote, relegating grizzlies to Alaska is about like relegating happiness to heaven: One may never get there.) In a great outdoors state like Wisconsin, elk, marten, wolverine, and caribou have all but disappeared. The moose barely survives in one or two counties after being on the brink of extinction for years. The wolf is gone. Sharptail grouse, northern shrike, bluebirds, many species of hawks, owls, and woodpeckers, and some of the ducks and shorebirds may soon be on the endangered list. Green Bay, which only twenty-five years ago was one of the great waterfowl areas of the world, is now sterile and virtually beyond repair.

Although hunting plays a valid role as an outdoors experience, the rightness of one being to kill another for sport is now extremely moot. The need to hunt for food is gone. Much of sport hunting has scant relevancy to primitive instincts or old traditions. It does little to instill a conservation conscience. Blasting polar bears from airplanes, hunting the Arabian oryx—or deer—from automobiles, trail bikes, or snowmobiles, tracking a quarry with walkie-talkie radios, killing for the sake of killing annihilate the hunt's essential character. There can't be much thrill to "the chase" when there is little chase. At one end of the spectrum, "slob hunters" shoot farmers' livestock, road signs, and each other. At the opposite end are the superpredators: jet-set gunners whose greatest goal is to mount on their walls one of everything that walked Noah's plank. Some of this breed pay thousands for a trophy, whether shot illegally, out of season, or even by someone else.

The hunter is told that he serves beneficently as a "management tool," cropping surplus game without diminishing the population, but many management plans fail to selectively cull overpopulation through elimination of the old or crippled or through selection of females, the only way a herd can be reduced. One may wonder whether it's really necessary to defend hunting by preaching that wildlife must be killed for its own good, or whether there would be no wildlife left if the emphasis was placed on protection of ecosystems with their own built-in balances rather than on the production of moving targets. Wilderness has its own natural ways. If we are wise enough to permit them, natural wildlife and occasional insect and disease outbreaks will kill off the climax vegetation, set back ecological succession, and thereby achieve about the same result as some techniques of intensive management. There is less likelihood in wilderness of unbalanced game populations that sometimes result from attempts to increase favored kinds and to suppress others, with the monoculture in game inviting the spread of disease, parasites, and starvation.*

In wilderness at times there is apt to be less game, since mature forests, with bigger trees and shady forest floor, do not provide an abundance of feed, but the quality of the hunt will be better for it. Hunting at its finest involves environmental satisfactions: an authentic immersion in nature, with hard efforts in tracking, scenting, and pinpointing the game for hours or even days when necessary. The quality of the hunt is scantly measured by the size of the bag but rather by the experience of woodmanship, living with the animals and thinking like them, perceiving surroundings from the viewpoint of the animal. The hunter conservationist imposes limitations on himself in order to create the earlier day moods of a Natty Bumpo or Lewis and Clark. He strives to preserve a world safe for leopards and bison, a world for rocks and all nature.

Crouching on the forest floor, the serious hunter does not have so many advantages over the game. The prey is scarce. It is fleet, alert, deceptive, unlike a chicken or a cow, a preserve-bred quail or semitame deer. It smells and hears better than the predator, particularly where it benefits from the presence of

---

* Elk and deer, in particular, thrive in young brushy forests, with numerous scattered openings. Many foresters, range managers, and biologists insist that timber-cutting, chaining of pinyon and juniper trees, controlled fire, and use of herbicides are essential techniques to increase the growth of herbs and shrubs for game. Yet they also warn against the dangers of over-browsing as a result of irregular buildups, followed by drastic die-off.

The key idea in forest wildlife management is diversity of habitat for food and cover, yet vast areas that once supported mixed forests have been reduced to "even-aged" stands with few plants desirable for game. When this leads to destruction of young trees by deer, sportsmen are subjected to demands to "bring the deer into balance." Likewise, though livestock exceeds its carrying capacity in large portions of the public range of the West, as it has for a hundred years, management requires reduction in numbers of game, rather than of livestock.

so-called "undesirable" or "competitive, nongame" species, such as coyote, wolf, wildcat, mountain lion, eagle, hawk, and owl. It lives on its artful protective instincts, developing the very qualities hunters admire. There is an inverse relationship between hunting prowess and intensity of management, as Leopold warned: the more of the latter, the poorer the former becomes. Wilderness demonstrates that management is more than manipulation of food cover and reduction of numbers through killing and transplanting; it is also protection from the influences of man to allow nature to manage its own affairs.

Wilderness game includes elk, grizzly, moose, caribou, mountain sheep, and mountain goat, but their range is vanishing. The California condor and birds of prey are creatures of wilderness, too; many kinds of birds, in fact, need inviolate areas for feeding and breeding. Management has failed to stress their total needs or the full range of the threats against them. This is particularly so in reference to the nation's timberlands. Hardwood forests have declined steadily; the mature, dying, and dead trees have vanished, and with them the fallen trunks and other litter from the forest floor. The result has been a decrease in ecological niches and in biotic diversity.

One principal victim, the ivory-billed woodpecker, the shy, wild bird with shining black plumage and great scarlet crest, is either extinct or nearly so. It was last seen in 1967. Destruction of the vast forests of the South, especially the luxuriant hardwood forests of swamps and river valleys, apparently has doomed this largest of our woodpeckers by removing its feeding niche of recently dead trees supplying its most important food, the larvae of wood-boring beetles. Though never abundant, its survival was assured as long as there were dead trees of the proper age scattered in the forest. No doubt biologists can succeed in breeding or stimulating quail, turkey, elk, deer, and other game species, but the ivory-bill is wholly dependent upon wilderness.

Nor can anyone breed a seal, whale, walrus, or sea otter. The latter are dependent on the extensive kelp beds and tidal currents in which they feed on sea urchins, oysters, clams, snails, and fish, constantly kneading and rubbing the lustrous fur that is their protection against sea and cold. Another is the manatee, or sea cow, docile, harmless, and ungainly (by human standards), shy by nature, impossible to breed in captivity. Once found along the coast from the Carolinas to Mexico, one species, the sea cow, has completely disappeared as the result of intensive slaughter for meat. The Florida species is reduced to a few relict populations in sequestered backwaters, but even there it faces new dangers in water contaminated by herbicide spraying, dredging, and invasion by numbers of humans in motor boats.

At one time a million Attwater's prairie chickens are believed to have ranged over the coastal prairies of Louisiana and Texas. Today, as the result of pollution from oil drilling, rice farming that destroys grasslands, and drought, only a few thousand remain. There is an Attwater's Prairie Chicken National Wildlife Refuge near Eagle Lake, Texas, but the future existence of this splendid game bird demands that it be provided soon with additional areas in which it will have tall grasses, fresh water, and protection from shooting.

Few species are threatened by the gun. The hunter kills one at a time. The entire environment in which all animals live is threatened by pollution, population pressures, and massive technological alteration. The alteration or destruction of habitat is more subtle than shooting, and equally deadly, though on a broader scale. Wildlife cannot continue to contribute to our way of life unless we set aside adequate living space, in wilderness, with the emphasis directed at conserving not game per se but adequate portions of the total life community—the arctic, oceanic, estuarine, prairie, marsh, high desert, low desert, forest, tropical, and the several other land forms in between.

Chapter Six

Recreation for Everyone...

While vacationing in the Adirondacks in August 1871 the celebrated Horace Greeley arose one morning at sunrise, but not to fish as was his custom. He sat thoughtfully, admiring the lake and absorbing the quiet environment. Presently his guide joined him, but neither spoke. They preferred to share in silence the blaze of fresh sunlight spreading across the waters. "John," Greeley said finally, "I suppose when the season ends, like John of old, you will be left alone in the wilderness. But, bear this in mind, God and John French will not be as isolated as Horace Greeley in the living wilderness of New York City."

The essence of wilderness recreation is in the individual freedom that Greeley sensed and expressed and that countless others have sought both before and since his time. Primeval country in his century was superabundant in comparison to urban concentrations such as New York. Now the ratio is reversed. Little wonder, therefore, that steadily increasing numbers of people are fleeing the cities to pursue the singular kinds of travel available to them in wilderness—hiking, backpacking, horseback riding, walking with pack stock, canoeing, kayaking, and the simplest pleasure of all, contemplation. There are now 10 million backpackers in America, or possibly 20 million, depending on the source of the estimate. The use of wilderness has been growing at a faster rate than any other form of outdoor recreation, to such an extent that many areas are already overcrowded, despite their seeming spaciousness.

There is a place for crowds and shared activity, but there should also be a place where one can be alone, to commune with himself and to dream freely and boldly. The artist appears entitled to claim his sanctuary in order to be creative. But wilderness recreation is an essential of democracy, open to all, and all are able to respond to it. Primeval nature has been a factor in the search for happiness since man began, perhaps even more so now that it has become so rare.

The right to choose a type of recreation deserves respect, but the choices are virtually all alike, focused on crowds, noise, and the presence of mechanical contrivances. Wilderness offers the principal alternative. Unlike some other activities that establish their own exclusivity through cost, wilderness recreation is open to everyone. Several thousand dollars or more are needed to acquire a pickup camper or travel trailer complete with water, light, heat, sewage, and air conditioning, but hiking requires only the place, and backpacking can be enjoyed with even a gunny sack or denim packs.

Wilderness assures the freedom of silence and the right to listen to silence and to the small sounds of nature. It doesn't involve investments in "development"—neither roads, gas stations, tramways, restaurants, nor souvenir concessions. You don't have to build anything to enhance natural beauty, all that is needed is receptivity, and a facility of perception, in the human mind. With the right outlook, anyone can appreciate the inspiration of wilderness. It isn't a question of how extensively, or expensively, one travels but of how much one absorbs. When civilization is brought no closer than the fringe of wilderness areas, even invalids can enter the sacred precincts to experience wonder and beauty.

It's never too late, and really never too early, to take to the priceless natural environment. Best of all, the experience, once tried, opens new and expanding vistas that go on forever.

I have encountered people from all walks of life on America's wilderness trails who have shown this to be the case. In the Grand Tetons of Wyoming there was a couple in their late fifties who had never backpacked before. They had camped widely but had never climbed. Yet through careful planning and preparation, they made it to the top of the Tetons, where they slept under the stars close to heaven. They said it was one of the greatest thrills of their life together. In the Southeast Reverend Rufus Morgan was over eighty and nearly blind, but he never missed a year without hiking the hills and hollows of the Great Smoky Mountains. As for getting started early, every year the Sierra Club conducts a series of family wilderness trips, one of which is limited to families with all children *under* eleven years. I've also seen young parents, instead of engaging a sitter, toting a child in swaddling clothes, papoose-style.

Time in the wilderness never hangs heavy; no two days are ever alike. I recall a trip as member of a horse party in the Bridger Wilderness, on the western slope of the Continental Divide in Wyoming. The trail led through a natural kingdom of tall timbers and a thousand clear lakes, weaving at times among massive rock formations almost as large as those in Yosemite Valley, alongside living glaciers and flowery alpine meadows, into a world of snowy starkness glittering in the bright summer light high above the timberline. No resort ever was endowed with better landscaping nor ever afforded a more refreshing change of pace from routine.

Given a road we probably could have driven the same route of ten or twelve days in three hours and seen virtually nothing. Driving through a wilderness is like watching a movie without sound: You're trying to perceive a landscape without its vitals, pretending that nature is represented by waterfalls but not stagnant swamps, by butterflies but not black flies, and by clear moonlit nights but not bone-chilling darkness and drenching downpours. Providing the mechanisms to fulfill these notions has helped to alienate a people from the natural world. On the other hand, the seeming slowness of transportation allows one to appreciate the fullness of what lies at hand. Walking is even better than horseback riding, (and less damaging to the terrain), a natural way for man to fit into the outdoors, whether to hunt, fish, hike, or picnic. The idea is not geared to moving from one point to another in the shortest possible time. Never mind the straight-line mile, if the crooked mile seems more appealing.

The trails followed those of Jim Bridger and the fur trappers, of General John C. Frémont and Kit Carson, his guide in 1842. We came upon the very scenes painted by Alfred Jacob Miller in 1837, the Wind River places that he had found "as fresh and beautiful as if just from the hands of the Creator." The lakes were crystal clear, the rare kind you can drink from or swim in, when the temperature is warm enough. At Trapper Lake we encountered company, a pair of fishermen, who had hiked in. Always, where the water is clean and cold, favorable to wild fish, there are fishermen; no matter how remote the setting, they will search it out. And, soon after, we came on a handful of young people, of high school or college age, boys and girls together, with canoes and the least expensive kind of camping gear, half of it that they must have made or pieced together themselves. Always, wherever there is wilderness young people are found. Apparently, in the search for identity they resort to places kept free of man's handiwork and neuroses, places still touching the mystery and complexity of living organisms.

We rode along rocky crests up precipitous switchbacks into the country explored by General Frémont, camping at the base of the mountain that he climbed and named for himself. We were surrounded by a concentration of great peaks just under 14,000 feet flanking the Continental Divide. Frémont was drawn by their shiny icecaps and determined to scale what he thought was the highest. He and five companions rode beneath a perpendicular wall of granite working their way to the summit, then dismounted and climbed on foot in thin moccasins made from buffalo skin. He miscalculated in judging himself to be at the highest point in the Rockies, but anyone who makes it this way will understand why he was overcome by "the concourse of lakes and rushing waters, mountains of rock, dells and ravines of the most exquisite beauty, all kept green and fresh in the air and sown with brilliant flowers."

In such an arena there are no social values to conform to; all individuals become essentially equal, benefiting from cooperation rather than competition, as did our group, in camping at Fremont Crossing, then hiking up to Indian Pass, from where we could see the Dinwoody Glaciers, the forested trough of

Wind River Valley calling from the east side of the divide, and the bright peaks of the Grand Tetons, far off northwestward.

A psychologist might explain that such a sweeping scene is more lively and lovely because it doesn't contain evidences of man's critical or harmful actions, or that, through one penetrating moment of unshared solitude in the primeval, an individual feels liberated of strain and stress. In the face of sheer power of stillness, of the artistry and complexity of earth, and of the lasting quality and independence of nature quite beyond understanding, the individual acquires a sense of scale, conceding to himself there is something larger and longer lasting than anything he has known before and feeling that he belongs at the bosom of a much greater whole—at peace. He has at hand an environmental model from which to measure the restorative impetus he and others need under current circumstances of alienation from nature. Or as Shakespeare summed it up in *As You Like It,* "And this our life, exempt from public haunt,/ finds tongues in trees, books in the running brooks,/sermons in stones and good in everything." *

In recent years wilderness trips of one type or another have become available for the uninitiated in all parts of the country. The idea among preservationists has always been to share treasures rather than to hoard them. Thoreau's hopefulness and generosity, for example, are spread across the pages of "The Maine Woods": "What a place to live, what a place to die and be buried in! There certainly men would live forever, and laugh at death and the grave." [1] So he exulted following his exploration of Katahdin. In the appendix he advised the potential tourist of his day on what to wear, carry (in the way of compass, axe, pocket map, and the like), the fee of an Indian guide, and the cost of the 12-day excursion starting from Moosehead Lake.

Likewise, it was John Muir himself who conducted the first Sierra Club wilderness trip, or outing, into Yosemite Valley in

---

* Spoken by the banished Duke Senior (in Act II, Scene 1), these lines are used by Shakespeare to strike a contrast between virtuous country life and the decadence of the court. The Duke clearly finds nature's reality a singular comfort and spiritual guide.

1901. Muir focused the viewpoint of the Club on faith and belief in people, all people; he wanted them to admire the wonders of the wild country and to be absorbed by them, and thus better equipped for pursuit of their normal activities. From that beginning the program has blossomed to encompass more than 250 trips a year, appealing to people of varying interest and outdoors competence, in all seasons and virtually in all parts of the globe. Members take turns with camp and cooking chores; they must be prepared to do their share in a cooperative venture.

For trips sponsored by the Wilderness Society, the only prerequisites are good health and a desire to learn firsthand about the wilderness. And all the Society hopes to derive is that participants, following an enjoyable experience, may wish to support the preservation cause. On this principle, guided trips are taken by horseback, hiking with pack stock, backpack, and canoe. Family participation is encouraged. There are trips for teenagers only, combining adventure with study of ecological values.

What it all means is that wilderness is for everyone, not for a "handful of elitists," as sometimes alleged by commercial interests that see no value to it. No program makes this plainer than the Montana Wilderness Walks conducted by the Montana Wilderness Association. The stated purpose is "to encourage people of all ages to use the wilderness and enjoy it; to show that backpacking and wilderness walking are available to people of limited financial ability; to teach use without abuse, and to insure the preservation of the resource for future generations." These trips are not led by professionals but by volunteers willing to show some of their favorite spots. Nobody makes any money, which may be another point hard to understand.

Rarely do critics deny the incomparable and inspirational qualities in wilderness recreation; they insist they only want to share them with all comers, to make the wonders of the outdoors more broadly available—to the elderly, infirm, poor, asthmatic, disabled, and lazy. Stated another way, a few roads won't harm the wilderness resources and will still leave enough to satisfy "those hardy souls who have the youth and strength to hike and camp their way to solitude." The roads would benefit private enterprise. Mr. Average doesn't hike anymore. If folks want to congest themselves in overcrowded camping slums, that's their privilege, isn't it? Why should a handful of wilderness hogs prevent them from doing so? The major reason our parks are so crowded is that 90 to 95 per cent of visitors are wedged into 5 per cent of the space, walling off the vast remainder to be visited by only one out of ten—and what's right about that in a democracy?

Some of the most persistent arguments come from resource administrators themselves. In the National Park Service the standard expression is that "Parks are for people." The focus is on human activity. Wildlife, forests and all their flora, and the running streams are assigned values as they relate to people. Budgets from Congress for each park and the entire park system are based on the numbers of people served in campgrounds, visitor centers, and counted at entry stations.

The same is true of pay levels of park personnel—these are determined not by acres of wilderness protected, endangered species of wildlife, or diversity of land forms but by the numbers of people served. The superintendent of a park with 2 million visitors is higher up the ladder than the man at another park with 2 million acres of wilderness and half as many visitors. It goes to the heart of the political system. "There are no votes in the Yellowstone Park for the Republican or Democratic Party," observed Senator George Graham Vest of Missouri, one of Yellowstone's rare friends during the struggle to save that park in the 1880s. "The result is that outside of those who are esthetic or sentimental, as we are told, in regard to the reservation, there seem to be few people who care anything about it." [2]

Much the same political presumption has prevailed over the years and applies today: that parks or forests or wildlife refuges in order to be valid must be used, demonstrably, by or for people, not in some future time, but now. Game must be produced and harvested, trees cut and transformed into cash crops, and visitors served; otherwise the areas are considered to be locked up and going to waste. Consequently, administrators find it convenient to support, or propose, construction projects designed to bring visitors in and to afford crowd-pleasing activities reduced to a low common denominator, rather than to hew to tough regulations joined with the values of the resource itself and its protection.

For example, in 1966 Stewart L. Udall, then Secretary of the Interior, wrote: "The continuing search for innovations that will make park visits more enjoyable has resulted in experimentation with such things as 'one-way loop roads' that give the visitor a sense of being the first person on the scene." [3] But no motorist can possibly feel like the first person on the scene; Udall's words, and the conception behind it, sound like inviting the people down a road into a blind alley, deluding them into a sense of false discovery where there is little to discover.

In the same year, 1966, the National Park Service presented its first proposal for wilderness designation under terms of the Wilderness Act of 1964. It related to the Great Smoky Mountains National Park, but, unfortunately, rather than presenting a design for safeguarding wilderness, the Park Service offered a plan for cross-mountain roads through primitive areas and for large new campgrounds in order to accommodate increasing numbers attuned to a mechanized age. It would have meant the end of a great wilderness.

The same philosophy was applied in North Cascades National Park in Washington state, where the National Park Service proposed a series of tramways in order to place visitors swiftly into the heart of the alpine zone. The idea is justified on grounds that tramways cause less damage than roads. Based on patterns of the past, however, with a tramway comes a concession, snack bar, restaurant, and overnight lodge; the need to keep the concession profitable then brings a cocktail lounge and souvenir shop, as well as electric power, water lines, sewage disposal, employees' quarters, and bulldozers, until the integrity of the resource is thoroughly disrupted. Moreover, it's unfair to park visitors to construct cable cars at high alpine elevations. Rarely do they recognize the dangers: Coming from lowlands in light clothing and thin shoes, they face the risk of abrupt weather changes and of finding themselves trapped in a blizzard or freezing weather. As between tramway and road access into the high places, the best solution is to furnish neither. Administrators would be at their best emphasizing protection of a fragile resource, with limited use by those who prepare themselves properly and make their way through difficult access.

The very character and purpose of wilderness limit its development—increased use undermines the values for which an area has been set aside. The seemingly generous procedure of letting people in by car, giving them a touch of wilderness from their window seat, is the first step to disaster. A road, such as the one proposed in the Great Smoky Mountains, appears to create jobs, open impressive scenery to more people, expedite the flow of traffic, keep people in their cars, and save the scenery. On the other hand, it splits a wilderness in two, altering the chemical constituents of streams and causing physical changes by siltation. Just because immediate changes are not visible does not mean there are no changes of consequence and significance. If a single species of salamander, or trailing arbutus, or birdfoot violet, or white-footed woods mouse should be eliminated in the Great Smoky Mountains in order to make way for a road or some other sort of development, then the public is being cheated of the wilderness promised to it.

In steep country, typical of the remaining wilderness, cuts and fills are commonplace in highway construction. They are expensive and difficult to maintain because of slides and earth faults. The cuts and fills need to be stabilized by plants, but those commonly used are exotic to the region, intruding into and disrupting the native life community. The road creates a barrier to the movement of animal species, providing avenues for introduction of new pests and pathogens into the adjacent wilderness—perhaps the equivalent of another balsam woolly aphid, Dutch elm disease, potato blight, or chestnut blight.

The injection of motor vehicles, together with their noise, exhaust fumes, and people, has predictable results: contamination, disturbance, refuse. And in due course the highway strip needs to be widened as park visitation increases, reflecting the increase of leisure time and shrinkage of wilderness elsewhere. Or, as the resource administrator might ask of himself, "If I remove that tree, do I admit more darkness than light?"

Those who direct the fate of the national parks, however, whether in Congress or the executive branch, are not ecologists by education or experience, and only occasionally so by inclination. On all fronts the national park heritage shows steady signs of dissipation without even being recognized.

In Yellowstone a small city named Canyon Village, with all the manifestations of urban blight, has been implanted in the heart of wild country. South along the loop road, the air is polluted by the exhaust from automobiles that bring viewers to Old Faithful, while the tens of thousands of visitors these cars disgorge compact the surrounding soil. They cannot hear the subterranean cannonading of the great geyser; but, of course, their experience in the park has already been altered from exploration to entertainment. Elsewhere in Yellowstone important hot springs and geysers have been destroyed, and others seriously marred or brought close to total spoliation. It is not much consolation to a visitor in search of the primeval life community to be told there are hundreds of square miles of "undeveloped" lodgepole pine forest.

Little is known about the ecological nature of wilderness. Botanists and zoologists have not recorded the distribution of any plant and animal species, let alone discovered the interrelationships of these organisms and their environment. Nevertheless, the ecosystem reacts as a whole. It is impossible to wall off one organism in nature and control it without affecting the remainder. Dead trees, disturbed forests, flood debris along stream banks, dead animals, and scars of natural erosion are inherent aspects of a dynamic primitive landscape. So are forest insects, lightning fires, and erosive forces, despite efforts to screen them out.

So too are grizzly bears. For centuries the grizzly was the dominant animal of the West. But hunting, trapping, and government "management" programs have been steadily pushing the grizzly to extinction. In 1967 two campers in Glacier National Park were pulled from sleeping bags, dragged off into the woods and killed by grizzly bears. These tragic events resulted in the summary execution of two bears, alleged to be responsible, but without significant evidence against them. Then followed several demands for total extermination of grizzlies in Glacier and Yellowstone, though the two parks are among the last major strongholds of these native animals that once roved the West. There were no declarations from administrators that man is far more dangerous to bears than bears to man or that visitors have been thoroughly beguiled and misled by the unrestrained opportunity to feed black bears along the Yellowstone roadsides, or that national parks deserve to be treated as wild places, rather than as zoos.*

Adolph Murie for years conducted wildlife ecological studies in the national parks. His approach was aimed at true research. This means living with the animals, trying to think as they do, and establishing an intimate relationship with the creatures that reveals their motivations in all they do. Such intimate, on-the-ground contact with animals, as his brother, Olaus Murie, commented, leads to an understanding of nature that is desperately lacking in this age of human exploitation of the planet.

On this basis, Adolph Murie, in his classic book *A Naturalist in Alaska* discussed recreation and grizzlies. As he related an incident, a friend was about to embark into bear country. When the friend inquired about the danger of bears, Adolph replied that a traveler had nothing to worry about: He could enter the wilderness with a light spirit; all he needed was faith. The chief difficulty would be to preserve one's faith. But if his friend did so, cautioned Murie, respecting the bear's potential for causing injury and keeping at a respectful distance, all would go well.[4]

As conditions now stand in Yellowstone and Glacier, grizzly-

---

* Bears have an uncommon predilection for human foods, whether in the form of garbage or groceries in a cabin, reports Adolph Murie on the basis of his extensive intimate observations. Accessible garbage is the chief cause of bear trouble. First it attracts bears, then it continues to hold them in an area so that they become unafraid and are soon breaking into tents, trailers, or cabins in search of more food. Human contacts follow, and incidents occur in which people are harmed, sometimes seriously. The bears become pests, no longer interesting wild creatures with natural habits. The usual ending of the story is damage of property, injury to humans, and death to the bear.

human confrontations are inevitable. They are apt to continue as long as visitor numbers continue to rise in bear country. Grizzlies habitually make shallow "day beds" from which they strongly resent being disturbed. It is extremely hazardous to approach a place where a grizzly has hidden food. When a grizzly is startled at close range, the animal is about as likely to charge as to run. The wilderness traveler who has studied bear habits knows enough to make his way cautiously. But the grave indication, based on recent trends and practices, is that Yellowstone and Glacier will be sterilized of the great bear in order to accommodate the mass of other travelers who are unprepared for that animal.

How best to serve the recreational needs of the majority of people? The U.S. Army Corps of Engineers has eliminated and altered entire river systems, which formerly constituted a living part of the national heritage, with civil works projects; yet it likes to cite statistics showing that its 300-plus artificial reservoirs are subject to a heavier volume of visitors than all baseball, football, basketball, soccer, hockey, and assorted other spectator sports combined. The figures showing use for motorboating, water skiing, and warm-water fishing are impressive, if you like numbers.

But almost all dams cause changes in flow patterns, water temperatures, the chemistry and quality of water, and the biological interrelationship with the clear-water streams below them. Fluctuating water levels periodically expose, then inundate, timberlands and scenery. Dead trees and silt are substituted for green plants and for plant and animal communities; beauty and quality are sacrificed. Mud, carried to the dam by its source waters, settles in the reservoir, where it accumulates in the form of silt and sediment. As the reservoir fills, its value diminishes, while the danger of flood increases. Dams and reservoirs may block passage of anadromous fish, such as salmon and steelhead, between sea and spawning grounds, damage the spawning areas, and upset oxygen and other water-quality conditions.

Amid the promotion and commercial clamor for such faulty technical delights, there is no revelation of recreation lost, such as the chance to listen to the murmur, roar, and rush of a native stream tumbling through a wild gorge or to get away from crowds and discover one's self for a little while, and certainly no revelation of the inevitable ecological damage.

In the case of the ill-conceived, ill-fated Cross-Florida Barge Canal (a politically inspired project that President Richard M. Nixon canceled in 1971, after the expenditure of $50 million), the Engineers painted an illusionary picture of expanded boating and camping but failed to say that swimming would be wretched because of weeds on the bottom and that fishing would decline inside a few years. Nor did they mention that the canal would drown out a natural stream, the Oklawaha River, whose rich, fast waters have created the dynamic conditions needed to maintain a productive sports fishery, or that they would be altering an unpolluted, free-flowing, spring-fed stream in a unique subtropical setting into a sluggish, slow-moving body of flat water. Is it laughable or tragic to hear people speak of "increasing the opportunities" when they are wiping out the most ennobling kind of recreation, the contemplation of nature?

Robert Marshall, a key figure in the modern preservation movement, was obligated, as an official of government, to consider wilderness in terms of democratic use. He reasoned that by opening up an area beauty can be tapped and bring joy into the lives of many who would never be able to see it as wilderness but who would still derive some thrill from the inferior version of the original—somewhat like the old lady who can never have the opportunity of seeing the real portrait of Whistler's mother but who still gets a thrill from the modified version on the postage stamp. Then Marshall completed his analogy. While the postage stamp of Whistler's mother did no damage to the original painting, the road or reservoir would wreck the values of wilderness.

"The Mona Lisa has given many people a supreme esthetic thrill," he wrote,

yet if you cut it up into little pieces one inch square and distributed it among the art galleries of the world so that millions might see it where hundreds see it now, neither the millions nor the hundreds would get any genuine value. Similarly, if the French government in order to augment its revenues sold to Pepsodent for a few million francs the right to paint a modest advertisement on just a minor fraction of the famous portrait, the Mona Lisa would be dead. Of precisely the same nature are the Unfinished Symphony and wilderness lakelets. All of them are destroyed by fragmentation or pollution. . . ." [5]

If it were decided that the most popular public activities should prevail in designating the use of every acre of public land and every public building, our metropolitan art galleries might be converted into metropolitan bowling alleys. Our state universities, which are used by a minor fraction of the population, might be changed into state Disneylands where hundreds could be exhilarated for every one person who may be either exhilarated or stimulated now. The Library of Congress might become a super-MacDonald's hamburger stand and the Supreme Court building a gigantic garage that could house a thousand autos instead of nine gentlemen of the law.

Wilderness can never justify itself on the basis of numbers, whether in terms of participants or tourist dollars generated. But why should it have to? If decisions were made on volume use, then everything of distinctive quality would vanish. Fortunately, society is blessed with provisions for the entire spectrum of individual tastes. Custom shops, restaurants, theaters, and television cater to all kinds. Public television was established to make up for the void in private television. Libraries and universities are maintained at public expense in the interest of the majority of people, though only a minority may use them. Some books may be read by only a handful, but by that reading they may serve everyone. That's how it is with mountain climbing. It takes an entire mountain slope, better yet a variety of slopes scattered everywhere, to accommodate the tastes of a relatively small number of climbers, yet society is better for having them and their awareness of the challenge, beauty, and fragility of the rugged environment.

If decisions on use of the land were taken one at a time, based on economics and numbers, in due course all the resources offering unique experiences would be extinguished. The builders of dams and roads would prevail as the foremost recreation purveyors on public lands, leaving the country impoverished in diversity and configuration of land forms. Democracy should accommodate a great variety of tastes, but this should be done by viewing land as a total system rather than piece by piece. Wilderness recreation, by its very nature, depends upon an input of space, which is why a small percentage of visitors use a large percentage of the land. Auto campgrounds, on the other hand, depend much more on inputs of money and work. In one 10-year period, the Forest Service doubled the capacity of its campgrounds and picnic area, but the sum total of the developments added up to 100,000 acres, or one-twentieth of 1 per cent of the whole National Forest System. This suggests that campgrounds could be managed more efficiently, with varied types clustered in particular areas to provide real choices; if they were cleaned up thoroughly and worn vegetation reseeded, there should be no need to demand intrusion of wilderness to meet the ordinary recreation activities.

The portion of lands preserved in wilderness is small. These areas become increasingly attractive as the population expands and becomes better educated to the implicit recreational and scientific values of the natural system. Many have ten people traveling in them in the early 1970s for every person who traveled in them twenty years ago. Some are overcrowded. The best restraints are the natural ones: remoteness, difficulty of access, and types of use that do the least damage. We are also moving into an age of limitation of numbers. There is need for more wilderness everywhere. We have no idea of public demand still to come or of fitting recreational uses to be devised. Ski touring, virtually unknown in the United States until the 1960s, has blossomed into an established national sport, one of the safest, most versatile, and least expensive winter recreations yet discovered. It's the best means of absorbing a natural winter environment without spoiling its beauty—a sport anyone can enjoy and one compatible with the resource.

Still, the demand that looms over us can never be satisfied. Slow attrition follows development like its shadow. Whenever there is a road or dug trail or shelter facility, there is slowly spreading damage. The primitive areas next to developments become littered, eroded, and threadbare from heavy use and abuse.

No further developments of any character should take place in what little wilderness remains. This means no more roads, no expansions, extensions, or additions to existing facilities. To protect what is left we must learn to live with facilities we now have. In order to ensure individual freedom within the wilderness, the hardest action will be the decision to exercise discipline and restraint outside of it.

Chapter Seven

... But Not Everyone at Once

The wilderness resource is for everyone—but not everyone at once, or in ways that are harmful, or that limit the experience of others to come, whether tomorrow or years hence.

John Muir was actually a promoter of recreation, encouraging people to come for their share of wilderness, providing they accepted it on its own terms. At Yosemite in 1912, when the major question on the agenda of the conference of national parks superintendents was "Shall automobiles be allowed to enter Yosemite?" Muir was reduced to despair. "It overshadowed all others and a prodigious lot of gaseous eloquence was spent upon it," he wrote a friend. "But the Yosemite Park was lost sight of, as if its thousand square miles of wonderful mountains, canyons, glaciers and songful falling rivers had no existence. Good walkers can go anywhere in these hospitable mountains without artificial ways."

Verily, wilderness is for people, not automobiles. There are places where Americans have agreed not to drive, such as cathedrals, concert halls, art galleries, up the Capitol steps into the halls of Congress, and private bedrooms. Why, then, should motor cars, motorcycles, snowmobiles, highways, and parking lots be accepted in the remaining refuges?

All over the world, once glorious corners have been reduced

to a level of sameness and monotony—monotony that is as great an enemy of human civilization as pollution. Honolulu, once characterized by natural colors, flowers, and uncluttered beaches, has deteriorated into a congested mixture of high-rise hotels, pancake houses, cheap restaurants, and ice cream parlors, with beaches that look like mob scenes. The same has happened at Miami Beach, San Juan, and St. Tropez. All are cut from the same mold, holiday ghettos to which vacationers flock from urban ghettos.

The same throngs are at historic museums, cathedrals, art galleries, and cultural centers—everywhere people standing in line as part of the compressed humanity, instead of exercising themselves as individuals in a stimulating environment. Yet once inside they are given a mere instant for each painting, since the mass must proceed to make way for the mass.

"But people like people and people like crowds! Why should we interfere with their choice?" a park administrator or chamber of commerce manager is apt to say in defense, or advocacy, of unrestricted numbers. Nevertheless, the tourist brochures and advertisements dwell on natural attractions, such as the "unspoiled" beaches, rather than on the synthetic and congested. The extent to which people flock to the prettiest lakes, the most attractive scenery, and shadiest glens emphasizes their desire to enjoy natural settings of quality. In the sum total of all motivations there is a common denominator: the urge to be free, to find an antidote to a frenzied supercitified age. There is need to fully interpret features of wilderness that make it worthwhile, a need for something like the trained guide in the gallery who explains great works of art, opening the visitor's eyes to a new dimension of sensory perception.

Unfortunately, resource administrators, instead of providing new interests and new experiences that contrast with urban lives, pour concrete for more highways and "motor nature trails" and congest visitors on treeless, barren, camping suburbias. In the process they destroy the features that visitors come to enjoy.

A heavily used wilderness is no wilderness at all. A lake or valley may be rich in appeal with ten people present. It may retain most of that appeal with 50, or even 250. But at some point sheer numbers alone transform a wilderness into a housing colony and ultimately an outdoors slum. When five campers per summer use an area, building a campfire is a harmless delight. When 500 campers build fires, they provoke an environmental catastrophe. The only way the area can be maintained in natural conditions is to limit access and development at the outset.

The effect of a single wilderness traveler is very small, but as the number is multiplied it becomes large and lasting. The least impact is probably caused by a single research scientist. There is some damage, but it is slight. That of a few Boy Scouts is probably not very damaging, but a steady stream of Scouts is something else again. As the number of visitors rises, so does the need for waste disposal, privies, garbage pits, and maintenance personnel. Remoteness and the sense of discovery are shattered when one finds many footprints along the bank of a beaver pond, or indelible evidence of campers' axes, the remains of campfires, beer cans shining at the bottom of a clear stream, or a trail deep in horse manure. You know people were there yesterday and that more will be added tomorrow.

Some activities are more compatible with wilderness than others, and some with more places than other places or time of year. Hiking, fishing, hunting, and canoeing are examples of generally compatible uses. They provide experiences the visitor cannot find elsewhere. But even canoeing may become incompatible when it diminishes nesting success of waterfowl by close and disturbing approaches to nest sites.

Mountainous environments, despite their grandeur, are quite fragile, easily susceptible to damage, slow to recover. The potential of soil erosion is great due to high rainfall, steep slope, lack of trees whose roots stabilize the soil, and thinness of soil. Soil formation is slow due to retarded growth of vegetation and gradual decomposition of any organic matter. Trails were built originally where people chose to walk, and shelters were placed in scenic areas; no thought was given to the ability of the land to sustain heavy use in these areas. Consequently, many trails and shelters are located in areas that cannot accommodate today's numbers. A trail up a steep incline may be the most direct route to the summit; however, when this trail is traveled by too many, erosion becomes a problem. In many cases, the location of shelters close to roads has encouraged heavy use. It becomes especially detrimental in early spring, when vegetation is at a delicate stage of growth and the ground is damp and more easily chewed.

Dr. Bettie Willard Scott-Williams undertook ecological studies at Rocky Mountain National Park, reported in 1963, with significant implications for all wilderness areas containing alpine vegetation. She found walking on tundra to be the most destructive activity of visitors. These effects had been observed in 1958, when the National Park Service opened a new parking area but constructed no adjacent paths. Visitors wandered away from their cars in two directions and within two weeks after the parking area was opened on May 30, distinct paths were visible on the fell-field environment. The tiny tundra plants were matted, flower stalks broken, and attrition of the cushion plants was beginning. By August 25 the attrition had destroyed two-thirds to three-quarters of the surface area of the cushion plants. The Park Service then installed black-topped trail, routed so as to link the features attracting the visitors. It was successful but only to an extent. People stayed on the trail for the most part but short-cut across the tundra when returning to their cars. The following summer the shortcut area was also black-topped, thus diminishing the natural resource still further.

An exclosure was installed at the beginning of the 1959 season to gain information about the rate of recovery of alpine plants from visitor trampling. The plants were observed numerous times during the season and seedlings were marked as they appeared. But the exclosure attracted so much visitor attention that the adjacent tundra was heavily trampled, and after two seasons it became necessary to install a second exclosure to cover this area, where the vegetative cover had been reduced from 70 per cent to 25 per cent. The remaining plants responded positively to release from trampling immediately, but continued observations revealed that time needed for recovery is many times greater than the time involved in causing the damage.

Elsewhere on the alpine ridge it was observed that the effects of intense visitor use for thirty-eight seasons had been total destruction. All plants were gone, except the few protected by large boulders. Five inches of topsoil were eroded, leaving a bare mineral soil surface. It was estimated, based on various observations of growth rate in alpine plants and on comparison of successional stands, that a minimum of 500 years will be necessary for the restoration of the climax tundra ecosystem.

The same conditions apply in wilderness areas everywhere. Only the degree varies; in some it is worse than others. All the outdoor clubs have been deeply concerned and are developing various guidelines and codes of ethics for their members. They urge wilderness travelers to try not to disturb the forest floor; to try not to tread unnecessarily on delicate plants that make up fragile alpine communities; to walk or climb on the bare rocks of streambeds, slides, and mountaintops, where possible, to reduce damage; to camp in designated areas only; to leave camping and hiking areas cleaner than they found them; to respect the natural environment and treat it gently. These efforts are not enough.

Overuse results not solely from increased popularity but from the decline in areas available. There are only a little over 100,000 miles of trail in the United States, less than one yard of trail per U.S. citizen and, not counting Alaska, only about fifty yards per square mile. Most U.S. trails are relics of past programs, mainly fire protection, rather than the product of serious recreational planning; despite the 1968 National Trails System Act, there are still few active programs to establish and maintain truly recreational trails.

Actually, there are more adverse than positive trends. Total trail mileage has not kept pace. Over half the mileage is in national forests, where trail mileage has dropped over one-third since 1945. Hiking has plainly occupied a low priority.* In addition,

---

* Why should hiking hold a low priority? Robert C. Lucas, Principal Geographer and Project Leader in Wilderness Management Research, Intermountain Forest and Range Experiment Station, believes hiking may be neglected because it does not produce any income and because it is inconspicuous as a result of being dispersed. In contrast, camping and skiing are concentrated, conspicuous, and often produce income. Hikers also are not as well represented by voluntary organizations as are many other types of recreationists. He discusses this in some detail in "Hikers and Other Trail

Forest Service practices of clear-cut logging and road-building have rendered vast areas useless for recreational pursuits. A "clear-cut," in which virtually all trees and other vegetation are removed, becomes valueless for a long time. The wild, scenic resource may be utterly shattered for as long as fifty years or more, whereas in a forested area left standing, or selectively logged, two generations could enrich their lives in the same period.

Logging and hiking can be compatible, when foresters build a certain number of trunk roads away from hiking routes, then log selectively from low-standard spurs that are "put to bed" when the harvest is complete. The trails are thus out of use only for several years, a small part of the 50- to 80-year growing cycle. However, no such multiple use is possible within the networks of high-standard, permanent roads that the Forest Service has been building. In the Pacific Northwest, for example, officials of Snoqualmie National Forest constructed a permanent road next to the north boundary of Mount Rainier National Park. In one fell swoop, they turned 3-day hikes into afternoon walks and eliminated a wilderness within the park. Gifford Pinchot National Forest has been so thoroughly criss-crossed with roads that little remains of the magnificent trail country of twenty years ago.

The same is true in national forests throughout the country. As public interest in wilderness recreation has risen, the space available has declined. More hikers, backpackers, canoeists, and cross-country skiers are crowded in smaller areas.

The hour of decision is plainly at hand to ration recreational uses of the back country if the back country is to survive. The destruction of animal communities, plant communities, the soil, and watershed of wilderness through overuse by recreational

---

Users," a paper from *Recreation Symposium Proceedings, 1971,* Northeast Forest Experiment Station, U.S. Department of Agriculture Forest Service, Upper Darby, Pa. In "Financial Planning Advice," a bulletin issued by the Chief of the Forest Service on May 14, 1973, relating to the President's budget for fiscal 1974, field offices in the national forests were advised to consider eliminating programs with low-volume use. Implementation of Project Hiking (an educational program on back-country use) was specifically deferred.

visitors has posed as much a threat as the bulldozer or commercial logger or miner. Wilderness, in common with other areas, has a "use capacity" that should not be exceeded.

Certain actions have already been taken by federal and state agencies. A permit system has been in force in the Boundary Waters Canoe Area of the Superior National Forest in Minnesota since 1966. Permits or voluntary registration are required to designated wilderness areas in California, Oregon, and Washington national forests, although without limitation on numbers. Several national parks require special permits for overnight back-country camping, with the number of permits based on the estimated capacity of trails and campsites to accommodate use without environmental damage. On the Colorado River, flowing through the Grand Canyon National Park and Grand Canyon National Monument, the Park Service has instituted limitations on commercial raft trips covering the number of passengers, number of boats, and maximum horsepower allowed for each steering engine. The Okefenokee National Wildlife Refuge requires permits for canoeists and for use of designated overnight shelters. A quota and permit system are in force at Mount San Jacinto Wilderness State Park, the only wilderness area in California's state park system.

It isn't solely through restrictions in numbers that recreational resources can be saved but in types of use as well. Shuttle buses, designed so visitors can enjoy the wonders without disruptions and pollution caused by heavy traffic, have replaced cars in portions of Yosemite, Grand Canyon, Mesa Verde, and Mount McKinley national parks. Still, extensive space is given over to trailers and large luxury vehicles and to concessions operations, consuming valuable real estate. At one national park alone, Shenandoah, in Virginia, over 700,000 pounds of garbage—including styrene plastic cups, paper plates, throw-away beverage cans, and sewage from the storage tanks of camping vehicles—are disposed of each year at five landfill dumps inharmoniously placed in wilderness. At this rate, how long will it be before there is no wilderness left?

There is nothing more natural than man resorting to his own physical efforts. Outdoorsmen who do so share a common bond, and conflicts between them have been almost nonexistent. It is hard to find activities more compatible than hunting, fishing, hiking, camping, and canoeing; the same outdoorsman may, and often does, engage in them all. Perhaps this harmony comes because these activities are re-enactments of how men lived, fought, obtained their food, and moved about in earlier times. Or because wilderness symbolizes permanence, stability in an unstable age, appealing values that it earns again and again by defending itself against intrusions and alterations.

No one can really justify his presence in the wilderness, unless he goes there on his own power. When a man enters the wilderness in a machine, he relegates himself to being a cog in that machinery; he detracts from nature and natural recreation, rather than contributing to them.

Off-road vehicles (Orvs) and all-terrain vehicles (Atvees) embrace a wide range of mechanical marvels—snowmobiles, dune-buggies, 4-wheel drives, 6-wheel drives, motor scooters, motorcycles, trail bikes, airboats, and hovercraft—that are incompatible with almost all other recreational uses. Atvees include the aggressively nomenclatured Terra-Tiger, Mini-Brute, Renegade, Cat-a-Gator, and Amphi-Cat, variously designed to "make the impassable passable" and to "go through hell and high water—and everything in between." Such vehicles render an area unsuitable for hunting, camping, fishing, bird-watching, nature study, wildlife, and wildlife habitat protection. Whether used on or off trail, Orvs and Atvees cause erosion, compaction, and displacement of soil, as well as siltation of streams; they result in contamination of streams with oil, grease, and scum; they present recurrent threat of fire due to their fuels and hot engine parts.

In the beginning of the snowmobile era, when there were few machines, their use was confined primarily to transportation by game wardens, timber cruisers, and search-and-rescue teams. The potential threat to the environment was minimal. Most operators were well trained. The modest horsepower of the engines precluded the capability of the early machines being able to run down game. Today, however, large, high-powered machines are capable of matching speed with many automobiles.

They are operated by a relatively untrained public, often by children. They present a threat not only to wilderness but even to urban areas incapable of absorbing the great number of vehicles on the market.

They're fun to ride, of course. The user feels a sense of power, excitement, control. But his focus of attention is on the activity of riding the machine, as a game, an end in itself, rather than on nature or the scenery. He's unmindful of shattering silence on a wintry day or night, of polluting clean air with exhaust fumes. The presence of the machine symbolizes that natural areas have lost their defenses. Even if it made no track or sound or released no odor, a mechanical sports vehicle is still misplaced in a natural setting, an intrusion where technology does not belong.

There is a considerable difference between using a vehicle for transportation on transportation routes and using it for off-road, all-terrain recreation. Proponents of Orvs and Atvees insist that rules and regulations are violated only by a few irresponsible users in their ranks. Possibly so, but one man can wreak havoc in a short time to private property and public lands. Wildlife in winter retreat has been a special target, though in that time of year most browsing and grazing animals are in poor physical condition. They live largely on the body fat stored during summer months and cannot tolerate extreme exertion. An hour's exposure to harassment by snowmobiles drains these animals of as much exertion as a week's normal existence.

Even when rules are respected, Orvs affect breeding, drumming, and spawning grounds, nesting and calving areas, winter range, feeding grounds, migratory routes, resting sites, and habitat for rare and endangered species. All wildlife is affected to some degree. Snowmobile treads snip the terminal buds off snow-buried evergreens, disfiguring trees and retarding spring growth. Compaction destroys the snow's capacity to insulate against the cold and to accommodate the burrows of rodents and other small mammals living beneath the snow's surface. Snowmobilers might not notice the disappearance of mice, but eagles, hawks, coyotes, bobcats, and foxes would.

Little wonder that snowmobiles are not allowed to roam the

national wildlife refuges. The national parks and national forests have not been as well protected. During the 1972–73 winter, more than 26,000 snowmobiles were in Yellowstone (presumably limited to roads, but with scant ranger supervision and control). The Forest Service has welcomed trail bikes to once peaceful valleys, lakeshores, and ridge crests. Public domain lands in the West, administered by the Bureau of Land Management, are in the poorest position of all to withstand the Orv and Atvee passion. Spectacular sand dunes, hundreds of feet high, have been worn down under the dune buggy and motorcycle tracks. Desert shrubs and cacti have been obliterated or removed; so have Indian ruins.

Regulations have been proven superficial at most, since enforcement officers can handle only a small fraction of Orv violations. The best regulation, of course, is to restrict Orvs and Atvees to established roads with all the rest of the mechanical marvels and save the back country while there's still some worth saving.

Much of the appeal of wilderness is embodied in the enjoyment of scenery that can't be viewed from a car, the physical challenge of doing something on your own that demands hard work, and the feeling of self-sufficiency away from the civilized world. Wilderness puts a person into a biologically healthy situation. Taking along too many items of civilization nullifies the benefits of the escape.

Even the best intentioned of hikers tend to be more concerned with the brand of their backpacks, boots, and sleeping bags than with the pleasures of the trail. Keeping the equipment simple helps achieve harmony with nature's rhythms and identification with wild places. There is no better goal in wilderness recreation.

Part II

SAVING THE WILDERNESS

President Lyndon B. Johnson signs the Wilderness Act at a White House Rose Garden ceremony, September 3, 1964. Immediately behind President Johnson from right are Stewart Udall, Secretary of the Interior; Rep. John Saylor, Pennsylvania, principal sponsor of the Wilderness Bill in the House of Representatives; and Orville Freeman, Secretary of Agriculture. The two women in the picture (front row) are Alice Zahniser and Margaret Murie.

Chapter Eight

Saving Wilderness by Law— The Ancient Creed

In 1934 and 1935 Robert Marshall dispatched a series of memo-randa to Secretary of the Interior Harold L. Ickes on the wilderness theme. His efforts during this period appear to be the first steps that ultimately led to the Wilderness Act. Marshall pleaded that roads be kept out of the undeveloped areas in Ickes's jurisdiction and warned of the threat of New Deal public works projects to overrun wild country.

When Marshall proposed setting aside parcels of wilderness,* he conceived of doing so as part of the process of democracy, with public understanding and due protection by law. Thus, in one report he recommended establishing a wilderness planning board, whose duty would be to select areas for protection

---

* Marshall defined wilderness in words that were strongly reflected in the Wilderness Act of three decades later: " 'Wilderness areas' are regions which contain no permanent inhabitants, possess no means of mechanical conveyance, and are sufficiently spacious for a person to spend at least a week of active travel in them without crossing his own tracks. The dominant attributes of such areas are: first, that visitors to them have to depend exclusively on their own efforts for survival; and second, that they preserve as nearly as possible the essential features of the primitive environment. This means that all roads, settlements, and power transportation are barred. But trails and temporary shelters, features such as were common long before the advent of the white race, are entirely permissible." *The People's Forests* (New York: Harrison Smith and Robert Haas, 1933): pp. 177–78.

by congressional designation in the same manner as national parks.

In his book, *The People's Forests,* published in 1933, he had already proposed a national network of numerous primeval reservations to be located in all sections of the country, both to make them readily available to people and to avoid overuse. As a forester he urged saving specimens of each timber type, on the grounds that each has its charm and beauty, whose possible destruction would distinctly lessen the esthetic enjoyment of nature. His interests cut across narrow bureaucratic boundaries of federal lands; when Marshall suggested recreational-use zoning, he employed categories such as "Superlative" for places like Yellowstone and Yosemite, "Primeval" and "Wilderness" for uninhabited forests, plus "Roadside," "Camp-site," "Outing," and "Residence."

Following World War II Howard Zahniser took up the call where Marshall had left off, stressing consideration of wilderness as part of civilization. Early in 1955 Zahniser delivered a speech before the National Citizens Planning Conference on Parks and Open Space for the American People in behalf of the Wilderness Society, in which he proposed protection of wilderness by law. The speech was entered in the *Congressional Record* on June 1, 1955. The circulation of a reprint brought nationwide interest, followed by introduction of the first wilderness bill in 1956.

Preservation, however, has an ancient history both as theoretical concept and legal doctrine. It represents the essence of Greco-Roman *usufruct,* or public trust, whereby perpetual use of common properties was "dedicated to the public." Under Roman law, for example, the shore was not owned by individuals but was treated like property of the Roman people, who were entitled to rights of use and enjoyment.

Preservation also embodies the environmental ethic: that no landowner may rightfully control use without regard for what his actions do to others. Fragile resources, such as mountain meadows, stream sides, and steep slopes, no matter in whose ownership, must be essentially *preserved,* not solely from abuses of exploitation but occasionally even from extensive human visitation, if they are to be retained for the use of generations to come. For intervention at one place in the environment, even on a minor scale, is likely to have far-reaching effects.

The creed of preservation is essentially the same as conservation and wholly compatible with it. There is no need to choose between them, despite the insistence of technicians that a resource must be exploited to be used or to be useful. Use means many things—such as conservation of water, scientific studies, and the sheer enjoyment of natural beauty—that are best done through preservation.

Saving the natural and wild from being civilized out of existence has in every case been aimed at protecting the people's own estate. In the settlement of the New World, open squares and commons were set aside in villages growing into cities. This idea reached its peak in New York in the nineteenth century after William Cullen Bryant started editorializing in the *Evening Post* for a major natural park. Frederick Law Olmsted, the landscape architect in charge, did not turn his back on the process of American urbanization; rather, he took the Jeffersonian rural idea and carried it into the heart of New York, humanizing the city, softening its hard edges through nature. "The main object and justification," he wrote, "is simply to produce a certain influence in the minds of people and through this to make life in the city healthier and happier. The character of this influence is a poetic one and it is to be produced by means of scenes, through observations of which the mind may be more or less lifted out of moods and habits into which it is, under the ordinary conditions of life in the city, likely to fall." [1] For Olmsted, recreation and the contemplation of scenery were synonymous; he felt the pastoral beauty of the park would bring refinement and happiness to the city's inhabitants.

California gave Olmsted another opportunity to apply the philosophy of land use for the public good. In 1865 he was appointed by Governor Frederick Low to head a commission to make recommendations on management of Yosemite as a public preserve. Congress had just withdrawn the area from the public domain and deeded it to California "for public use, resort, and recreation"—the first area to be set aside for such purpose. After exploring the Yosemite country, Olmsted became convinced that it was "far the noblest park or pleasure ground in the world." His preliminary report on *The Yosemite Valley and the Mariposa Big Trees* is a landmark document enunciating the individual's right to enjoy public scenery and the government's responsibility to protect him in the exercise of that right.

In 1870 the first step was taken for the nation to preserve its treasures unimpaired, when the Doane-Washburn-Langford party agreed around a campfire in Yellowstone that the area should be shared for the benefit of all people. The northwest corner of Wyoming, including Yellowstone, was then part of the Montana Territory. Jim Bridger, tough, rawboned "Old Gabe," had been trapping and prospecting the entire region since coming there with General William Ashley's Rocky Mountain Fur Company in 1823. Except for John Colter (who had passed through in the winter of 1807–08) Bridger was the first to make known the fantastic wonders of Yellowstone, and for many years his stories of the spouting geysers and boiling springs were known as "Jim Bridger's lies." Nevertheless, in 1859 Bridger was summoned to guide the first government expedition into the area, led by Capt. W. F. Raynolds of the Corps of Topographical Engineers, with the distinguished F. V. Hayden as geologist. Other expeditions followed, gradually building up a picture of the wonders and beauties of Yellowstone.

One group that came to verify the frontier stories set out from Fort Ellis on August 21, 1870, led by Henry D. Washburn, surveyor-general of Montana, Judge Cornelius Hedges, and Nathaniel Pitt Langford. Lieutenant Gustavus C. Doane, of the U.S. Second Cavalry, commanded its military escort. With the complement of soldiers, the party consisted of nineteen in all. By September 19 they had covered an amazing amount of ground while roaming amid the high mountains, majestic waterfalls, plunging canyons, and thermal features. They had mapped known wonders and discovered more: Tower Falls, Grand Canyon of the Yellowstone River, hot springs at the East Fork, Crystal Falls, and new geysers. They gave many of the region's features, including Old Faithful, the names they bear today. Around the campfire that cool September night, at the junction of the Firehole and Gibbon rivers, it is presumed that members of the party discussed what they might do with the wonderland they had explored. The talk apparently focused on the possibilities of profitable speculation; then Judge Hedges (as the chronicler of Yellowstone, Hiram M. Chittenden, relates)

. . . interposed and said that private ownership of that region, or any part of it, ought never to be countenanced, but that it ought to be set apart by the government and forever held to the unrestricted use of the people.

This higher view of the subject found immediate acceptance with the other members of the party. It was agreed that the project should be at once set afoot and pushed vigorously to a finish.[2]

On their return home, several members of the expedition broadcast the message widely through printed and spoken words. Nathaniel Langford, for instance, wrote in *Scribner's Magazine* and lectured in Helena, Minneapolis, New York, and Washington, carrying the expression "national park" all over the continent. N. P. (for "national park") Langford, as he became known, subsequently was appointed Yellowstone's first superintendent, serving five years without pay. Lieutenant Doane wrote a masterly official report, in which he declared, "As a country for sightseers, it is without parallel. As a field for scientific research it promises great results. In the branches of geology, mineralogy, botany, zoology and ornithology, it is probably the greatest laboratory that nature furnishes on the surface of the globe."[3] His report passed through military channels and reached Congress in early 1871; in that year F. V. Hayden led a scientific expedition, this time in behalf of the Geological Survey, to authenticate the findings.

Hayden's enthusiastic endorsement was buttressed by a superb set of photographs taken by William H. Jackson. Consequently, Representative William Horace Claggett of Montana introduced his park bill before 1871 was out. It was enacted forthwith. The language of the law, which President Ulysses S. Grant signed on March 1, 1872, reads as follows:

Be it enacted by the Senate and House of Representatives of the United States in Congress assembled, that the tract of land in the territories of Montana and Wyoming, lying near the headwaters of the Yellowstone River . . . is hereby reserved and withdrawn from settlement, occupancy, or sale under the laws of the United States, and dedicated and set apart as a public park or pleasuring ground for the benefit and enjoyment of the people; and all persons who shall locate or occupy the same or any part thereof, shall be considered trespassers and be removed therefrom.

How could such a sense of responsibility have arisen and spread in Western society, at a time when free enterprise, never quite blind but seldom far-seeing, was on the march? Some say that Congress created the national parks, starting with Yellowstone, in a spirit of concession to zealous knots of wilderness enthusiasts, out of a seemingly limitless public domain and only out of those parcels of land scorned by commercial interests. Still, it would have been easier to let the Yellowstone go to the prospectors and squatters and ranchers and lumbermen. The establishment of this first national park, protecting a 2-million-acre wilderness, appears in the context of time as an overt act of idealism—the opening wedge of a conservation era that gradually spread the world over.

Meanwhile, John Muir was leading the fight to preserve the Yosemite grant lands from destruction of giant sequoias and devastation by sheep-grazing. Congress responded in 1890 by reserving 1,500 square miles surrounding Yosemite State Park as a national park (and fifteen years later accepted return of the valley from California). The new national parks—Sequoia, General Grant, Mount Rainier, Crater Lake, Wind Cave, and Mesa Verde—established between 1890 and 1910 were not merely outstanding scenic areas or the locations of natural curiosities but reservoirs of true wilderness.

The same was the case in the heart of Washington, D.C., where some 1,600 acres were purchased as Rock Creek Park in 1890 by a Congress vowing to safeguard "its pleasant valleys and deep ravines, its primeval forests and open fields, its running waters, its rocks clothed with rich ferns and mosses, its repose and tranquility, its light and shade, its ever-varying shrubbery, its beautiful and extensive views."

Muir's primary concern, which he repeatedly stated, was to prevent the destruction of wilderness for narrow, short-term goals. In 1912, in the wild Kern River Canyon country of central California, Stephen Mather, who four years later was to become first director of the National Park Service, encountered Muir, distraught, full of alarm about what the timber, mining, and power barons were doing to the wilderness. Two years later, when he returned to California, Mather saw where private operators had taken over sequoia groves on the slick thesis that because each spring when the snows melted the big trees stood on soggy ground, they came under the Swamp Land Act, a measure designed to unburden the federal government of substandard bogs. Mather saw cattle grazing inside the parks. The National Park Service became to him an instrument of direct action to save wilderness. This he demonstrated in opposing construction of a cable crossing of the Grand Canyon and an electric steam elevator alongside the 308-foot Great Fall of the Yellowstone. Throughout World War I he blocked the efforts of the meat, wool, mineral, lumber, and power interests to get their hands on park resources, though these groups relentlessly played on the public's emotions about war as a time "not to worry about the flowers and wild animals." In 1925 Mather approved construction by the Great Northern Railroad of a sawmill beside Lake McDermott in Glacier National Park in order to implement building of a hotel at Many Glacier. But the mill exceeded its operating deadline and kept cutting timber. After due warning Mather personally headed a brigade to blow it up with thirteen charges of TNT.*

From the start the national parks were subjected to a precarious existence by the special interests. Railroads and commercial boomers pushed a bill through the House of Representatives during several consecutive sessions to permit a rail line through Yellowstone. Each time the Senate failed to cooperate, but to show they meant business the railroad boosters

---

* Mather was in Glacier with his daughter Betty on August 10, 1925, which happened to be her birthday. He personally lighted the first of the TNT charges. With each detonation, his mood lightened. When people inquired into his motives, he replied: "Celebrating my daughter's nineteenth birthday." Quoted in Robert Shankland, *Steve Mather of the National Parks* (New York: Knopf, 1951): pp. 209–10.

induced Congress to shut off funds during the 1880s for adequate protection of the park. Such was the pattern everywhere. The Southern Pacific owned over 10 million acres and held California in the hollow of its hand. Millions of acres intended for homesteaders passed over to the special interests. The loggers picked up the heaviest stands of timber through fraud and deception.

During the 1960s timbermen may have pleaded the cause of dear old private enterprise in attempting to thwart rescue of a few surviving stands of redwood wilderness through the means of a new national park, but they overlooked mentioning the historic land steals by which the properties were acquired. "The waste and destruction of the redwood . . . and the big trees . . . of California have been and continue to be so great as to cause apprehension that these species of trees, the oldest and noblest in the world, will entirely disappear unless some means be taken to preserve at least a portion of them," Secretary of the Interior Carl Schurz warned as early as the early 1870s and 1880s. He called for a reversal of the tide of public opinion, "looking with indifference on this wanton, barbarous, disgraceful vandalism; a spendthrift people recklessly wasting its heritage; a Government careless of its future." [4]

John Wesley Powell expressed the same idea. He urged preserving the country's natural wealth against exploitation and monopoly control. He opposed the cattle trusts and disposition of the public domain. The western livestock grower, according to Powell, was "a trespasser on the public domain, an obstacle to settlement, and at best a crude forerunner of civilization." He urged safeguarding timberlands from fire, protection of streams in public ownership, and cooperative labor and capital for development of irrigation.[5]

Similiar forces were at work in the East, evoking a public response for protection of nature. In New York citizens campaigned for years to preserve the Falls of the Niagara as a public park and to rescue the area from private exploitation; their efforts culminated in 1885 in the authorization of the New York State Reservation at Niagara. In that same year the state legislature established the Adirondack Forest Preserve in portions of the Adirondacks and Catskills and reinforced its sanctity with a constitutional amendment of 1894. The amendment declared: "The lands of the state, now owned or hereafter acquired, constituting the forest preserve as now fixed by law, shall be forever kept as wild forest lands. They shall not be leased, sold, or exchanged, or be taken by any corporation, public or private, nor shall the timber thereon be-sold, removed, or destroyed."

The amendment was adopted by the constitutional convention in reaction to scandals of fraudulent land deals and bribery in Albany and to illegal logging on state forests. It combined a growing awareness and support of wilderness values with opposition to a steady stream of proposals in the legislature to permit cutting in the preserve, "nearly all of which," as the *New York Evening Post* reported, "are directly to the advantage of the timber land sharks."

In further reaction to such destruction, the Society for the Protection of New Hampshire Forests was organized in 1901 by Governor Frank West Rollins and Philip Ayres. They were inspired, according to Sherman Adams, a former governor and forester, by "pilferage of the lumbering bandits" plus tragic major fires. For eons these predominantly red spruce forests had stood unmolested in an inaccessible mountain wilderness. With the first Crown grants in the 1760s, land had become a commodity. It went first to rural speculators, then to large holding companies, and from them to operating or timber companies that slashed, burned, and denuded the resources. Adams called Rollins and Ayres revolutionaries, "the activists of their time." They began to see and express the values of wilderness in woods and trees, in streams and mountains, that were not measured in dollars or in board feet.

In one 15-year period the society and the state acquired by gift and purchase some of the most cherished wilderness in New Hampshire: Crawford Notch, Sunapee, Lost River, and Grand Monadnock. "The preservation of these and other gems in New Hampshire's diadem may not seem epochal in the events of forest history," Adams comments. "But here began the first firm steps to make the opportunity to enjoy wilderness areas of great charm available to all the people at no more cost than the maintenance of the attractions themselves." [6]

As public interest grew, the federal government moved a little faster to save the land from exploitation. In 1891, when timber resources were being consumed and wasted at a disastrous rate, Congress authorized President Benjamin Harrison to make withdrawals from the public domain and establish a new entity called forest reserves. He set aside 13 million acres, to which his successor, Grover Cleveland, added 21 million more, no small feat in the face of severe western opposition. Theodore Roosevelt, during his six years in office, signed proclamations for another 132 million acres (including 16 million acres between the time Congress voted to deprive the President of this authority and the final deadline when the power expired), very likely Roosevelt's most important and enduring contribution to the nation.

Roosevelt had been to the Grand Canyon, where he proclaimed, "Do nothing to mar its grandeur. Keep it for your children, and your children's children, and all who come after you, as the one great sight which every American should see." He knew and admired John Muir and had camped with him in Yosemite, where they lay on beds of fir boughs among the giant trunks of the sequoias, listening to the hermit thrush and the waterfalls down the sheer cliffs. "It was like lying in a great solemn cathedral," Roosevelt wrote, "far vaster and more beautiful than any built by the hand of man." However, he was most influenced by Gifford Pinchot, an apostle of use rather than protection or, as he would say, of "preservation through use." Pinchot, for example, had objected to the New York constitutional amendment forbidding timber-cutting in the Adirondack Forest Preserve.

Use aspects of the land were a fetish with Pinchot. Although at first a friend and admirer of John Muir, these two parted company over the disposition of Hetch Hetchy Valley on the Tuolomne River in Yosemite. As early as 1882 city engineers of San Francisco, 150 miles distant, had scouted the possibility of damming Hetch Hetchy's narrow lower end to make a reservoir for water storage, then of using the fall of the impounded water to generate hydroelectric power. The establishment of Yosemite National Park in 1890 as a wilderness preserve appeared to head that off. But the city politicians refused to quit. They pressed the issue for years, from one administration to another. John Muir knew every part of Hetch Hetchy. "These sacred mountain temples are the holiest ground that the heart of man has consecrated," he wrote, "and it behooves us all faithfully to do our part in seeing that our wild mountain parks are passed on unspoiled to those who come after us, for they are national properties to which every man has a right and interest." Muir and followers looked to Theodore Roosevelt, when he took office in the White House, to defend the integrity of the park; Roosevelt, however, looked for guidance to Pinchot, who recommended utilitarianism and convinced Roosevelt to support conversion of Hetch Hetchy, on the grounds that the greatest good for the greatest number would be to furnish good water to hundreds of thousands rather than to save a scenic valley for a few hundred. Muir conceded the need of an adequate water supply but insisted it could be secured without disrupting the wild mountain parks. The idea that no part of a national park should be violated for commercial purposes, however, was still in the dim future, except in the minds of preservationists such as Muir and the Sierra Club, the American Civic Assocation, and Robert Underwood Johnson, editor of *Century Magazine*. In 1913 the battle was lost in Congress, and the dam was built, flooding a valley that many have said compared in beauty with Yosemite itself.

Pinchot was not the only leading figure to disappoint the preservationists. Another who endorsed the dam was his Yale classmate Representative William Kent, a progressive Republican from California, who had been as active as any person in the fight to save the redwoods and who had purchased the tract to be known as Muir Woods and presented it as a park to the state without benefit of tax write-offs.

But Pinchot was far more than a technical forester devoted to timber harvest or the sustained yield syndrome. In one sense, he was the vanguard of applied ecology and environmental activism. In another, he was a leader of a social movement in an age of social reform, along with Jane Addams, Lincoln Steffens, Ida Tarbell, the trust busters and muckrakers. Ancient primitive peoples prospered in a given habitat for hundreds of years, or even a thousand, because they used nature without abusing it; they became part of the ecological balance instead of destroying it. This is the type of approach Pinchot had in mind.

The conservation movement began in earnest when he battled the lumber industry to stop exploitation of timber on public land and to save our forests for future generations. No generation can be allowed needlessly to damage or reduce the future general wealth and welfare by the way it uses or misuses any natural resource, warned Pinchot. He believed in free enterprise—freedom for the common man to think and work and rise to the limits of his abilities with due regard for the rights of others. But he did not believe in what concentrated wealth means by free enterprise—freedom to use and abuse the common man. The earth, he felt, belongs by right to all its people and not to a minority, insignificant in number but tremendous in wealth and power. Pinchot insisted the public good must come first.

In his autobiography Pinchot told how the inspiration had flashed into his mind that many separate questions concerning the nation's resources "fitted into and made up the one great central problem of the use of the earth for the good of man." He defined conservation as "the foresighted utilization, preservation, and/or renewal of forests, waters, lands, and minerals for the greatest good of the greatest number for the longest period of time." When he put conservation into practice, he made it plain that it could not be limited only to protecting areas untouched. It had to become part of life, part of the way in which resources devoted to production of commodities—whether timber, minerals, livestock, or water—were used and developed. Still, he did not disassociate wilderness from wise use.

Pinchot had joined the federal government in 1898 as Chief of the Division of Forestry, which, in 1905, became the U.S. Forest Service. During its early years, under Pinchot and his successors, the Forest Service engaged in instituting controls over logging, grazing, and mining, in launching reforestation, fire control, and protection of wildlife. Although the emphasis was on use, at the same time it safeguarded many millions of acres in wilderness in the National Forest System, which would become the most important stronghold of this resource remaining in the country.

The question arose in due course, as the national forests became a little more accessible, about whether, and how, to develop the untamed places, presumably for recreation. There were no plans, policies, or funds. In 1897 the organic act had defined the forest missions simply and directly, to protect watersheds and furnish a continuous supply of timber, though leaving the door slightly ajar to other values by these words: "The Secretary will make such rules and regulations . . . to regulate occupancy and use." The forest products industry, then as now, supported appropriations from which it would benefit, opposed funds for recreation, and considered the wilderness an abhorrence. Nevertheless, the idea of classifying wilderness, of protecting and managing the resource, of translating Thoreau's vision into a functional plan, appeared early, at least in a few minds.

Between 1917 and the end of World War I, the Forest Service conducted a survey of recreation resources and potential. It concluded that the forests should be opened, leasing of summer homesites encouraged, and that men trained in landscape engineering be employed. The first landscape architect hired was Arthur Carhart.

Carhart worked for the Forest Service from 1919 to 1923 before going on to a career of city planning and conservation writing, but he left a lasting influence. His first assignment was in Colorado, choosing a location for a cluster of summer homes along the shore of Trappers Lake in White River National Forest. Dutifully, he undertook extensive surveys and found that many applications for homesite permits already were pending. But Carhart concluded *any* development would mar this choice beauty spot of the high Rockies. He convinced his superiors that the Trappers Lake area should remain roadless and the homesite permits not be honored—a definitive step to protect a national forest scenic resource.

Carhart's second assignment then took him to the Superior National Forest in northern Minnesota. He traveled through the country along the Canadian border, now called the Boundary Waters Canoe Area, in order to devise a recreational plan based on proposals for roads and a great number of lakeshore homes. Instead, he wrote a report declaring, "The first logical step in any work of this type is to plan for preservation and protection of all of those things that are of values great enough to sacrifice a certain amount of economic return so there may be a greater total return from the esthetic qualities." [7]

His 1921 recreation plan noted there was "so little wilderness left where natural conditions are supreme that the Superior stands somewhat by itself in this type. . . . The whole place should be kept as near wilderness as possible, the wilderness feature being developed rather than any urban conditions." Portions had been well worked over by loggers and miners, but Carhart recognized the area could become in time "as priceless as Yellowstone, or the Grand Canyon—if it remained a water-trail wilderness." His was a minority viewpoint; there was already the master plan to build roads. But he joined with Sigurd Olson of Ely, a town at the gateway to the canoe country, and a handful of others, in blocking mass development and holding, as Carhart puts it, "a thin line of defense protecting this exquisite wilderness until help could rally to save it." Together they achieved success with designation of the Superior Primitive Area in 1926 and a declaration that "No roads will be built as far as the Forest Service can control the situation, and no recreational developments will be permitted on public lands except waterways and portage improvements and such simple campground improvements as may be needed to prevent the escape of fire or to protect sanitary conditions."

Olson had come north from Chicago in 1922 as a young biologist and scientific researcher to join the staff of Ely Junior College (of which he later became dean) and to guide summer canoe trips. For many years to come he went from one major battle in defense of the canoe country to another. In the mid-1920s he joined Ernest C. Oberholtzer of Rainy Lake, Minnesota, and friends in facing a powerful opponent, E. W.

Backus, a lumber and power magnate, who proposed to construct a chain of power dams across the Rainy Lake watershed. This would have converted all the lakes east of Rainy into four reservoirs, submerging islands and waterfalls, leaving the shoreline a morass of stagnant water and dead trees. Backus had influence, affluence, and money; his battle to transform public wilderness into private use and profit continued till 1934, when the International Joint Commission, which adjudicates boundary disputes, set it to rest by ruling, "It is impossible to overstate the recreational and tourist value of this matchless playground. Its natural forests, lakes, rivers and waterfalls have a beauty and appeal beyond description and nothing should be done to destroy their charm."

As early as December 1919, when Carhart was headquartered in Denver, he received a visit from Aldo Leopold, a Forest Service colleague from the Albuquerque office, who was interested in the former's experiences and outlook. Following their conversation Carhart wrote a supplementary 4-page memorandum. His immediate concern was summer-home sprawl, and he listed four types of areas that should be free of it altogether: the superlative area, the unsuited high ridge of a mountain range, the area that should be for the group rather than the individual, such as lakeshore or stream bank, and the area of greatest use for preservation owned by the federal government. "There is a definite point in different types of country where man-made structures should be stopped," he wrote.

Leopold agreed and went on from there. He reasoned that large undeveloped sections of the national forests were as much an asset as the timber, water, forage, and minerals. He explained in articles and memoranda that the very fact of being compelled to use negative terms like "undeveloped" demonstrated the newness of the concept. In looking across the Southwest, where he had arrived when Arizona and New Mexico were still territories, Leopold had seen six immense roadless areas, each larger than half a million acres, providing refuge for wild creatures and wilderness sportsmen. These were the Jemez and Datil-Gila in New Mexico and the Kaibab, White Mountains, Blue Range, and Tonto Rim in Arizona. Leopold considered the timber famine, of which Pinchot had warned, a matter of quality rather than quantity. As he watched wilderness continually cut by roads, he warned, "The existence of a wilderness-recreation famine has emerged as an incontrovertible fact," and therefore proposed a detailed new kind of management plan for the national forests. Logging under intensive forestry and sustained yield would be restricted to the richest and most accessible forest regions, which were capable of producing high-quality timber, while the remaining regions of the total land organism would be dedicated to varying forms of recreation, game management, and wilderness.

Leopold outlined a concept of wild areas for the Southwest to fulfill four objectives: (1) prevent annihilation of rare plants and animals, like the grizzly; (2) guard against biotic disruption of areas still wild; (3) secure recognition, as wilderness, of low-altitude desert generally regarded as valueless for recreation because it offered no pines, lakes, or other conventional scenery; and (4) induce Mexico to cooperate in wilderness protection. "We have no faunas or floras which have not been abused, modified or 'improved,' " he wrote, "but in the Mexican mountains the whole biota is intact with the single exception of the Apache Indian, who is, I fear, extinct." [8]

Specifically, he sought to establish a wild area embracing the hazy Mogollon Mountains above the Mexican border at the head of the Gila River in Gila National Forest. On his initiative, and based on boundaries he had drawn, the regional forester approved the designation in 1924, safeguarding the area from both timber-cutting and road-building. Leopold wanted the Forest Service to go further. He foresaw that, unless concerted action was taken, the new Federal Highway Act would doom the remaining wild areas. His prophecy has come all too true: Of all the extensive wilderness Leopold first knew in the Southwest, only the Gila remains of any significant size, and it has been split down the middle and pared at the edges.

In the mid-1920s, however, since most western forests were relatively undeveloped, there was ample opportunity to implement his proposal. William B. Greeley, the Chief of the Forest Service, not only indicated approval of the Gila designation, but encouraged other regions to follow a similar course with comparable areas. "The frontier has long ceased to be a barrier to civilization," he wrote in 1927. "The question is rather how much of it should be kept to preserve our civilization." At his direction, Assistant Chief L. F. Kneipp undertook an inventory of available wilderness areas for use in formulating a service-wide policy. (See Chapter One.)

On the basis of this report, Greeley issued, in 1929, Regulation L-20, providing for the establishment of "Primitive Areas." * Under RL-20 and the succeeding more definitive and tighter "U" regulations some 14 million acres were administratively classified as primitive—thirty areas over 100,000 acres in size, and forty-two areas of less than 100,000 acres, plus three units in Minnesota classified as "Roadless Areas." The Forest Service, however, did not anticipate reserving the primitive areas indefinitely from commercial use. Many of the remote portions with outstanding scenic and recreational qualities were being kept from haphazard road-building and commercial development until a time when more intensive study was needed. It is also conceivable that the Forest Service was trying to keep one step ahead of its "sister agency," the National Park Service (headquartered across the city of Washington in the Department of the Interior); by demonstrating active concern for wilderness, it was better able to block establishment of new parks out of old forests.

Another practical development in the evolution of wilderness protection was contributed by Benton MacKaye. Trained as a

* Until then, designation, as in the case of the Gila or the Superior, had been at the option of regional foresters, but the new regulation stated: "The Chief of the Forest Service shall determine, define, and permanently record . . . a series of areas to be known as primitive areas, and within which, *to the extent of the Department's authority,* will be maintained primitive conditions of environment, transportation, habitation, and subsistence, with a view to conserving the value of such areas for purposes of public education, *inspiration,* and recreation. Within any area so designated (except for permanent improvements needed in Experimental Forests and Ranges) no occupancy under the special-use permit shall be allowed, or the construction of permanent improvements by any public agency be permitted, except as authorized by the Chief of the Forest Service or the Secretary of Agriculture." (Italicized passages were deleted and the phrase in parentheses added by an amendment of 1930.)

forester, first at Harvard, then under Pinchot early in the century, he was primarily engaged in reclaiming and improving the forests of America. But like his superior he was also concerned with wider issues applied to all basic resources.

In an article published in 1921, which he titled "An Appalachian Trail—A Project in Regional Planning," MacKaye envisioned "a 'long trail' over the full length of the Appalachian skyline from the highest peak in the North to the highest peak in the South." Few proposals in regional planning have fired the imagination more. Almost at once scattered groups and individuals began to work and in a few years the Appalachian Trail became a reality, representing a choice expression of wilderness. Or as MacKaye wrote: "The old pioneer opened through a forest a path for the spread of civilization. His work was nobly done and the life of the town and city is in consequence well upon the map throughout our country. Now comes the great task of holding this life in check—for it is just as bad to have too much urbanization as too little." He foresaw the trail as an application of Thoreau's philosophy, the backbone for a whole network of wild reservations and parks, linked together by feeder trails, constituting a reservoir for maintaining primeval and rural environments at their highest levels, and where practical man could go to learn new lessons from the balanced system of nature.

Robert Marshall was twenty years younger than MacKaye, but they were close friends and collaborators during the 1930s. Marshall spent most of his career in the Forest Service, with time out for trips to Alaska and four years, 1933–37, as Director of Forestry for the Office of Indian Affairs at the Department of the Interior.

In 1933, after returning with enthusiasm from Alaska, where he had collected data on tree growth under severe conditions and charted new territory ("of rivers unvisited by man, deep canyons and hanging valleys glimpsed from a distance but never explored, great mountains which no human had ever ascended"), Marshall published *Arctic Village*, a book that became a best seller. This he followed in 1933 with *The People's Forests,* in which he advocated public ownership of all forested land. It was written when there was little evidence of private forestry applying conservation principles, when destruction of wilderness timber for profit was in vogue. But Marshall was unique among foresters in that he understood and praised the noneconomic—indeed, the artistic—qualities of forests.

In August 1934, while on a field trip in the Appalachians, Marshall stopped in Knoxville and conferred with Benton Mac-Kaye, who was working as a regional planner for the Tennessee Valley Authority, and Harvey Broome, lawyer, wilderness enthusiast, and activist in the Great Smoky Mountains Hiking Club. The three set out for a day-long trip to the nearby Great Smoky Mountains National Park, the component lands for which were then being assembled by the government. They discussed their common concern that skyline drives in a variety of New Deal projects would overrun the best unspoiled mountain areas in the East—they had only to look at the new Shenandoah National Park and the Great Smokies, where the threat was real—and therefore considered the need of a new organization to protect the Appalachian Trail and other established footpaths. By late afternoon they agreed on a project, but it was based on Marshall's broader suggestion for uniting "all friends of wilderness."

Thus, in the Great Smokies, the foundation was laid for the Wilderness Society. In October Marshall returned to Knoxville for a speech before the annual meeting of the American Forestry Association. During a field trip he, Broome, and MacKaye were joined by Bernard Frank, associate forester of TVA, in outlining a statement of principles for their new movement. A letter dated October 19, 1934, enrolled the four other founders of the Wilderness Society, Harold Anderson, Aldo Leopold, Ernest Oberholtzer, and Robert Sterling Yard, who defined their goals: "to secure the preservation of wilderness, conduct educational programs concerning the value of wilderness, encourage scientific studies, and mobilize cooperation in resisting the invasion of wilderness." Yard was chosen as the first president; a brilliant writer and a former editor of *Century Magazine,* he had worked closely with Stephen Mather in setting up the National Parks Association to promote public support of the National Park

Service in its early years. But Marshall was the prime mover. He launched the Wilderness Society with financial support, climaxed by a bequest of $400,000 to a trust fund named the Robert Marshall Wilderness Fund after his death. In 1935 he wrote,

It is imperative that all friends of the wilderness unite. If they do not present the urgency of their viewpoint, the other side will certainly capture popular support. Then it will be only a few years until the last escape from society will be barricaded. If that day arrives, there will be countless souls born to live in strangulation, countless human beings who will be crushed under the artificial edifice raised by man. There is just one hope of repulsing the tyrannical ambition of civilization to conquer every niche on the whole earth. That hope is the organization of spirited people who will fight for the freedom of the wilderness.

Marshall at this time was working as Chief Forester for the Indian Service. His superior, John Collier, a former teacher and social worker, had been appointed Commissioner of Indian Affairs at the beginning of the New Deal and was responsible for returning to the Indians a sense of right to their own culture. He believed in the Indians, and he believed in Marshall. Thus, in an order approved by the Secretary of the Interior, Collier established, in October 1937, twelve roadless and four wild areas on the Indian reservations. He felt the Indian folk life had not shredded away, as had other folk cultures of our country, in the face of a commercialism ruthless towards man and the wild creatures and toward the land. Yet he found the Indian increasingly encountering the competition of the white race and acquisitive society. Collier envisioned the roadless areas as a means to save for the Indian some places that are all his own but also to save for the nation some fragments of commercially unexploited wilderness.

Little of this system remains today, but it sparked interest and activity. Marshall was called back to the Forest Service in the Department of Agriculture, where he was offered the chance to operate on a wide front as Chief of Recreation and Lands. At this time Ickes was running a campaign to show that Interior was the only department qualified to administer wilderness and that the national forests belonged under his jurisdiction. Marshall was considered the man to prove him wrong. With approval of Ferdinand A. Silcox, Chief of the Forest Service, he pursued at once the cause of wilderness protection as a consistent element of intelligent forest management. A democratic society, he insisted, ought to respect the preference of the few, in this case the preference for wilderness. To him, the National Forest System was uniquely fit to provide two distinct recreation environments: one, the comfortable and modern; and two, "the peaceful timelessness where vast forests germinate and flourish and die and rot and grow again without any relationship to the ambitions and interferences of man."

Marshall's crowning achievements came in September 1939 with issuance by the Forest Service of the "U" regulations, which established a procedure for expansion of wilderness and for excluding developments previously permissible in primitive areas.

Regulation U-1 provided that the Secretary of Agriculture, on recommendation of the Forest Service, could designate unbroken tracts of 100,000 acres or more as wilderness areas, which could be modified or eliminated only by the Sectretary on the basis of a record of public hearings. Commercial timber-cutting, roads, hotels, stores, resorts, summer homes, camps, hunting and fishing lodges, motorboats, and airplane landings were prohibited in all areas. Grazing was permitted to continue under both U-1 and U-2 regulations, "subject to such restrictions as the Chief deems desirable." So was mining, reflecting the power of a politically entrenched industry; exploration and development could not be ended by an administrative order, since the permissive mining law of 1872 superseded the various Forest Service laws. Regulation U-2 made a distinction in size, providing for wild areas of between 5,000 and 100,000 acres. Procedures for establishment and administration were the same as for the wilderness areas, although final action in modification or elimination rested with the Chief of the Forest Service, rather than the Secretary.

As for the primitive areas designated under the old Regulation L-20 prior to September 20, 1939, they would retain their status until revoked or modified by the chief. They could not automatically be reclassified as wilderness or wild, for the early boundaries had often been drawn hastily, imperfectly, sometimes encompassing uses said to be incompatible with the strong new regulations. Consequently, the Forest Service conducted reviews and public hearings, which led ultimately to changing thirty-eight primitive areas to wilderness or wild.*

This process continued over a period of years, and in December 1947 a directive was issued from the office of the chief to clarify administrative policy: "We wish to re-emphasize the importance of treating all Primitive Areas just as though they had been established under Regulations U-1 or U-2 . . . all existing Primitive Areas will be managed just as though they had been established under Regulations U-1 or U-2."

Bob Marshall died in November 1939, two months after announcement of the U regulations. (Silcox died in the same year—a double blow.) The following year the Forest Service gave Marshall's name to nearly a million acres of rugged Montana country in the Lewis and Clark and Flathead national forests. The serpentine backbone of the Continental Divide runs through the Bob Marshall Wilderness and at the escarpment called the Chinese Wall breaks away eastward in thousand-foot cliffs for a distance of fifteen miles. The Flathead Alps, an offshoot of the divide, challenge the best rock climbers, and the Bob Marshall Wilderness is home of a large elk herd, as well as bear, deer, mountain sheep, and mountain goat. It was a generous living memorial, but Bob Marshall doubtless would have preferred

---

* In addition, there were national forest areas called "Back Country" in West Virginia and "Limited" along the Cascade Crest of the Pacific Northwest, and others covering millions of acres without any classification, although embodying the qualifications of wilderness and protected as such. In West Virginia a portion of the Monongahela National Forest had been closed to the public since 1936 as a fire prevention measure, then designated as back country in 1945 simply because it was back in the woods as far out in the country as one could get. The popularity of the area was quickly established with hunters and fishermen. The future of these areas was insecure, but the Forest Service guarded them as wilderness. It made little difference at the time the regulations were placed in effect, for there was still plentiful wild country, or so it seemed.

his spirit and enthusiasm more fully infused into the Forest Service, his philosophy understood, if not accepted, by fellow foresters.

The National Park Service had no such criteria for wilderness protection as Leopold and Marshall had written for the Forest Service. Early national parks were "public pleasuring grounds" to be retained in a "natural condition"; consequently, laws establishing individual units deliberately left the way open for roads and tourist accommodations. The organic act established the National Park Service in 1916 with a seemingly contradictory dual role. The areas were intended to conserve the scenery, natural and historic objects, and wildlife. At the same time they were also expected to provide for the enjoyment of these resources by the people. The Act stipulated, however, that the enjoyment—or public use—must be undertaken in such manner and means as would leave the resources "unimpaired for the enjoyment of future generations."

Preservation was presumed by Mather and many administrators to be the transcendent purpose of the parks—preservation so that they might be enjoyed but by means compatible with preservation. For many years a number of areas were regarded as "wilderness parks" and most national park back country was administered as wilderness. Nevertheless, the parks have been thoroughly plagued by one attack after another. The most serious in the early days centered on the spectacular, high-walled Hetch Hetchy Valley. Then followed the threats of World War I, the cable car crossing of the Grand Canyon and of cable cars and tramways ever since, old authorizations for mining (which have burst into reality at the rim of the Grand Canyon and in Glacier Bay National Monument, Alaska) and grazing, the development of private holdings ("in-holdings") that have sprouted into subdivisions in the heart of Olympic, Yosemite, Sequoia-Kings Canyon, Clacier, Grand Teton, Rocky Mountain, and other parks.

During World War II the logging industry appealed for the right to harvest the wilderness of Olympic National Park. The supplication was cloaked in soul-stirring patriotism; the Olympic

Sitka spruce was said to fit exact specifications for military aircraft. The loggers lost their case, but the war was won anyway.

The Olympics were saved, the law governing the inviolability of national parks prevailed, and at the end of World War II the American wilderness was still a substantial estate. Robert Marshall's concept of a wilderness system established by law remained an idea. It had not yet become an urgency.

Chapter Nine

Saving Wilderness by Law— The Ultimate Showdown

The Olympic Peninsula is a marvel of the original America. Its steep-faced mountains, shaggy green with a million Douglas fir and other trees, bespeak the wild glory of the Northwest. The peninsula lies in semi-isolation, bordered by the waters of the Pacific, the Strait of Juan de Fuca, and the clustered cosmos of Puget Sound. In times past its rugged mountains and dense forests resisted the intrusions of modern civilization more stoutly than the rest of the Pacific Coast, and it is still quite possible to observe the course of nature undisturbed. In some ways the Olympics are like the Great Smokies in the East; their isolation, the lush development of their forests, the preservation of a portion of each within a national park, and the use of surrounding lands as national forests. Additionally, the Olympic Peninsula presents a thrilling geological story, with more than sixty living glaciers in the high country, including six major glaciers on Mount Olympus alone, all vestiges of massive sheets of ice that plowed, scraped, and scoured the earth in at least four surges spread over millions of years.

In the years immediately following World War II the Olympics became the scene of a renewed attack on wilderness, the first of many everywhere. Large timber companies already owned a considerable part of the peninsula and held logging contracts on the Olympic National Forest. But then there was the national park, beyond their reach. Theodore Roosevelt had set aside a portion of the virgin forest by establishing Mount Olympus National Monument in 1909. When the national park was established by Congress in 1946, it occupied 890,000 acres in the heart of the peninsula, while the bordering national forest covered but 628,000 acres. The park represents a last glorious opportunity to preserve an estate of giants—trees, elk, bear, and all wild things, free to follow their natural course, but the ratio was disturbing to timbermen, chambers of commerce, and foresters, who set out to rectify the mistake.

Their interest was in the Douglas fir, third only to the giant sequoia and redwood in size of all trees on the continent, a stately, wonderfully proportioned tree growing to heights of 250 or 300 feet with the larger trees ranging in age from 400 to 1,000 years. As a timber source, the Douglas fir is the most important tree of the Northwest, prized for its strength and immense size and free of knots and other defects. Then there are other valuable species, such as Sitka spruce and hemlock. The commercial interests simply couldn't stand to see all that beautiful timber within the park "locked up" and "unmanaged."

Legislation was introduced each year from 1946 through 1969 either to reduce the size of the park, eliminating an appreciable volume of commercially valuable timber, or to restudy the boundaries with a view to transferring to the national forest the rain forests on the western slope—the Hoh, Bogachiel, and Queets—serene botanical gardens comprising the entire sweep of plant progression from fungi, mosses, and lichens to immense trees of a thousand years in age. These plans very nearly succeeded, except that timber interests made plain they were really determined to eliminate much more of the park following the opening blow. Conservationists rallied to block it, preserving the wilderness park intact.

The next major battle over wilderness arose in the early 1950s. It was another Hetch Hetchy, this time in Dinosaur National Monument, Utah, where the Bureau of Reclamation proposed to erect a dam across the deep, narrow gorge of the Green River at Echo Park as one of ten dams in the billion-dollar Colorado River Storage Project. In 1950 Secretary of the Interior Oscar L. Chapman considered the positions of both the reclamation and parks bureaus in his department and of their respective public supporters; then he ruled in support of the dam. Coming at a time of rising population and accompanying material demands, the issue represented far more than an isolated case on its own. Rather it was a test of the integrity of the whole National Park System; for after Echo Park which gorge would be next with the ideal dimensions for water storage?

The battle was fought for more than five years in Congress. At one point wilderness appeared headed for a decisive defeat, but the Wilderness Society, Sierra Club, and other groups worked as they had never done before, appealing to the nation with articles, editorials, and open letters, arousing an outburst of concern and protest. Finally, when the Colorado River Storage Project bill was enacted on April 11, 1956, it carried a proviso that no dam or reservoir would be constructed within any national park or monument under terms of the Act.

Still another dam crisis confronted the park system in the 1960s, at the Grand Canyon, of all places. In what is the nation's most renowned wilderness landmark there were to be two dams, at Bridge Canyon and Marble Canyon. Congressmen, chambers of commerce, Arizona newspapers, and, of course, the Bureau of Reclamation all pledged that raising the water level would improve the natural beauty of the Grand Canyon and make it accessible to many more people. It took another extensive nationwide campaign to convince Congress that the canyon needed no improvement.

Citizen conservationists had cause for concern over unceasing threats to the national parks and inadequacy of the organic act to protect undesignated wilderness zones. Who could tell what might come next, once given a precedent? Harnessing the Yellowstone geysers, perhaps? Using Yosemite Falls to generate electric power? Permitting the cutting of the granite in Half Dome for building blocks and the drainage of the Everglades for commercial housing developments in order "to meet the needs of a growing nation"?

Meanwhile, all was not well for wilderness in the national forests, even with criteria and designated areas. Preservation policy had been based essentially on administrative decision, subject to change at any time by Forest Service personnel. Following the death of Bob Marshall, policy toward wilderness shifted, first gradually and then more decisively after World War II. It reflected the emergence of an emphasis on timber production inside the agency, with a pressing sense of urgency about it.

Although citizen groups had long supported the Forest Service as an agency concerned with scenic resources and wilderness, they lost their place as a key part of its constituency. The timber-first policy came to the fore in response to several factors, one being the political pressure of the timber industry, which, having intensively cut its own private lands without adequate concern for sustained yield, became reliant on public lands, including the remaining virgin forests, to keep its mills going. Another factor was the change in forestry education. Until World War II students had received heavy doses of the early conservation idealism, along with silviculture, management, and forest administration. Most graduates had gone to work for state and federal conservation agencies, whose leaders had considered themselves part of a social movement, relating land to the progress of the common citizen. Although ecology as a science was little known, the early stress was on protection rather than production or intensive utilization. But the new industrial demand for foresters had its impact on college faculties; the schools placed more emphasis on training technologists and engineers with their orientation shifting from growing trees to harvesting them.

Methods of logging changed, too. For many years foresters had preached the virtues of "selection-cutting," or all-aged forest management, in which individual trees are logged when they reach maturity and younger trees continue their growth. Following World War II, however, lumber-company foresters in the Pacific Northwest applied research reports that claimed that partially cut stands of Douglas fir and hemlock would revert in second growth to the less valuable hemlock. They claimed that Douglas fir, a species relatively intolerant of shade and requiring sunlight to reproduce, should be clear-cut in patches, followed either by natural seeding or by artificial planting.

From the Northwest the clear-cutting method spread through the national forests, closely paralleling the rising demand of the industry for timber. Such pressures had been light, considering the industry had available to it an estimated 70 per cent of commercial forest lands (those suitable for growing of continuous timber crops) held in private ownership and generally more accessible. However, the steady depletion of resources on millions of private acres had driven the operators to press for greater productivity in national forests. And the Forest Service responded. In 1950 the annual "allowable cut"—a figure designed to balance growth with harvest in order to ensure a perpetual yield—was 5.6 billion board feet. Ten years later it was up to 10.6 billion. The industry demands for increased cutting were greatest in the West. In California the allowable cut rose from 1,205 million feet in 1950 to 1,384.4 million in 1960, then soared to 1,977.2 million in 1965. In the Pacific Northwest, it climbed from 2,450 million feet in 1950 to 3,898 million in 1960 and to 4,105 million in 1965.

In response to criticism or serious questioning from their old supporters among the public, the answer given by Forest Service officials was that "foresters know best." Charles A. Reich, best known as the author of *The Greening of America,* touched on this question in a monograph published in 1962. The great danger, he wrote, is that entrenched professional bureaucracy will become short-sighted in its perception of the public good. It may care so much about today's balance sheet that it forgets tomorrow's heritage. He placed the original responsibility on Congress for granting sweeping powers of legislation and policy-making to the agency. Congress told the Forest Service to "best meet the needs of the American people" but left it entirely up to the service to determine what these needs are. As a consequence, according to Reich, professional bureaucracies have grown up to do the work of management and planning, and decisions touching the vital interests of the commonwealth are made in rooms insulated from the voice of the people.

The forester who had protected wilderness now became instead a prime threat, coveting the forest preserved in dedicated areas, even though it would barely meet demand for saw timber. They used insect outbreaks as a reason to save the forest from itself, to interrupt the forces of succession that made the forests possible and durable. High-quality, virgin timber is now almost always spoken of by the professional forester as "old and decadent." Low-grade, second-growth timber is "young and productive," even while these young stands are understocked and producing far below their potential. Foresters say the virgin stands are "ready to cut," which means they can be logged profitably and therefore should be cut *now*. If left alone, as they have been since the ice age, they would be ready to cut in another hundred years, too. And then they would be much more valuable. In the meantime, the public could be enjoying all other uses and values of a public forest.

The wilderness the Forest Service had protected for years began to go. For more than three decades the Selway-Bitterroot Primitive Area, for example, had covered an immense area of almost 1.9 million acres astride the border of Montana and Idaho. The primitive area embraced steep, rugged river-break terrain and forested mountainous country to over 10,000 feet, much of it impassable, and remaining as in ages past. The region was noted for one of the largest elk herds in the world, mountain sheep high on the slopes, and challenging sport fishing for steelhead trout and salmon in the wild waters of the Selway and Salmon rivers and their tributaries.

In 1961, however, the region was split in two through administrative action; the northern portion was established as the Selway-Bitterroot Wilderness and the southern portion as the Salmon River Breaks Primitive Area. The presence of a gravel road passing between them with a couple of short and minor spurs was held to be inconsistent with wilderness criteria, and, consequently, the Magruder Corridor, about 200,000 acres (a strip eight to ten miles wide), was left for "general forest administration."

A multiple-use plan was prepared. The preliminary ground-work involved upgrading the old road, marking proposed timber sales, and surveying logging roads. The latter were to accommodate hunters, picnickers, and other recreational users, constituting a veritable network to replace the one lone road that had been held as the justification for withdrawing the corridor from its long-term protected status.

Following protests received by members of Congress from sportsmen, naturalists, and other citizens of Idaho and Montana (as well as the game and fish departments of the two states), Secretary of Agriculture Orville L. Freeman appointed a special advisory committee to examine the Forest Service plans. This committee, composed of six citizen experts in various natural resource fields, including forestry, issued a report questioning the need of a logging road and the economic feasibility of logging. The committee report stressed, instead, the importance of protecting from erosion the watershed and fisheries values in the upper Selway River drainage, the spawning ground of Chinook salmon and steelhead trout. "The Forest Service was preparing to initiate timber road building and timber cutting in this area without clearly stated limitations or restrictions to this use or to other values," the report declared. It noted also that wildlife resources had not received consideration commensurate with roads and timber-cutting in the plans.

The ultimate showdown that convinced citizen conservationists that the Forest Service could not be trusted to preserve wilderness on the basis of administrative regulations came in the North Cascades of the Pacific Northwest. In 1938 Bob Marshall had proposed that 795,000 acres between the North Cascades Primitive Area and Stevens Pass be studied for possible wilderness classification. It was one of the finest natural areas in North America, a network of hanging glaciers and icefalls, ice aprons and icecaps, hanging valleys and waterfalls, a rough, tall country with fine mountaineering opportunities, interlaced with varied plant communities ranging from rain forest through subalpine conifers, green meadows and alpine tundras, back down to pine forests and sunny dry shrublands; it was a great refuge for wildlife, including mountain goats, wolverines, grizzly bears, fishers, cougars, and large numbers of bald eagles congregating along the streams in winter to feed on salmon.

In 1940, after the death of Marshall and Silcox, the Forest Service set aside not 795,000 acres but only 352,000 acres—and not as a Glacier Peak Wilderness Area, but as a Glacier Peak Limited Area, a peculiar classification that seemed to suggest there were too many commercial trees not yet ready to be harvested. In 1951, with demand for public logs growing, the service began preliminary studies for reclassification of the limited area as wilderness. But these were dragged out or delayed, while logging proceeded in valleys that conservationists felt deserved inclusion in any permanently protected area.

At first the citizens felt wilderness was an inexhaustible resource; if one valley was logged, or two or three or a dozen, they could always escape to what seemed uncountable virgin valleys remaining. But this is not how it worked. Roads were gouged out of steep hillsides. Skidding with heavy equipment and clear-cutting in massive patches overrode watershed soils and covers, scraping stream bottoms and silting fisheries habitat. Tons of debris, called slash, were burned on the ground, covering the woods with a pall of smoke; sometimes the fires got away and spread. Until 1960, nevertheless, conservationists hoped to gain protection of the North Cascades under Forest Service administration and placed their hopes for the area's protection in a Glacier Peak Wilderness of sufficient dimensions. They were most concerned with saving the low-country virgin forests and wild rivers as respectful entryways to the high-country meadows, glaciers, and peaks. The response of the Forest Service in 1959 was the disappointing "starfish proposal" of 422,925 acres—confining the wilderness to tentacle-like ridges of rock and snow, of "wilderness on the rocks," with the intervening valleys devoted to commercial development.

It was following this development that conservationists realized that only by transferring the area to the jurisdiction of the National Park Service could they assure protection of the timbered valleys. The issue became a virtual national crisis in conservation, with supporting editorials in newspapers across the country, reaching its climax with passage by Congress of the

North Cascades Act of 1968, transferring 671,500 acres for the establishment of a new national park.

That was not the only battleground. In Oregon, the Three Sisters Primitive Area had been established in 1937, embracing almost 250,000 acres astride the Cascade Divide. It included a portion of the Skyline Trail, beautiful lakes with unexcelled fishing and forested habitat of big game and birds. But the Secretary of Agriculture, on recommendation of the Forest Service, knocked out 53,000 acres when the area was reclassified as a wilderness in the early 1960s. Similarly, the agency policy of road-building and timber sales rendered impossible proposed enlargement of the Mount Jefferson Primitive Area, centered on snow-capped Mount Jefferson, the second highest peak in Oregon, which abounded in wild mountain flowers, unusual geological formations, and spectacular glacial scenery, a favored objective of wilderness hiking clubs since 1900. In fact, of the numerous limited areas in the Pacific Northwest, only Glacier Peak has to date been classified as wilderness (and that as a congressional proviso in the North Cascades Act), although there may still be an Alpine Lakes Wilderness and a Cougar Lakes Wilderness, both smaller than originally envisioned.

In 1960 Congress enacted the Multiple Use and Sustained Yield Law, redefining the purposes of the national forests as the enhancement of recreation, soil, range, timber, watershed, wildlife, fishing, mining—based on the "most judicious use of the land for some or all of these resources." The law was a measure whose passage the Forest Service had tried to secure several times before and which, in effect, gave it legislative carte blanche to do almost anything it wished under the mantle of professional expertise. Given a law of this kind, the Wilderness Society had pressed for protection of wilderness as one of the principal and legal missions of the national forests. In a last-minute compromise between no mention of wilderness and what the Society had urged, the new law stated: "The establishment and maintenance of areas of wilderness are consistent with the purposes and provisions of this Act." But the survey of wilderness undertaken the following year by the Wildland Research Center of the University of California showed only 17 million acres of wilderness remaining in the National Forest System. This survey used essentially the same definitions as the study of 1926 by the Forest Service, which had found 55 million acres of wilderness. The rate of loss over a 35-year period was in excess of 1 million acres per year.

There was no letup in sight. Industrial civilization appeared destined to occupy all the unoccupied lands. The saving of wilderness had become a responsibility of the public through such groups as the Wilderness Society, as much as of the federal agencies, perhaps more so.

At the Sierra Club's Second Biennial Wilderness Conference, held at San Francisco in 1951, Howard Zahniser spoke of a national wilderness preservation system. His thrust was different than it had been at the first conference two years earlier; then he had discussed wilderness "as an intellectual concept as well as a type of physical environment," but his subject in 1951 was "How Much Wilderness Can We Afford To Lose?" Zahniser saw test cases of civilization everywhere—"of the public interest with reference to wilderness preservation when in conflict with other enterprises"—cases so widespread that citizen conservationists were continually on the defensive, without time or energy to pursue a positive program to prevent recurrence of many controversies. Therefore, he called for a bold offensive to enlist public support and congressional action to establish something new and different; a national wilderness preservation system, based on legislation to be drafted through cooperation of federal land-management agencies and conservation organizations.

Zahniser suggested that areas to be included in the system be specified in the bill, while additions to the list could be provided by executive order or formal designation by the secretaries of Agriculture or of the Interior, with removal of any area from the system effected only by Congress. No changes in jurisdiction would be involved, and no new land-administering agency established. Each component area of the system would continue to serve its particular purpose, but the agency in charge would be responsible for preserving its wilderness character. In addition, a commission or council would be set up to recommend to Congress any necessary adjustment in the program and to coordinate preparation of maps and other materials on the wilderness system for public information.

The first wilderness bill, written largely by Zahniser, was introduced in Congress in 1956 by one Democratic senator, Hubert Humphrey of Minnesota, with nine co-sponsors, and one Republican House member, John P. Saylor of Pennsylvania. They listed eighty areas in the national forests, forty-eight in national parks and monuments, twenty in national wildlife refuges, and fifteen on Indian reservations to constitute the wilderness preservation system.

Between June 1957 and May 1964 eighteen hearings were held on the wilderness proposal, both in Washington and the West. Howard Zahniser attended every one of them, impressing enemies as well as friends with his belief that "we deeply need the humility to know ourselves as the dependent members of a great community of life." Zahniser, or "Zahnie," had been a key figure in the fight to save Echo Park. He was studious, soft-spoken, and patient, both persuasive and persistent, a man of love for his fellow men, and highly principled. He knew the government from the inside, having been a writer and editor for the Fish and Wildlife Service and in the Department of Agriculture. The bill was written and rewritten again and again. With the passing of time the proposed national wilderness preservation council was dropped, largely because the Park and Forest services did not want private citizens looking over their shoulders. Another draft specified that only classified wilderness and wild areas of the national forests would be included in the system—fifty-four areas instead of eighty.

The forest products industry fought the bill from beginning to end. So did the oil, grazing, and mining industries. Few opponents denied the validity of the wilderness concept. In principle, they were all for it, but it was in the wrong place, and there was too much of it. The Park Service, Forest Service, and most of the forestry profession were against it at first too. Broad powers have been granted to the agencies not simply for administration but for determining the character and use of the land, and administrators prefer not to share their prerogatives with the public. Professionals technically trained do not like to have their expertise challenged. The Department of Agriculture outlined the objection of the Forest Service in a 1957 letter to the Senate Committee on Interior and Insular Affairs. "This bill would give a degree of congressional protection to wilderness use of the national forests which is not enjoyed by any other use. It would tend to hamper free and effective application of administrative judgment which now determines, and should continue to determine, the use or combination of uses to which a particular national forest area is put." [1]

In the long struggle to get the bill passed, the wilderness cause was aided by Senator Clinton P. Anderson, Chairman of the Senate Committee on Interior and Insular Affairs, who many years before had been an intimate friend of Aldo Leopold and had walked in the New Mexico wilderness with him. The bill was bottled up year after year, however, by Anderson's opposite number in the House, Representative Wayne Aspinall, a highly skillful Colorado politician responsive to western economic interests. Finally, however, the groundswell of public support, expressed through congressional hearings, hundreds of newspaper editorials, and thousands of letters directed to congressmen from all sections of the country, became decisive. On April 10, 1963, the Senate passed the bill by a vote of 73 to 12; action could no longer be delayed in the House. When it passed there on July 30, 1964, only one negative vote was cast, but the House version was different, with special dispensation to permit mining exploration in wilderness. In the Senate-House conference where differences were ironed out, Aspinall had insisted on the mining provision as his price for the compromise, a final thrust of old power against the spirit of the new law.

When the President signed the bill on September 3, 1964, Leopold and Marshall were long gone and could not share the joy of the hour. Zahniser was gone, too. He had given the final years of his life to working for the wilderness bill and then at fifty-eight died in May, on the eve of the historic victory.

Chapter Ten

Hearing the People's Case

During the fight over the wilderness bill, the *Seattle Times*, published in the stronghold of the Pacific Northwest forest-products industry, derided the proponents of wilderness as "a powerful lobby of extreme conservationists." It was rather a compliment in its way. For certainly it was the upsurge of a concerned citizenry that overcame indifference and antipathy of congressional leadership to push the Wilderness bill through. The same "powerful lobby" rescued the virgin redwoods of California by means of a new national park and saved the Grand Canyon from being flooded.

"It was not so much a victory for the Sierra Club as it was for common sense," commented Stewart L. Udall, then Secretary of the Interior, following resolution of the Grand Canyon issue. Common sense prevailed, however, despite Secretary Udall's support of the dam project and the extensive campaign in its behalf by the Bureau of Reclamation, which he had approved. An aroused public had brought common sense home.

"Nothing great is ever accomplished without enthusiasm," wrote Ralph Waldo Emerson. Virtually every happening associated with wilderness, both before and after passage of the Act, demonstrates that only the enthusiasm of people can make it work. An enlightened and involved public stands as the hope between the remaining parcels of wilderness and oblivion.

Federal agencies responsible for administration cannot muster the required spark of genius, certainly not by themselves. For one thing, agency leadership is reluctant to cross swords with the economic-political power structure. The stomach for fighting and thirst for martyrdom are rare. Within the ranks individual enthusiasm to accomplish greatness is stifled; conformity is the rule. For another, technical experts, whether foresters, game biologists, or park planners, deal largely with men experienced in their own fields. Competence is judged to a great extent within the bounds of their professions. This goes back to their training, which is often limited in scope.

As the resource agencies are learning, no land-use plan or program will succeed or long survive in the age of environmental awareness unless it has public support and is judged consistent with public interest. This idea is at the heart of the Wilderness Act, which delineates a process for participation and understanding. When the law was passed in 1964, a little more than 9 million acres, administered by the Forest Service as wilderness and wild areas and a Boundary Waters Canoe Area, were at once protected as part of the National Wilderness Preservation System. The Act gave a clear direction and firm legal foundation to federal agencies responsible for protecting wilderness. In addition, it provided for public hearings on the feasibility of including other areas of national forests, national parks, and national wildlife refuges. At first this seemed like a complicated procedure, not what the conservation organizations had originally hoped for. Yet now the issues must be debated, area by area, before the people, and the people must be heard. If the ultimate decisions are based on the active participation of more people clamoring for understanding, refusing to settle for political promises or platitudes, this in itself represents an achievement in the course of democracy.

The full text of the Act appears in Appendix A of this book, but its contents deserve to be spelled out here. The Act states its mission clearly: "to secure for the American people of present and future generations the benefits of an enduring resource of wilderness."

It recognizes wilderness, in contrast with those areas where man and his own works dominate the landscape, "as an area where the earth and its community of life are untrammeled by man, where man himself is a visitor who does not remain."

In the opening section the Act declares establishment of a National Wilderness Preservation System, with component units to be designated by Congress and administered for the use and enjoyment of the American people. But use and enjoyment must leave these units unimpaired for future use and enjoyment as wilderness.

The fundamental uses are listed as: recreational, scenic, scientific, educational, conservation, and historic. In order to provide for them fully, administration must be designed to protect and preserve the wilderness character and to gather and disseminate information regarding use and enjoyment of wilderness.

A component of the wilderness system must be an area of undeveloped federal land "retaining its primeval character and influence, without permanent improvements or human habitation, which is protected and managed so as to preserve its natural conditions." It must also meet the following criteria:

1. Generally appears to have been affected primarily by the forces of nature, with the imprint of man's work substantially unnoticeable
2. Has outstanding opportunities for solitude or a primitive and unconfined type of recreation
3. Has at least 5,000 acres of land or is sufficient in size to make its preservation and use in an unimpaired condition a practical matter
4. May also contain ecological, geological, or other features of scientific, educational, scenic, or historical value

Some uses are specifically prohibited, including permanent roads, temporary roads (except as necessary to meet minimum requirements for administration of wilderness under the Act), motor vehicles, motorized equipment and motorboats, landing of aircraft, other forms of mechanical transport, and permanent structures and installations.

The restrictions are subject to certain exemptions. The most disturbing of these authorizes continuation of prospecting for minerals until January 1, 1984. For claims filed until then, only the mineral rights can be patented; the land itself remains under government title. While machinery and motors can be used to develop claims, methods of access are subject to reasonable regulation. Moreover, the Secretary of Agriculture can require that areas on claims disturbed by mining be restored as near as practicable to a natural condition. No new claims can be filed after the beginning of 1984. Representative Aspinall of Colorado, aware of the incompatibility of mining operations with a wilderness environment when he forced the concession into the Act, was constrained to advise his mining constituents to proceed with caution.*

Other exemptions authorized by the Act are: existing private rights, grazing where already established, subject to reasonable regulations considered necessary by the Secretary, and use of aircraft and motorboats where they have already become established. Although the Act *permits* motors to be used where established, it does not *require* their continued use. The language is perfectly clear on this point: The Secretary of Agriculture can decide whether to permit or prohibit motors in national forests. But the Forest Service has taken a timid stand, particularly in the Boundary Waters Canoe Area, where it has dodged the need to phase out motors, perpetuating a chronic major problem. In addition, the President is empowered to authorize prospecting for water resources, establishment and maintenance of reservoirs, power projects, transmission lines, and other utilities should he find them in the best interest of the nation.

The wilderness system became a reality with the law itself. It

---

* On January 5, 1973, U.S. District Court Judge Philip Neville, sitting in Minneapolis, issued a permanent injunction to halt mining and mineral exploration in the Boundary Waters Canoe Area (BWCA) of the Superior National Forest in northern Minnesota. Basing his decision on the Wilderness Act of 1964, Judge Neville held it was the court's responsibility to keep the popular north-country wildlands area in the most natural condition possible. "To create wilderness and in the same breath to allow for its destruction could not have been the real Congressional intent, and a court should not construe or presume an act of Congress to be meaningless if an alternative analysis is possible," his opinion stated. The decision was the result of a suit filed in December 1969 by the Izaak Walton League of America. The suit sought to enjoin anyone allegedly holding mineral rights in the BWCA from entering the area for mineral exploration or mining.

designated for inclusion at once all areas of the national forests previously classified as wilderness (a total of eighteen covering 6,898,014 acres) and wild (a total of thirty-five covering 1,355,034 acres), and also the Boundary Waters Canoe Area of Minnesota (886,673 acres).

In addition, the Secretary of Agriculture was directed by the Act to review the status of all thirty-four primitive areas, covering 5,477,740 acres (which had been administratively classified prior to the Wilderness Act), within ten years, based on a regular time schedule with reports on one-third of all areas to be ready for presentation to Congress within three years after enactment (by 1967), a second third within seven years (1971), and the remainder by 1974. The same pattern and schedule were defined for the Secretary of the Interior to report on suitable roadless areas in the national parks and national wildlife refuges. The stipulated procedure requires the Secretary to report to the President whether or not they are suitable for preservation as wilderness and the President, in turn, to submit his recommendations to Congress.

In each case a public hearing must be held, convenient to the area involved, and allowing testimony by state, county, and federal officials and by concerned citizen groups and individuals. A record of the hearing is required in each recommendation to the President and Congress. The same process applies when disestablishment of a wilderness may be proposed due to new needs; Congress may restudy any area, but there must first be a full record of discussion in the public forum before it acts.

Other wildlands in unclassified status, or *"de facto* wilderness," are not required to be reviewed but under a broad interpretation could be considered for the wilderness system and added to it. Likewise, though only the holdings of three agencies are mentioned, nothing appears to prevent Congress from adding those of others, such as the Bureau of Land Management. This agency of the Interior Department was excluded because of its historic role in disposal of the public domain. However, in 1964, the same year the Wilderness Law was passed, a sense of permanence was invested; Congress adopted the Classification and Multiple Use Act (which remained in effect until 1970) authorizing the BLM to classify lands either for disposition or for retention in manners that "best meet the present and future needs of the American people." The bureau was given the right to manage retained lands for grazing, occupancy, industrial development, fish and wildlife, timber, outdoor recreation, mineral development, watershed, wilderness preservation, or preservation of public values "that would be lost if the land passed from Federal ownership." The 175 million acres in public domain of the western states that might be classified for retention include choice native grasslands and desert of the very types Aldo Leopold had hoped to save.*

In determining minimum size, the provision for units of less than 5,000 acres that can feasibly be preserved in unimpaired condition permits protection of islands and other relatively small areas. The National Wildlife Refuge System alone listed nearly fifty island refuges in 1969 that qualified for study. These islands contain some of the most diverse and fragile environmental features of the nation. Though many are small, their values cannot be measured in size but rather in the ecological, biological, scenic, scientific, and historic features they contain. Many are vitally essential to the preservation of rare flora and fauna, while some represent ecological features that will be preserved as wilderness nowhere else in this country.

At the time the law was passed, it appeared the National Wilderness Preservation System could encompass in time 50 to 60 million acres from these potential sources: about 22 million acres in national parks and monuments, 24 million acres in national wildlife refuges, and between 15 and 20 million acres in national

---

* The issue of wilderness on the public domain came sharply to the fore in early 1974 with serious congressional consideration of an organic act granting the BLM permanent status and defining specific objectives for the lands under its administration. In view of vast oil shale and coal deposits on the public domain, the advocates of energy exploration sought to keep the bill weak and without any wilderness review provision. Conservationists, however, insisted that the organic act must require the BLM to identify and protect areas qualified under the Wilderness Act as standard inventory procedure. "If Congress fails to allow for the possibility of wilderness protection for those BLM lands deserving of it," editorialized the *New York Times*, "the bureau's reorganization will have been tainted at the outset by the sordid influence of special interests."

forests. That was before the roadless-area review and evaluation revealed a much broader potential. In any event, the full dimension can be developed only through expression of public desire, for the agencies will not press the issue, at least if we judge on performance to date.

As an illustration, consider the wilderness hearing on the Great Swamp National Wildlife Refuge conducted, as prescribed by law, at Morristown, New Jersey, in December 1966. One thinks of wilderness in other terms—of the western domain and of a few large, clearly established eastern areas like the Okefenokee and Great Smokies—yet here was a prospect lying within the otherwise suburban-industrial complex of New Jersey, fifteen miles from downtown Newark and a mere thirty miles from Times Square.

For generations swampland has been drained, filled, flooded, logged, and burned without restraint. Now the question was being asked, "What are we destroying that truly deserves saving?"

The Great Swamp represents the remnant of an ancient lake, created when the Passaic River was dammed by glacial action during the last ice age. When William Penn acquired the area from the Delaware Indians, it was a giant bowl or trough, some three by seven miles in size. Although man has been pushing back its borders and has made sporadic and deep intrusions, about 8,000 acres still remain in natural forest, marsh, and meadow.

The Great Swamp is never dull or repetitive; the life forms change continually with moisture, setting, and elevation. The lucky visitor is apt to catch sight of a belted kingfisher, always a solitary traveler, fishing for his meal in one of the pools. At least 175 species of birds have been identified and 75 are known to nest and rear their young in this vicinity. Den trees reveal the homes of raccoons, foxes, and other small mammals. In another section of the swamp waterfowl rest during migration on the Atlantic flyway. Here one appreciates the value of the vestigial native swamp as a nesting ground for black ducks, wood ducks, and teal, especially since the massive destruction of wetlands along the mid-Atlantic Coast.

The southwest end of the swamp, the setting of a county park, serves effectively to eliminate the need of any recreational development within the refuge itself, other than nature trails and boardwalks. The Nature Education Center, run by the park commission, offers classes and guided walks for children, enabling them to learn the total complex of swamp life—the kind of spot that every community in America ought to have for the benefit of botanists and biologists of all ages.

The nature center, with capacity of about 200 persons, had originally been scheduled as the setting of the wilderness hearing, but more than a thousand turned out—a tremendous outpouring of urbanites in support of wilderness. Officials of the Bureau of Sport Fisheries and Wildlife in charge of the proceedings appeared to be overwhelmed, dismayed, a little helpless. But presently the local citizen conservationists showed the way, arranging to move the proceedings to the grand ballroom of a Morristown hotel, then heading the throngs in the right direction.

A regional director opened the hearing without the faintest trace of enthusiasm. Still, the day marked the first proposal for a wilderness of less than 5,000 acres, a significant step. At that time the government owned 4,500 acres in the refuge and expected to acquire an additional 1,500. It would, the director said, establish a "roadless island" of 2,400 acres, leaving the balance subject to manipulation, such as artificial dikes and ponds, to enhance use by migratory and nesting waterfowl.

The effort to preserve the swamp was started in 1956; 450 acres were acquired by a local group and set aside as a sanctuary. In 1959, when the Port of New York Authority placed its finger on the Great Swamp as the ideal site to fill with earth and level with concrete for a jetport, many were stirred; over 7,000 individuals and organizations throughout the nation contributed $1.5 million to save the swamp.

They purchased some 3,000 acres, which they deeded to the federal government as the nucleus of the national wildlife refuge. But almost on the eve of the wilderness hearing they had reason to wonder about the safety of their gift. The Port Authority had never given up; it had renewed its position that the area offered the ideal site for a jetport—after all, to the engineer trained to build highways, dams, and airports, what more is a swamp than a void awaiting transformation into something useful?

At Morristown, the Wilderness Act was the medium of promise. "It is hard to underestimate the importance of wilderness area designations," as U.S. Senator Clifford Case declared in a statement that he had sent to the hearing. "These are established by Congress, therefore can only be reversed by Congress. In contrast, wildlife refuges are created by a special commission. Subsequently, the Secretary of the Interior has independent authority to permit invasions of these preserves where he sees fit to do so." And the senator cited two current instances, one nearby in New Jersey, the other in Alabama, that showed that federal administration of a refuge is no guarantee of lasting sanctity.

All kinds of people came to testify, from representatives of the Wilderness Society to those of the Staten Island Greenbelt Preservation League, whose representative said, "Our wilderness is gone. We need the Great Swamp and to know it is there." Some talked about the value of the swamp as a natural regulator of water supply, holding runoff and releasing it gradually into the Passaic River. Spokesmen for nine colleges and universities accented the importance of the living laboratory for faculty members and students. Almost all regarded the official wilderness proposal of 2,400 acres as inadequate; they insisted on a thousand acres more, which would still leave 1,600 acres for diking and ponding in waterfowl management.

In the end the Great Swamp Wilderness was established by Congress with the extra thousand acres included. The emphasis was as the people wanted it: on the balancing provision of green areas and wildlife preserves to stimulate awareness and appreciation of nature at the fringe of a great urban area.

Another example, of a different agency, lies in the very first proposed national forest addition to the system, the San Rafael Wilderness in Los Padres National Forest, in the brush-covered hills of the Coast Range in California. The Forest Service published its preliminary proposal August 7, 1965, and held field hearings in Santa Barbara November 8, 1965. Conservationists applauded the initiative, knowing that the agency had to move quickly to meet the Wilderness Act deadline of submission to Congress of one-third of the administration's recommendations concerning the thirty-four primitive areas.

The wilderness originally proposed had included only 110,403 acres—the 74,854-acre San Rafael Primitive Area established in 1932, plus some 36,000 acres of contiguous land, as compared with 158,000 acres that the citizens had felt justified in proposing at the hearing. But Associate Chief Arthur W. Greeley, testifying before the House Committee on Interior and Insular Affairs on June 19, 1967, conceded that the agency had come up with "a poor preliminary boundary" in this initial proposal. Conservationists gained encouragement from this candid appraisal as Greeley spoke in behalf of a much-improved proposal totaling 142,722 acres. They also felt that they could accept in good conscience a reduction of some 13,000 acres in their original proposal and still preserve a priceless living museum, with its deer, bears, mountain lions, eagles, trout streams, sugar pines, and rare lilies. A difference of 2,200 acres between the proposals of the Forest Service and the California Citizens Committee for the San Rafael Wilderness was all that remained after the give-and-take on both sides. Conservationists anticipated this approach toward middle ground and the resolution of differences would continue during the congressional portion of the wilderness review process.

But this was not to be. The Forest Service was unyielding when the issue came before the Senate; on May 3, 1967, the agency's proposal of 143,000 acres was adopted by voice vote under the unanimous consent procedure. The citizens committee felt, however, that it must hold its ground and determined to make a fight to add the contested 2,200 acres through action by the House.

Anyone who has hiked into the area can well understand their position. For here are found examples of an unusual meadow life zone, highlighted by *potreros,* or grassy balds, dotted with rocky outcrops, components of a beautiful and unworldly scene. And inscribed among some of the rocks are prehistoric aboriginal cave art, considered among the best yet discovered in North

America, left by the recently extirpated Chumash Indians, the native people of the Santa Barbara Coast. In addition, the presence of California condors, an endangered species of extremely limited habitat, observed within these 2,200 acres as recently as October 1967, enhances the ridgetop's value in its natural state.

The citizens prevailed upon the House Committee on Interior and Insular Affairs to adopt a version of the wilderness bill adding the 2,200 acres, and so it passed the House on October 16, 1967. But when it came back from the Senate-House conference the acreage was eliminated, though two conferees (John Saylor of Pennsylvania and Laurence Burton of Utah) had sought to find a middle ground in the conference committee between the Senate and House positions.

The fight was still not over. Representative Saylor, ranking Republican member of the House Interior Committee and champion of wilderness legislation from the beginning, declared that he would move to recommit the conference report to the conference committee. The Forest Service, he noted, at first had sought to exclude a 4,500-acre proposed addition on grounds that it was needed for grazing. Then it had opposed the 2,200-acre addition, claiming its inclusion in wilderness would interfere with ability to fight and suppress forest fires. However, one of the outstanding firefighters in the Santa Barbara area, a retired Forest Service officer, had given evidence before the House committee that including the disputed area would not hamper fire control, in fact, that the natural *potreros* constituted adequate firebreaks in themselves.

The objection of the Forest Service was vehement and made widely known through its field offices. It was joined by the Society of American Foresters, presuming to uphold the prerogatives of the profession, and by the American Forestry Association, which had opposed enactment of the wilderness bill. Plainly, firebreaks were not the issue. When the vote came before the House, on March 5, 1968, one hour was given to debate, relating not simply to San Rafael but to the broad public role in the process of decision-making. The Forest Service had its way; it defeated enlargement of this particular wilderness but not before a number of members addressed themselves to the issue.

The Forest Service implementation of the Wilderness Act was highly institutionalized from the very first. The approach was carefully thought through and essentially constructive and far-seeing with reference to protection of classified wilderness. On June 1, 1966, when Secretary of Agriculture Orville L. Freeman directed preparation of individual plans for each of the wilderness units already incorporated into the system and for others to follow, he defined the basic management principle, based on terms of the law, as follows: "National forest wilderness resources shall be managed to promote, perpetuate, and, where necessary, restore the wilderness character of the land and its specific values of solitude, physical and mental challenge, scientific study, inspiration and primitive recreation."

The agency prepared lengthy field regulations and supporting guidelines, comprising no less than sixty double-spaced pages. The administrative handbook for internal use comprises a small book. In certain respects the manual reflects economic considerations. It goes beyond the intent of the Act by introducing the concept of availability. In the name of public interest areas are considered "unavailable" if they contain some economically minable minerals or high quality timber. But in others it shows a strong attempt to respond to the spirit of the new law. In a speech on "National Forest Wilderness Under the 1964 Wilderness Act," delivered before the annual meeting of the Soil Conservation Society of America on August 22, 1965, Associate Chief Arthur W. Greeley listed three basic assumptions of the agency that were not specifically stated in the Act itself:

1. The intent of the Wilderness Act is to ensure an enduring resource of wilderness for the Nation. Hence the nonconforming uses which the Act authorizes need to be carried on in such a way as to minimize adverse impact on the wilderness character of the areas.

2. Wilderness values must be given priority in the many kinds of decisions that must be made about how wilderness areas are to be used.

At several points the Act is quite specific about saying that the rules governing nonconforming uses must be "reasonable." But administrators must also so manage each area as to "preserve its wilderness character." We do not see how to preserve wilderness character except by finding reasonable ways to give priority to wilderness values.

3. Wilderness areas have different characteristics. They are not all alike. Some differences are the products of nature. Others are the result of human attitudes or of traditional patterns of use of a particular area. So, we do not expect to have one rigid set of directives that will cover all situations in all units of the Wilderness Preservation System. Rather, within a generalized set of guidelines, the control will be a plan of management for each area which sets forth specific objectives and says how these objectives will be reached.

The Forest Service set a firm schedule for classification work on primitive areas, based on conducting field work and field hearings within seven years, and it kept to it throughout. From the inception of the wilderness system, it directed its concern to conflicts and nonconforming uses, such as with prospecting and mining and the place, if any, of machinery in wilderness. It endeavored to look ahead to the inevitable problems of recreational overuse and to provide answers at a relatively early stage.

In short, the agency committed itself to impeccable compliance with the letter of the law and fulfilled it thoroughly insofar as the primitive areas and wilderness areas are concerned. Its attitude toward potential additional areas, or even to consideration of any, is quite another story, one of consistent resistance to proposals of new wilderness, endless confrontation with citizen groups in virtually all parts of the country, often ending with officially sanctioned intrusion and commercial exploitation of the contested regions so as to render the wilderness invalid.

The Alpine Lakes country in the Pacific Northwest represents one bitter example. This rugged area astride the jagged crest of the Cascades was long protected by inaccessibility, even though close to the population center of Puget Sound. The marvel is that so much survived into modern times. For years its high lake basins and meadows have been enjoyed by visiting Boy Scouts, horseback riders, hunters, hikers, and fishermen, and efforts to protect its natural beauty extend from before World War I.

In 1946 the Forest Service itself, in recognition of potential wilderness value, set aside a 256,000-acre Alpine Lakes Limited Area for further study, but the designation omitted a number of key scenic locations regarded by citizen groups as integral parts of the wilderness. In the late 1950s extensive plans for logging became known, which evoked first a request for deferment, then the submission, in 1963, of a formal proposal for an Alpine Lakes Wilderness of 278,000 to 334,000 acres, depending on the feasibility of including private inholdings on some peripheries. This proposal was sponsored by all the leading northwestern conservation groups, as well as the Wilderness Society and Sierra Club.

Despite repeated citizen protest, logging advanced in the 1960s into the prime scenic and wilderness valleys of the Alpine Lakes. The first timber sale into the rain forest of the East Fork Miller River required construction of a 6-mile road far up the valley. The Forest Service justified it on the grounds of needing to develop the Miller River for motorized recreation. That parcel of wilderness is gone now, its place taken by clear-cuts and a high-grade road. What hurt most was the pattern of the Miller River timber sale, the same design of "wilderness preventive logging" that had been adapted to national forests in Washington, Oregon, and elsewhere. In such cases the logging does not creep up a wilderness valley in small steps, year after year; rather, the typically new logging road penetrates from two to seven miles, leapfrogging virgin forests before opening new cutting units.

Sound forestry management? To conservationists the practice has seemed a deliberate attempt to commit unprotected wilderness to timber management before Congress had the chance to pass on proposals for classification. Once a road is in place, once the cutting is done, the Forest Service considers the question of the wilderness status resolved—negatively, of course, for in the agency's viewpoint any such area cannot qualify as wilderness because of the existence of a road.

With passing of time, timber sales in large clear-cut units were

pressed onward and upward, over strenuous protests and repeated pleas for deferment, penetrating the boundaries of the
proposed Alpine Lakes Wilderness. In early 1968 Brock Evans,
spokesman for the Sierra Club and Federation of Western Outdoor Clubs, warned that another 150,000 acres of prime *de facto*
wilderness in the Alpine Lakes faced dismemberment in pursuit
of the Forest Service policy of "trees for the loggers, rock and ice
for the conservationists."

Evans complained bitterly:

> No one seriously questions its extremely high scenic, wilderness, and
> recreation value, right in metropolitan Seattle's backyard, but in spite
> of this it seems we are to be left only with rock and ice not wanted
> for commercial exploitation. We can attribute this unhappy state of
> affairs mainly to the attitude of the Forest Service that areas containing
> substantial amounts of commercial timber must not be included in wil-
> derness. It has been this attitude of that agency that has led to the dis-
> enchantment of Northwest conservationists with the Forest Service.[1]

But who was to hear the complaints of the citizens? A letter
from Evans to the Secretary of Agriculture, Orville L. Freeman,
had brought a response dated July 13, 1967, from Acting Chief
of the Forest Service E. M. Bacon. "There are many thousands
of acres of presently undeveloped land throughout the National
Forest System," wrote Bacon. "A large percentage of these have
been at one time or another recommended for Wilderness status
by some organization or individual. To defer development of
all such areas pending a Congressional determination would be
to abdicate our responsibility for administering the National
Forests in the public interest."

This same point was made by Charles Connaughton, Regional
Forester for Oregon and Washington, at the Northwest Wilderness Conference, conducted by citizen organizations in Seattle
in February 1970. He maintained the Forest Service would only
manage as wilderness those areas that the agency itself believes
should be so classified, while multiple-use management would
be practiced in all other areas, regardless of any wilderness proposals by citizen groups, or whether Congress had an opportunity
to consider the issues. Conservationists lamented that in the

preceding twenty years at least 10 million acres of wilderness in the Pacific Northwest had been lost due to roading and logging under the multiple-use program.

The Forest Service alleged other reasons than timber-cutting for its management programs. As Bacon had explained in his letter to Evans about the Alpine Lakes: "It is undoubtedly true that improved access to the general area will encourage use and cause a more rapid increase in administration problems. However, use would continue to increase whether or not roads are built; and maintenance of the primitive character of the land around Enchantment Lakes can only be accomplished through proper administration and control of use and not through extension of the recommended boundaries."

Such tortured reasoning was given on a broad front. Forest officials everywhere have insisted that wilderness boundaries could not, and would not, be expanded. They would make the considerations and judgments. But they would maintain primitive environments and enhance recreational quality—by cutting trees, building roads, and making remote areas accessible to greater numbers of people.

Sometimes the foresters have had their way, but sometimes the people's enthusiasm for wilderness has prevailed. In the case of the Lincoln-Scapegoat Country, in west central Montana, conservationists for more than half a century have sought protection for this beautiful area of high mountain snowfields, rushing streams, and narrow valleys carpeted with wildflowers. The Lincoln Back Country and Scapegoat Mountain area, covering about 240,000 acres, have been a source of attraction and enjoyment since the Lewis and Clark expedition and the days when early fur trappers and early hunters came into the region. Yet the area had never received special attention by the Forest Service; its protection was built in by inaccessibility, lack of significant timber, and other commodity resources. Much of it lies in high-elevation zones, with steep gradients and shallow soils, the watersheds protected by nonuse. This is not to say the Lincoln-Scapegoat was idle; it was used by campers, hikers, hunters, and fishermen, and by a wide variety of fish and wildlife, including such rare and vanishing species as native cutthroat trout, wolverine, bald eagle, grizzly bear, and mountain lion, that were wholly dependent upon the wilderness environment.

Against this background the Forest Service in 1963 announced plans to develop the area for combined timber production and intensive recreational use. Citizen groups, joined by the Montana Game and Fish Department, objected; they asked for legal protection of the area as wilderness. Consequently, the Montana state senate in 1967 unanimously memorialized Congress to take such action and appropriate legislation was introduced by the Montana delegation into both houses.

On September 25, 1968, hearings were conducted in Washington on Senate bill S. 412. Edward P. Cliff, Chief of the Forest Service, presented the agency position in opposition. The effect of passage, he warned, would be to combine the Lincoln-Scapegoat Back Country with the 950,000-acre Bob Marshall Wilderness, which lies contiguous on the southeast—as though a large dimension of wilderness resource should be considered undesirable. "In our studies of the Lincoln-Scapegoat Back Country," Cliff continued, "we have found that a very large part of it has unusual potential for 'back country' recreation use—including some activities and facilities for recreation use not permissible under the Wilderness Act, and yet different from the use and facilities provided in the intensively roaded and highly developed portions of the national forests."

One of his suggested alternatives was to devote three-fourths of the area to primitive-type recreation, while holding the land in a natural, unroaded condition. Another was to develop a system of scenic highways and timber-harvesting. But Senator Lee Metcalf countered that the area appeared so fragile that heavy recreation and highway development might cause serious erosion. The Forest Service did not have its way. In 1969 the Senate took favorable action on the Lincoln-Scapegoat Wilderness bill. The legislation was blocked in the House that year by Representative Wayne Aspinall, chairman of the Interior Committee, on grounds that a pending mineral survey had not been completed. Two years later, in 1971, the survey was at last completed (showing nonproductivity among 131 mining claims); the Senate again voted favorably and action was imminent in the

House. In the meantime the Forest Service responded to political reality (notably the concern of Senator Lee Metcalf and Senator Mike Mansfield), announcing in December 1971 that it could now report favorably on the pending wilderness legislation, which was enacted forthwith.

A variation on the pattern is found in the proposal for a St. Joe Wilderness in northern Idaho, located within a few hours of population centers in eastern Washington. In that region tragic results of widespread roading, clear-cut logging on erodible, steep slopes, and mass recreational developments of recent years had focused concern on the future of a 200,000-acre roadless area, the last major possibility for wilderness north of the Lochsa River. Elevations range from 3,000 to 7,000 feet, providing interesting changes in vegetation and opportunities for ecological study. High mountain lakes and unaltered streams, including the wild upper reaches of the St. Joe River and the Little North Fork of the Clearwater, furnish excellent fishing for rare cutthroat and Dolly Varden trout, while the surrounding slopes and forests constitute habitat for mountain goats, elk, black bears, moose, grouse, beavers, and other animals.

In 1968 citizen conservationists outlined their concept of saving the wilderness. "The major obstacle," wrote Morton R. Brigham, chairman of the North Idaho Wilderness Committee, the following summer, "has been the disinclination of the Forest Service to discuss such a proposal." [2]

What the agency did, instead, was to proclaim, on May 16, 1969, a roadless "Pioneer Area" of 30,500 acres, without benefit of public hearing and with scant public discussion, then to project a network of roads and timber sales throughout the remainder of the 170,000 acres of *de facto* wilderness. The pleas of wildlife organizations for time to conduct field trips for various proposals fell on deaf ears. At first so did the proposal of the Idaho Fish and Game Department to add the Collins Creek drainage to the pioneer area; a road up the mountain along this stream would have ruined cutthroat trout fisheries, invaded elk range, endangered mountain goats, and effectively cut the proposed St. Joe Wilderness in two, making it more difficult to gain approval of Congress for any genuine protection. Additional protest came from Clifton R. Merritt, Western Regional Director of the Wilderness Society, who demanded a "comprehensive study and full consideration of the special recreational, fishery and other fragile resources involved in the greater area." Ultimately, the agency relented on this point, deferring the Collins Creek Road but substituting another through the saddle west of Pole Mountain, into steep, erosive soil. By early 1970 roads had been built, and it was clear that logging would proceed in the only major stand of primeval forest left in the drainage of the Little North Fork of the Clearwater. It was also planned to widen a jeep road along the St. Joe River, despite pleas for protection of the cutthroat trout fishery and the possibility of gaining inclusion of the St. Joe in the National Wild and Scenic River System. It was not a very happy prospect.

In the face of these repeated episodes of confrontation, one may properly inquire whether the citizens could dare to be right, or whether the foresters, with their broad charter from Congress and presumption of professional expertise, could dare to be wrong. In the case of East Meadow Creek, a part of White River National Forest in Colorado, the decision was rendered not by the bulldozer or chainsaw but by court of law.

East Meadow Creek lies adjacent to the Gore Range-Eagle's Nest Primitive Area, approximately eighty miles west of Denver and just east of the ski resort of Vail. It contains some of Colorado's spectacular mountain country, including seventeen peaks over 13,000 feet in elevation; the high country is dotted with numerous alpine lakes tucked in glaciated cirques and snowfields, while the lowland creek drainages are covered by forests of Englemann spruce, lodgepole pine, and scattered aspen groves. Elk, deer, black bear, mountain goats, and bighorn sheep are found throughout the area. Under terms of the Wilderness Act, the Forest Service recommended, in 1968, classification of 71,785 acres, an increase of 10,510 acres over the original primitive area. Conservationists agreed with the recommended additions but proposed significant increases of 53,000 acres for a total wilderness proposal of 125,000 acres.

Certain units were felt required to "take wilderness off the rocks," to round it out with timbered, lower-elevation recreational areas, to protect the scenic foreground of the Gore Range, and to furnish the cushion needed to withstand increased use. These areas include the 20-mile-long Gore Range Trail, a superb walking and riding route along the east side of the range. Another unit was suggested as an integral ecological component of the whole wilderness. Then there was the East Meadow Creek drainage, one of the main access routes for the thousands who visit the primitive area each year. Its wilderness campsites have been used for years by hunters, fishermen, and hikers, while the surroundings have served as summer range and habitat cover for an important herd of elk.

But the Forest Service had other plans for East Meadow Creek. In 1968 it agreed to sell 4.3 million board feet of spruce, pine, and fir to an Arizona timber company, Kaibab Industries, dispensing with any wilderness consideration on grounds that a single old access road running three-quarters of a mile inside the sale area disqualified it as either primitive or wilderness. This announcement spurred the first citizen suit to restrain the Forest Service in its design to eliminate potential wilderness units from consideration via the logging route. The action to stop the sale was entered by a combination of the town of Vail, Eagle's Nest Wilderness Committee, Sierra Club, and *Colorado Magazine.* In April 1969 U.S. District Judge William E. Doyle handed down a preliminary injunction prohibiting the sale. In late February 1970 he ruled that the injunction "be continued indefinitely or until a determination has been made by the President and Congress that East Meadow Creek is predominantly wilderness in character and should be made part of the Gore Range-Eagle's Nest or that it should not be."

The judge warned that the Forest Service must not ignore the Wilderness Act, which declares the President may recommend to Congress for inclusion as wilderness "any contiguous area of national forest lands predominantly of wilderness value." If the proposed sale were to proceed, the judge wrote, it would frustrate the purpose of the Act, which leaves the ultimate decision as to classification up to the President and Congress, rather than to the Forest Service and Secretary of Agriculture.

"Under the Multiple Use Sustained-Yield Act, this authority

of the Secretary of Agriculture to preserve wilderness was specifically recognized," observed Judge Doyle.

However, prior to the Wilderness Act, the issue of what areas should be designated as wilderness, wild or primitive, and what uses might be made of such areas was entirely within the discretion of the Secretary of Agriculture and the Forest Service. Thus, the administrative decisions with respect to the suitability of an area for wild, wilderness or primitive classification, the need for preserving the natural state of such an area, and the relative values of various resources in the particular area were final and unreviewable. One of the major purposes of the Wilderness Act was to remove a great deal of this absolute discretion from the Secretary of Agriculture and the Forest Service by placing the ultimate responsibility for wilderness classification in Congress.

Despite the existence of the East Meadow Creek Road, Judge Doyle ruled that the region "meets the minimum requirements of suitability for wilderness classification and must, therefore, be included in the study report to the President and Congress." With the exception of the road (which he noted to be substantially unnoticeable from approximately 100 yards away), the judge declared East Meadow Creek drainage "untrammeled by man," with outstanding opportunities for solitude and a primitive and unconfined type of recreation.

The judge's decision made clear that citizens who had brought the suit were on the right side of the law. This means, then, that the federal agency, the adversary in his court, was pressing an unlawful position with legal talent underwritten by citizens of all the nation. Where agencies have failed to meet their responsibilities to make the Wilderness Act work, the citizens have had to fill the gap, whether in court or Congress, in one section of the country and then another. Should the burden of upholding an act of Congress be borne by the public when public servants presumably are paid to furnish this specific service?

In late 1971 the Forest Service finally turned its attention to the roadless areas, the *"de facto* wilderness" of unmeasured dimensions. Until then the agency had insisted that it must first complete the study of primitive areas, which would take until 1974, before giving consideration to the unclassified lands. Conservationists had no objections so long as all options were preserved—that is, so long as the areas were not eliminated through roading and logging. Under such pressures as the Lincoln-Scapegoat congressional action and the East Meadow Creek legal decision, the Forest Service advanced its schedule.*

The results of the roadless area inventory were announced in January 1973. A total of 235 areas was nominated for possible further study "based on their suitability, availability and need" for potential inclusion in the wilderness system. These new candidate areas covered 11 million acres. Only two were in the East and one in Puerto Rico; the remainder were in the West and Alaska. Actually, sixty-one areas containing 4.7 million acres had already been committed to study either through Forest Service decision (Cougar Lakes, Mount Aix, Alpine, and Enchantment in Washington state and Tracy Arm-Ford's Terror, Granite Fiords, Russell Fiords, and Nelly Juan in Alaska), congresional statute (Indian Peaks, Colorado; Lower Minam River, Oregon; and Dunoir Area, Wyoming), or judicial direction (East Meadow Creek and other adjacent areas), so that the agency had developed a new schedule of only 174 areas totaling 6.3 million acres.

How many roadless areas that might qualify for wilderness were actually identified, however? The inventory revealed no less than 1,448 areas, encompassing 55.9 million acres. Almost 1,000 areas of potential wilderness were arbitrarily eliminated based on "other resource values which might be lost or diminished if the area were classified as wilderness." The emphasis for further study was plainly on "mountaintop" acreage; the lower-level forests, where accessible commercial timber trees grow (notably

---

* Members of the Council on Environmental Quality drafted a Presidential executive order to grant interim protection to *de facto* wilderness areas pending review. "Such an order would be a vitally important step in stopping the further decimation of the wilderness on our public holdings until the Executive branch and the Congress can act on permanent protection for these lands," declared Senator Gaylord Nelson on August 12, 1971. Failure of the President to sign the executive order was attributed to the resistance of the Forest Service. In addition, the Sierra Club introduced further pressure through a law suit to halt logging in the roadless areas.

the prized old-growth stands in Oregon), were generously deleted.*

Later in 1973, the Forest Service announced that it would study for possible wilderness designation a total of 274 areas, covering more than 12 million acres in 14 states and Puerto Rico. The review program will span a period of 10 to 20 years. The areas involved will be managed in the meantime to protect their wilderness values. Additional roadless areas not designated for review will be subject to provisions of the National Environmental Policy Act (including preparation and publication of environmental impact statements) in advance of roading, logging, or other developments.

The roadless inventory, whatever its shortcomings, signaled that the early estimate of a wilderness system of 50 to 60 million acres was low—low by far. No one would demand that all 55.9 million roadless acres be included in the system, but before being assigned to other uses certainly the nation should be able to weigh benefits gained versus benefits lost.

The year 1974 was originally conceived as the end of the wilderness review period. The second stage, challenging citizen activism, is only beginning.

---

* The Forest Service asserted that each region had gone to the public in order to solicit opinions—through workshops, public meetings, and mailings of maps and brochures—and that these were reflected in the new study areas ("Proposed New Wilderness Study Areas," Current Information Report No. 9, Department of Agriculture, January 1973). Conservationists complained, however, that the review had been superficial and hurried, conducted during the winter season when citizens could not make adequate field surveys, that opportunity for citizens to be heard at public meetings was extremely limited, and that their protests were ignored.

Chapter Eleven

Any Wilderness in the East?

The wooded, rocky region bordering the Sipsey Fork of the Black Warrior River first came into public attention in 1969. That was the year the Alabama Conservancy undertook its research for remaining natural areas that might contain virgin forest to propose for inclusion in the National Wilderness Preservation System. The hunt inevitably led to the Sipsey, embraced within the Bankhead National Forest of northwest Alabama, a naturally hardwood area, threaded with streams and waterfalls in deeply eroded valleys that fall away abruptly into towering perpendicular sandstone cliffs.

The conservancy had been organized by concerned citizens in order to cope with Alabama resource issues, including air and water pollution, strip-mining of coal, and the disruption of many natural streams through construction of dams and technological channel-straightening, or "channelization." Then there was the challenge presented throughout the state by conversion of millions of forested acres of hardwoods and pines, capable of supporting diverse flora and fauna, into tree farms of pine only, designed strictly for production of pulp and paper.

The area suggested for wilderness review covers 11,000 acres. It includes the Bee Branch Scenic Area, a 1,240-acre tract of rough gorges, which had been protected administratively by the Forest Service for a number of years. In this region the Forest Service was engaged in a program of "stand conversion": spreading toxic chemical herbicides (usually 2,4 D and 2,4,5-T), bull-dozing, and clear-cutting to kill the natural hardwood forest in order to replace it with even-aged pine plantations.

Here the southern tip of the Cumberland Plateau meets the ecological influence of the coastal plain. In times past the Chickasaw and Cherokee Indians roamed among the towering trees, in company with mountain lion, bear, and beaver, where the abundant water and sheltering walls now enclose an island of the past.

The hiker descending into the deep gorges finds the rimrock cliff exposed in grayish and yellow hues, while waterfalls tumble over monstrous boulders to the valley floor. Only a remnant of the original forest survives in the 30-mile chain of gorges, but it is a distinctive forest. Deep shade, a constant supply of moisture, and cool summer temperatures provide a southern refuge for plants normally found farther north. Alabama's largest tulip poplar tree, nearly twenty-two feet in circum-ference, grows in the box canyon of Bee Branch. In the same setting are eastern hemlock and sweet birch, crowned with its gracefully symmetrical round top, ferns, flowering shrubs and plants, and mountain laurel climbing 100 feet on the steep slopes.

The proposed wilderness represents only a small portion of the Bankhead National Forest—only 6 per cent—and an even smaller portion of all private and public forest lands in the state, one two-thousandth of 22 million acres. Nevertheless, the Forest Service responded categorically that no forest land meeting wilderness standards could possibly exist in Alabama. The Sipsey area, in particular, was disqualified because por-tions had been briefly farmed by man and a few wagon roads built.

In November 1969 the agency showed members of the con-servancy its management plans. Only the canyons and the scenic area were to be exempt from clear-cutting and stand conversion. The gorges were to be preserved, because it was economically unfeasible to cut them, but the ridges (which provide moisture and protection for the gorges' ecosystem) were to be clear-cut and converted. The conservancy requested and was granted a year's moratorium in order to conduct a wilderness feasibility study.*

The conservancy then undertook to survey the wildlife, plants, geology, speleology, and history, with the foremost authorities in these fields contributing their time and talent. The report on the Sipsey was completed before the moratorium ended. The conservancy investigators found there are still deer, squirrels, otters, mink, beavers, and raccoons in the area. Many fish driven out of major rivers by pollution, siltation, damming, and ditching are found only in remaining natural rivers like the Sipsey and its tributaries. These include not only popular fishing species, such as bass and sunfish, but two kinds of darters, colorful little minnows, previously unknown and unnamed. There are no less than eighty species of birds, ranging from northern whippoorwill to southern chuck-will's-widow, of which more than half depend upon the hardwood environment to survive. Because birds are so mobile, ecological conditions of the Sipsey may affect populations of birds hundreds or thousands of miles away which depend on the kind of food and cover they find during migration or while wintering down South.

There is not a cranny in such rocks, not a foot of the Appalachian wildwood but harbors something lovable and rare. Turn over any rock or log and something unusual is apt to be exposed. Perhaps a red-backed salamander, its fox-red dorsal strip contrasting with a mixture of dark and light spots on its belly, or a seal salamander, or one of the lungless group, living without gills or lungs under the moist, mossy floors of the mountain forests. Many salamanders are endemic to the Appalachians, found in their own special corners and nowhere else. Of what use are they? Possibly none at all, at least not to man, or not in practical terms to man. They're part of a living community, whose members don't go around destroying their

---

* The Forest Service conducted a study of soils in the proposed wilderness, examining the cliff slopes and stream bottoms, and reported them to represent "the ultimate in hardwood sites to be found in Alabama." The study also concluded that 65 per cent, or 7,000 acres, of the suggested wilderness area was "poorly suited" for intensive forestry management such as clear-cutting and that it would be hazardous to construct roads, due to danger from erosion.

own homeland or poisoning their food and water; they evolve and adapt within a given environment and, to the extent that man learns from them, that becomes a use, too.

The committed citizens of the Alabama Conservancy felt they had located an area providing "outstanding opportunities for solitude, and the primitive unconfined type of recreation" as prescribed, or required, by the Wilderness Act. Legislation to establish a Sipsey Wilderness was introduced by both of Alabama's senators, who obviously concurred. It was endorsed by the governor, the Alabama Department of Conservation, the Alabama legislature in a joint resolution, major national conservation organizations, and by a petition bearing the signatures of 20,000 Alabamians.

Despite this outpouring of public expression, the Forest Service remained unmoved, insisting in May 1971 that the scars of human use borne by the Sipsey gravitate overwhelmingly against it. Four months later Associate Chief (and soon Chief) John R. McGuire expounded the official position that there was no wilderness left east of the Rockies to qualify under terms of the Wilderness Act.

Is there any wilderness in the East?

This region of America is pictured throughout the world as a massive urbanized web, overpopulated and overpolluted. The view is quite correct, of course—which makes the last wild fragments worth clinging to: those bits and pieces of original seacoast, estuarine salt marshes and inland fresh-water swamps, the primeval forests that have managed, without benefit of "management," somehow through natural attacks by fire, insects, tornadoes, volcanoes, and hurricanes for millions of years, and the mountains, including some of the oldest on earth. Certainly every ridge, crag, and wooded ravine, such as those in the Sipsey of Alabama, will become more valuable in the flood tide of civilization around them.

The Forest Service administers approximately 23 million acres of federal land in the East, extending from the White Mountains of Maine and New Hampshire down through the southern Appalachians to the Florida plain and across the Ozarks and Ouachita Mountains and the states bordering the

Great Lakes. Unlike western national forests, which were carved out of the public domain, most of the eastern lands were formerly private holdings acquired through purchase under the Weeks Law of 1911. They include a variety of formerly remote and undeveloped areas, as well as many others that have reverted to natural condition through years of protection.

Conservationists have nominated scores of potential additions to the wilderness system, but the Forest Service has turned them all down. When interested and concerned citizens have inquired about saving what appears to them as wilderness, the answers uniformly have been either, "The works of man have marred it" or "It is less than 5,000 acres in size." As Chief of the Forest Service Edward P. Cliff declared at the Sierra Club Biennial Wilderness Conference held at San Francisco in 1967, "Personally, I hope very much that we will not see a lowering of quality standards to make aceptable some man-made intrusions or defects of other kinds simply for the sake of adding acreage." On this basis numerous areas throughout the National Forest System have been withheld from wilderness protection for purposes of multiple-use management, with foresters making all the decisions on their own.

The concept and spirit of wilderness are defined in the Act; two key phrases, "retaining its primeval character and influence" and "the imprint of man's work (must be) substantially unnoticeable," are used to describe wilderness. The Forest Service zeros in on the word "primeval," closing the options to anything but virgin forest, but there is no requirement that the forest must be virgin or that all evidence of man be absent. Conservationists believe that the phrase "substantially unnoticeable" provides leeway for interpretation, as Judge Doyle expressed it in the East Meadow Creek case, and opens the door to admissibility of recoverable areas.

This question was discussed in 1970 by the second session of the Ninety-first Congress. In reporting on H. R. 19007, a bill designating for addition to the National Wilderness Preservation System portions of several national wildlife refuges, national parks and monuments, and national forests, located in twelve states, the House Committee on Interior and Insular Affairs noted near the outset of its report that the areas range from over 50,000 acres down to 3 acres. "The areas have little in common except one very distinctive characteristic," the committee commented. "Each is an undeveloped tract of Federal land retaining its natural character and influences without permanent improvements or human habitation. Each can be managed and protected to preserve its natural conditions for the use and enjoyment of future generations. Each presents outstanding opportunities for recreation and solitude as well as having value for scientific study."

During consideration of these areas for wilderness designation, testimony had disclosed that some were not entirely free of man-made improvements. In most instances, the Department of the Interior and Department of Agriculture had recommended the exclusion of land immediately surrounding such structures or improvements. In a few other situations where improvements exist, the committee had been assured by departmental witnesses that these were scheduled for removal upon designation of the areas as wilderness. "The committee approves and accepts this position and wishes to emphasize its own conviction that these areas must be kept free of man-made intrusions and of nonconforming uses." But it did not say that it would not accept them into the system because of such intrusions or uses.

To the contrary, the report details the subvirginal qualities of the several areas in question. For instance, the Seney Wilderness, the 25,150-acre northwest section of the Seney National Wildlife Refuge in Upper Michigan, includes a varied mixture of tracts. Some lands, though never cut, in the late nineteenth century had been frequently swept by fires that followed logging nearby. The "string bogs," a subarctic formation rare this far south, with low ridges covered with tamarack, embraces two-thirds of the wilderness. The remainder was once a white pine forest, logged off before the turn of the century, then burned over many times, and now covered with large, charred pine stumps, second-growth aspen and jack pine, and a variety of other species. Likewise, in the Moosehorn Wilderness, within the Moosehorn National Wildlife Refuge in Maine, the Edmonds Unit had been logged over several times. "While not true forested wilderness in the strict sense of the word, the Edmonds Unit, if set aside as wilderness, will eventually become wilderness," the committee commented, in terming the Edmonds a "creative wilderness." Then it added, "There will be high interest in the changing ecology as years pass for the serious student and casual visitor alike."

No such expression has been heard from the Forest Service, only disclaimers of qualifications of *de facto* wilderness with the slightest blemishes and repeated assurances that multiple-use management will take care of everything. Yet one of the major purposes of the Wilderness Act was to remove the power of absolute discretion from the Secretary of Agriculture and the Forest Service by placing the ultimate decision and responsibility for wilderness classification in Congress.

Based on its policy of purism, the Forest Service has decreed that no areas in national forests east of the Mississippi River qualify as wilderness. Before passage of the Act in 1964, the service had cooperated with conservationists and designated as wild areas the 7,655-acre Linville Gorge and 13,400-acre Shining Rock tracts in North Carolina and the 5,400-acre Great Gulf in New Hampshire, even though the first two of these areas had been logged by railroad methods around the turn of the century, much the same as other Appalachian forests. In addition, however, other large areas within the eastern forests have regained their cover of mature trees, with fertile soil and high rainfall encouraging rapid growth. In the southern mountains, in particular, forests have the capacity to regrow and regenerate within thirty to fifty years to the point that trees provide the scenic beauty of wilderness. Railroad grades, too narrow and too temporary for use as more than trails, have reverted to the wild state, with overgrown banks and the few cuts into rock covered with moss, fern, and lichens. Nevertheless, the Forest Service has disclaimed wilderness qualifications of statutory and *de facto* wilderness with the exception of the Great Gulf. As John McGuire of the Forest Service declared before the biennial Wilderness Conference, conducted in Washington, D.C., in September 1971, "The areas with wilderness characteristics as defined in the Wilderness Act are virtually all in the West." McGuire told the conference that his agency recognized the pressing need in the East and South for providing primitive outdoor recreation opportunities and maintaining wildland values but insisted this must be done through alternatives to the Wilderness Act.*

The Forest Service has presumed to answer the desire for protection of primitive eastern forests through a variety of administrative designations, such as scenic areas, pioneer zones, and travel-influence and water-influence zones, within the multiple-use framework. But these have left much to be desired.

For example, in West Virginia, citizen groups, led by the West Virginia Highlands Conservancy, after studying the Wilderness Act, offered proposals for establishment of three units in the Monongahela National Forest: Dolly Sods, 18,000 acres; Otter Creek, 18,000 acres, and Cranberry Back Country, including two units of 26,300 acres and 10,000 acres. All were very choice locations for eastern America; the state of West Virginia, in fact, recommended that the Forest Service preserve "sizable primitive areas" in their natural condition, with these in mind.

The Otter Creek unit includes the complete bowl-shaped basin drained by Otter Creek and at least two contiguous areas of potential wilderness. Though almost completely stripped of timber during the harsh logging era of 1905–15, the area has remained almost undisturbed with hardwood and hemlock forests nearing maturity and is penetrated only by trails, including some on the old railroad grades. Otter Creek is considered outstanding for hiking and backpacking, while the basin is

---

* The Forest Service offered to support a concept of "wild areas" specifically designed to meet eastern needs. Under terms of congressional legislation to establish such a system (National Forest Wild Areas bill, S. 3973 in 1972, S. 22 in 1973), a component unit would be one that is "an area of outstanding beauty; is primarily primitive and natural in character although man and his works may have been present and wherein the marks of man's activities are subject to restoration to the appearance of a primitive and natural condition; is large enough so that primitive and natural values can be preserved; and the area provides outstanding opportunities for public use and enjoyment in a primitive type setting." Conservationists united to oppose this concept, which appeared to duplicate and undermine the wilderness system and to promote intensive recreation rather than preserve wilderness.

one of the few remaining West Virginia areas sufficiently remote to serve as breeding grounds for the heavily hunted black bear.

The Dolly Sods, a high, wild section of the Allegheny Plateau, also was logged over, but forests, including hardwoods and spruce, are slowly reclaiming the land. Many of the open, rocky higher ridges, known locally as "huckleberry plains," support a variety of heath shrubs, with blueberries summoning pickers when they ripen. Botanists find the sphagnum bogs, with a flora reminiscent of the Arctic tundra, especially worthy of study, while the diversity of plant communities supports many species of wildlife—bear, beaver, deer, wild turkey, and bobcat among them; the varying hare is quite common, a reminder of the Canada-like climate of the Dolly Sods.

The most attractive, varying, and important features of the Cranberry Back Country are its mountain streams rushing down from pine-capped heights, renowned not only for beauty but for their native trout populations. The tree species vary, too, from northern hardwoods at lower elevations up through hemlocks and pines on the mountain slopes to red spruce completely taking over the highest summits. Wildflowers follow a comparable progression pattern; naturalists, both amateur and professional, have no difficulty in identifying dozens of varieties. Trails offer possibilities for hikers of all degrees of competence, including one fifteen miles long completely crossing the back country atop a high ridge.

The Forest Service responded to the citizen wilderness proposals with something less than enthusiasm. On Otter Creek it countered with a plan whereby one-third of the area would be designated a pioneer study area and thus protected against timber-cutting and road-building. The rest of the area would be called a "Back Country," where logging would go on, but timber access roads would be gated against unauthorized vehicles. When conservationists entered a formal appeal against this management plan, the supervisor of the Monongahela National Forest announced the road-building program was going ahead. Furthermore, he granted access to a coal company to build rough roads for core-drilling to establish quantity and quality of coal underlying the area. On the Dolly Sods proposal, the

Forest Service agreed to designate a Dolly Sods Scenic Area, but deleted nearly all commercially valuable timberlands from the boundary.

"The Forest Service has administratively divided the Monongahela National Forest into small timber sales compartments, which eventually will have the effect of destroying the wilderness resource," advised George Langford of the West Virginia Highlands Conservancy in a March 31, 1971, statement. In the Gauley Ranger District, for example, the average size of the seventy-six timber sales compartments is 2,015 acres. The pioneer study units (the Forest Service version of local administrative protection of wild areas) in that district have sizes of 3,168, 1,110, 597, and 525 acres—not much different from the size of the timber sales compartments. For the whole Monongahela National Forest (outside of the Spruce Knob–Seneca Rock National Recreation Area, where three pioneer study areas are planned, totaling 21,300 acres), the average size of the ten pioneer zones is 2,430 acres (if the largest and smallest were omitted, the average size would be 2,030 acres).

"The sizes of these Pioneer Study Units," Langford went on,

are generally barely large enough to encompass the drainage basin of a single perennial stream and are too small to provide a wilderness experience or setting comparable with other de facto wildernesses within the same national forest. Because of the extensive system of roads existing or planned within the rest of the timber sales compartments, nearly every point within the Pioneer Study Units would be within an hour's walk of a permanent Forest Service road. This presents little obstacle to a poacher or to most other (legitimate) visitors. Solitude and the opportunity for an unconfined type of recreation are unlikely to be preserved in such small areas. The pressure of many casual visitors would probably soon overload all the primitive facilities and trails, as there would be little distance or challenge to filter and disperse the users. In the general forest (the rest of the timber sales compartments) the timber access roads would leave a patchwork of urbanized woodlots of homogeneous, uninspiring character and even smaller walking distances.

The Forest Service's Travel- and Water-Influence Zones are mere corridors having only a narrow veneer of wilderness encompassing the immediate sight distance or filter strip provided to prevent visual or particulate pollution. These corridors are confining, both esthetically and physically, as the adjacent timber operations are ugly and nearly impassable for periods measured in decades.

The reply from the Forest Service to citizen groups interested in designation of eastern wilderness has been consistently the same: (1) The area you propose doesn't qualify under terms of the Act; and (2) we can give it better protection anyway. But the latter proviso often doesn't work in practice. To illustrate, for the past several years conservationists in the southern highlands have sought a Joyce Kilmer Wilderness, combining Joyce Kilmer Memorial Forest, which covers 3,800 acres in western North Carolina, and the valley of Slickrock Creek, a roadless area of 10,700 acres adjoining it astride the Carolina-Tennessee border. The Kilmer unit is one of the few choice examples remaining of the primeval Appalachian hardwood wilderness, an area the loggers somehow overlooked. Among its diverse species of trees are patriarchs five and six centuries old, immense fellows, some measuring 20 feet in circumference and standing 150 feet tall, a rare collection showing what the past was like in sheltered coves throughout the hills.

In 1934 the Veterans of Foreign Wars petitioned the government for a living shrine to Joyce Kilmer, the author of "Trees." After a long study of possible areas throughout the country this portion of the ancient Cherokee hunting ground was chosen—not just a grove but an entire drainage, circled on three sides by steep ridges. It is probably as impressive as any woodland of its size on earth. As for Slickrock Creek, 3,000 acres of the upper slopes are composed of virgin timber, while the rest, logged years ago, has regained much of its wilderness quality. With fertile soil and up to eighty inches of rain a year, the forest has grown up with groves of poplars up to two feet in diameter. The old railroad ties have rotted and the railroad grade is now a hiking trail. It is one of the outstanding areas in the southern mountains for the enjoyment of quality sports, favored by boar, deer, turkey, and bear, and by hunters who follow these species. The creek is noted among fishermen

as one of the few choice clear-water streams where trout reproduce naturally, largely because of the stable, unroaded, and
unlogged conditions of the watershed.

But all has not been well on the Kilmer-Slickrock front.
When the memorial forest was established, the Forest Service
pledged to protect it forever "as a place of inspiration and a
treasure of native flora and fauna." When the citizens came
along with their proposal for wilderness, they were told the
area was too small to qualify. The Act, in fact, delineates wilderness as an area of at least 5,000 acres or one "of sufficient size
as to make practicable its preservation and use in an unimpaired condition." The Forest Service simply read as far as
the words 5,000 acres. Its pledge to protect the area "forever"
presently was proven to have its limitations; on June 10, 1964,
Chief Edward P. Cliff approved construction of a commercial
highway, designed to link Robbinsville, North Carolina, and
Tellico Plains, Tennessee, across steep terrain on the upper
portion of Joyce Kilmer. Of several possible routes considered,
this undoubtedly was one of the worst.*

The highway was also destined to violate still another "administratively protected" area, Falls Branch Scenic Area on the
Tennessee side; nothing was known about this until signs of
surveying were evident in late 1971 and could never have
happened if the Wilderness Act had been applied to areas of
less than 5,000 acres. The validity of Slickrock had, of course,
likewise been denied: The trees, except for those at the upper
end, were not virgin timber; trees only fifty years old symbolized
the mark of man's hand; the old railroad grade was a mark of
man's hand. Citizens have fought to save the wilderness, proposing that the highway be routed through another, now
roadless, valley and that the virgin forest of Kilmer be joined

---

* In a memorandum to Secretary of Agriculture Orville Freeman, Chief
Cliff said the road would "enhance access to the Joyce Kilmer area," but he
overlooked mentioning that it would divide and scar the wilderness, that
inevitable siltation would disrupt the ecosystem, that heavy tourist travel
would create pressure on fragile areas protected primarily by lack of access,
or that it would drive away hunters, fishermen, campers, hikers, and nature
lovers.

with the roadless valley of Slickrock to be given permanent protection as a unit of the National Wilderness Preservation System.

Until the roadless-area review and evaluation (discussed in the preceding chapter) were announced in early 1973, there had not been a single instance, whether in the East or West, in which the Forest Service had nominated an area for inclusion in the wilderness system or had publicly suggested that any be set aside for future study following completion of work on the primitive areas. With the list of new study areas accompanying the roadless-area review, the agency included two in the East (Joyce Kilmer–Slickrock, North Carolina, and Bradwell Bay, Florida) and one in Puerto Rico (El Cacique). In all other cases, however, the public itself has been obligated to make its interests known, both to the Forest Service and to Congress.

In 1973 the Eastern Wilderness Areas Act was introduced into both houses of Congress. It was intended to establish at once eighteen new wilderness units covering approximately 254,000 acres and to designate thirty-seven additional units covering 395,990 acres for interim protection pending further study. The fifty-two units all told are located in twenty states east of the foothills of the Rocky Mountains and Puerto Rico.

The Eastern Wilderness Areas Act, in whatever form it might emerge, is part of the second stage of wilderness protection through law. The total acreage it would set aside covers about 2 per cent of eastern national forests. Why, one might demand, settle for 2 per cent? Under terms of the Weeks Law these lands were purchased for protection of watersheds rather than production of pulp or timber. The basic function of eastern national forests should not be commercial but rather educational, recreational, and scientific, goals wholly compatible with watershed.

As to the responsiveness of the National Park Service— "Conservationists the world over are looking to our National Park Service for exemplary leadership in the field of safeguarding the beauty and character of natural landscape and sites. It would be most unfortunate if the Park Service were unable to fulfill this role in the Smokies."

These words, heard at the first public hearing on wilderness in the national parks, conducted at Gatlinburg, Tennessee, in June 1966, were spoken by Stewart M. Brandborg, executive director of the Wilderness Society. The subject under immediate consideration was the fate of the Great Smoky Mountains, but this also marked the beginning of scheduled reviews to be held in many national parks, monuments, and additional units of the national park system, preceding congressional action on each one. The expression of concern seemed to touch the heart of the historic issue with simplicity and directness. It made the listener conscious of the greatness of moment before the audience in the hall and before the vaster unseen audience. For as someone said during the flood tide of feeling and eloquence, "A wrong decision will be severely judged by untold millions still unborn."

Considering the interest of the Wilderness Society in the Wilderness Act and in making it work, Brandborg's comments were fitting. They might have been more fitting as part of a keynote delivered by a representative of the National Park Service, pleading for public support for a program designed to protect and enhance the Great Smoky Mountains, the largest mountain wilderness remaining east of the Great Plains.

Instead, a regional director of the service opened the program, reading carefully and without digression from an uninspired statement. He read it once in the auditorium at Gatlinburg, as the hearings began on the Tennessee side of the Smokies, and again two days later as they resumed in Bryson City, on the North Carolina side. The statement offered nothing new or consequential in wilderness philosophy or protection. It was, rather, more of a road plan intended to solve seasonal traffic jams, a plan outlining the location of a proposed transmountain highway plus corridors for additional inner loops. What was left over, 247,000 acres, or less than half the park, was offered for inclusion in the National Wilderness Preservation System—not in one contiguous unit, nor even in two, but in six broken blocks, ranging in size from 5,000 acres to 110,000 acres.

Congressmen and local office holders spoke first at both

Gatlinburg and Bryson City and, after hearing representatives of chambers of commerce and local promoters extol the Park Service plan, departed. Neither they nor officials in Washington could possibly have felt the pulse of those who followed, including schoolteachers, scholars, scientists, scouts and scout leaders, the hikers, trout fishermen, botanists, and bird-watchers, speaking up to defend the integrity of national parks. Over 300 witnesses presented oral statements; 6,000 letters from all over the country were later received for the hearing record.

Not one single national conservation leader, nor scientist, nor representative of a significant outdoors organization spoke out in support of the Park Service proposal. Leaders of the Appalachian Trail Conference, National Audubon Society, Izaak Walton League, National Parks Association, Nature Conservancy, and Sierra Club, as well as the Wilderness Society, endorsed a larger plan of at least 350,000 acres of the park safeguarded as wilderness, with the remaining 150,000 acres for reasonable development and traffic arteries. Scientists pleaded with passion for large expanses of primeval land for biological, botanical, and ecological studies. "No road on earth," warned one, "is important enough to destroy the values inherent in these mountains."

The finest hours of the hearings were derived from the enthusiasm of people. "I love the wilderness so much that I must oppose the transmountain road," said one. "As much as I like and admire the National Park Service, I just can't approve this plan," said another. They looked into the future, beyond the perspective offered by the Park Service, expressing hope for their children and grandchildren. "Wilderness is never idle land," reminded a young mother from Georgia. "Saving the wilderness may be one of the few worthwhile accomplishments of this generation." People spoke of the joys of wilderness, the spiritual exhilaration, the threats of a multimillion dollar political road-building boondoggle. They identified themselves with love of land, with idealism, representing the qualitative experience that must be the essence of our national parks.

The government plan for the Smokies clearly was a weak and poorly drawn document, designed only to solve short-range pragmatic and political problems. The justification was based on a 1943 legal agreement. In that year the Tennessee Valley Authority had decided to construct Fontana Dam on the Little Tennessee River as a source of power for the atomic energy plant then being built at Oak Ridge. This involved flooding a narrow mountain road and evacuating the residents of several towns between the south boundary of the national park and the high-water line of the future lake. Parties to the agreement included TVA, the National Park Service, the state of North Carolina, and Swain County, which held outstanding bonds in payment for the original state road. It provided for acquisition by TVA of 44,000 acres of land above the shoreline, which it turned over to the national park, thus filling in a logical topographical boundary, and the payment by TVA of $400,000 to the North Carolina Highway Department to be applied toward retirement of the county bonds. The Park Service, as its share of the agreement, pledged to provide a new road, a rural transportation artery linking the towns of Bryson City and Fontana, when funds became available after World War II. The state in fulfillment of its part of the bargain constructed the road upon the agreed route from Bryson City to the park boundary.

For a number of years following the war the Park Service sought to convince Swain County to accept improvement of Route 129, along the south shore of Fontana Lake, pleading that a road on the north shore would disturb large parcels of wilderness with choice trout streams. This proved unacceptable: After all, it was not transportation for local citizens that was at stake but rather the opening of a new tourist route for the commercial benefit of little Bryson City.

Thus, finally during 1963–64 the bulldozers were brought into the back country. Construction proceeded 2.5 miles into the park, at a cost of nearly $2 million. The result was disaster: Mountains were slashed, natural beauty destroyed, the landscape scarred with cuts and fills and with erosion that will require many years for nature to heal. A halt was called to the project.

At this point an observer might conclude the Park Service

had endeavored to fulfill the bargain and thus discharged its obligation. Competent lawyers, in fact, have questioned the validity of the 1943 agreement, although the Park Service has never put it to the test. In September 1965, to the contrary, at a meeting in Bryson City George B. Hartzog, Jr., director of the Park Service, offered officials of Swain County still another alternative: a major, multimillion-dollar transmountain route across the Smokies wilderness into Tennessee. There had been no advance notice of this proposal to citizen conservationists, no public hearings at which national conservation organizations might have been represented. And when they complained, the parks director and associates explained that hikers on the Appalachian Trail had been well considered; they were to be spared by the construction of a tunnel just below the mountaintop. Pollution of the environment and disruption of the ecosystem were not discussed.

By the end of 1965 the new agreement, providing for the transmountain road, had been signed by the parties in North Carolina and was only awaiting confirmation by Secretary of the Interior Stewart L. Udall. But he was having second thoughts, his mood reflecting, perhaps, the strong tide of protest, including editorials in major newspapers, against the road. "The proposed new transmountain highway is being offered as a 'substitute.' The wonder is why," commented the *Milwaukee Journal*. "It won't link the two communities. It will be enormously expensive. The sensible course is to scrap plans for both highways. Surely, an alternate route can be found *outside* the park." And from the *New York Times*: "The Park Service has put forward a road-building project that trangresses the spirit of the Wilderness Act and that would bring heavy automobile traffic streaming through the very area that needs to be protected. The proposal for this transmountain road reflects weariness rather than foresight and clear thinking."

The agreement had arrived on Secretary Udall's desk at a time when wilderness hearings were soon to be held for the Great Smokies. The proposed road would slice through one of the two areas in the park waiting to be delineated as wilderness zones under terms of the Act.

A review of events after 1965 raises the question as to whether the 1943 agreement was anything more than a device employed by the Park Service leadership to avoid fulfillment of the wilderness opportunities in the Great Smokies, whether its intent throughout *all* the parks was to keep wilderness small and unprotected by the Act. Director Hartzog gave strong evidence this might be the case when he addressed the Sierra Club Biennial Wilderness Conference on April 7, 1967, in San Francisco. "To assume that the Wilderness Act establishes new standards and new criteria for national park wilderness, replacing the old and time-tested wilderness standards and criteria, would jeopardize the whole national park concept," he declared. But exactly what standards and criteria did he mean?

"It is obvious that Congress could only have intended that wilderness designation of national park system lands should, if anything, result in a higher, rather than a lower, standard of unimpaired preservation," he explained. In other words, as with the Forest Service, the Park Service standard was the essence of purity itself; even though very few areas would pass the test of absolute purity and though the Wilderness Act's criteria insist only that wilderness appear to be affected primarily by the forces of nature with the imprint of man's work unnoticeable.

Hartzog defined three land zones within national parks: (1) the enclaves of development "for the accommodation of visitors" connected with roads, bridle paths, and foot trails; (2) transition zones between these developed sites; and (3) the untrammeled, primeval wilderness. This was one manner of possibly subdividing the parks into small wilderness areas and large facility areas.

Though pledging there would be no lowering of park values on the remaining park lands not designated as wilderness, Hartzog then revealed still another system for zoning or land classification (based on a formula prescribed for application to federal lands by the Bureau of Outdoor Recreation), with the following six separate classes: Class I—high-density recreational areas; Class II—general outdoor recreation areas; Class III—natural-environment areas; Class IV—outstanding natural areas; Class V

—primitive areas, including, but not limited to, those recommended for designation under the Wilderness Act; and Class VI —historical and cultural areas.

"Often, Class III and Class V lands both represent significant natural values," Hartzog conceded. Still, he said, the former are not considered lands that meet criteria for wilderness. "If we are to preserve the integrity of national park wilderness, we dare not lower its standard or compromise its integrity by the inclusion of areas that express in less than the highest terms the definition of national park wilderness."

Then he announced that Class III lands would be managed to provide the "transition" or "setting" or "environment" or "buffer" between intensively developed areas and higher classifications and "wilderness threshold" when they abut or surround wilderness. "The wilderness-threshold lands afford the newcomer an opportunity to explore the mood and the temper of the wild country before venturing into the wilderness beyond. Here in the wilderness threshold is an unequaled opportunity for interpretation of the meaning of wilderness."

While Hartzog insisted Class III lands were not "intentionally reserved for future intensive developments," he then spelled out the first steps in the process of inevitable development, including "one-way motor nature trails," small overlooks, and informal picnic sites. He pledged that, "Such limited facilities must be in complete harmony with the natural environment," but the relevancy or compatibility of roads and cars with a natural environment is certainly subject to challenge. So is the entire outlook. "We must come to grips with the use of the automobile," he asserted. "Shall we explore the possibilities of the monorail, the funicular, the shuttle bus or other means of mechanical transport, in an effort to separate the visitor from his car while he enjoys his parks?" Shall it be cars, trams, or trains? But no question is raised about the essentiality of enjoying the parks without mechanical transport, of exploration and enjoyment on foot as the basic element of "harmony with the natural environment."

Conservation leaders on the program of the conference criticized Hartzog's program on the very day it was presented.

Stewart Brandborg rejected the large Class III exclusions. Although peripheral to larger wilderness tracts, he said, they themselves are essentially wild in character and would qualify under the Wilderness Act definition. He raised the question as to whether any lands in the national parks should be designated for high-density, mass recreation purposes. Anthony W. Smith, of the National Parks Association, expressed a parallel idea. Warning later at the same conference that "threshold zones" could easily be used to accommodate increasing crowds in years ahead, he said there was little value in denying that Class III areas would not be used for development of facilities: "If they are not to be used for that purpose, then let them be protected as wilderness."

By the end of 1970 the National Park Service had fallen far behind in its schedule of wilderness reviews. Six years after passage of the Act, a total of only two areas (within Craters of the Moon National Monument in Idaho and Petrified Forest National Park in Arizona) with a combined acreage of 93,503, had been designated by Congress for inclusion in the wilderness system. Various reasons were given by the agency. One was the need to prepare and maintain a "master plan" to guide the use, development, interpretation, and preservation of each particular park. But the same need applied also to national forests and national wildlife refuges, whose administrative agencies had kept their schedules up to date and secured statutory protection of their areas while planning proceeded.

Another reason given was the lack of funds to conduct wilderness reviews, but even this might be questioned; in 1971, apparently, funds were available for publication of a booklet entitled "Back Country Travel in the National Park System," with scant mention of "wilderness" and no reference at all to the wilderness system or its benefits. Park Service wilderness proposals have continually recommended exclusion of large acreages from wilderness for threshold or buffer purposes. Then followed another concept of excluding "enclaves" within wilderness for purposes of development. In advance of the wilderness hearing on Bandelier National Monument, scheduled for December 18, 1971, in Los Alamos, New Mexico, the Park Service announced a recommendation for zero wilderness out of a total of 30,000 acres, on grounds that it would detract from study and preservation of archeological sites, but citizen groups pledged to fight for setting aside 25,000 acres.

And what happened, meanwhile, to the Great Smokies, the meeting ground of northern and southern forests, with an incredibly varied vegetation that has ever charmed naturalists, and where the Appalachian Trail follows the mountain crest for over seventy miles, the full length of the park? On June 23, 1969, a delegation of almost 100 conservationists, representing groups in Tennessee and North Carolina, came to present their case to Secretary of the Interior Walter J. Hickel.

He gave the group a serious reception—much more serious and straightforward than anything conservationists had received from officials of the Park Service. "I am impressed by your numbers and sincerity of your purpose," the Secretary declared. Then he assigned the Park Service to develop a new plan, with an 18-month deadline.

The new report, issued by the agency in January 1971, conceded that the Smokies comprise "a natural treasure of plant and animal life living in an ecological balance that once destroyed can never be restored." This document seemed to recognize the worst enemy of the parks as the automobile, proposing restrictions on traffic and gradual phasing out of Route 441, a main highway bisecting the park. In addition, the proposal of another transmountain highway, which had highlighted the plan of 1966, was withdrawn in favor of a scenic loop road around the perimeter of the park, as urged by citizen organizations.

Still, along the loop road the Park Service said it would locate no fewer than twelve visitor "clusters," complete with large campgrounds and "motor nature trails." It appeared to be the same old appeal for numbers, or, at best, a pragmatic solving of today's problems at the sacrifice of tomorrow's civilization.

Arno B. Cammerer, director of the Park Service in an earlier day, delivered a speech in Washington in 1938, in which he spoke of establishing a national park that might not measure up to all that everybody thinks of it at the present time, but that, 50 or 100 years from now, with all the protection we would give it, would then have attained a natural condition comparable to primitive condition. He reflected on how such an area might look 1,000 or 2,000 or 5,000 years hence. Cammerer had the Great Smoky Mountains specifically in mind. Even under the most destructive type of lumbering, the flowers, shrubs, and trees had grown back as if nothing of that kind had occurred. In another twenty to fifty years even the stumps would have rotted to furnish humus for the plant life to come, so that it would be difficult, even for the ecologist, to ascertain whether a certain area was cut over or not or that a certain mine had been worked years ago in a given location to the detriment of the park.

Such vision among administrators is rare, particularly in our time. The focus today is centered on expediency and immediacy, survivability in office, political realities, rather than on fundamental principles and issues of the long range. Under terms of the Wilderness Act the administrators are directed to gather and disseminate information regarding use and enjoyment of wilderness, but this has not been done, or has been done feebly at most, certainly not with enthusiasm or commitment. If it had been, there would be much better understanding, both inside and outside of government, of what the law means, and of all its rich potential.

Insofar as devotion to "purity" of wilderness and unwillingness to lower lofty standards are concerned, the Wilderness Act delineates more than a procedure; it outlines a point of view, a philosophy of land management. Considering the declared intention and uses it specifies—to provide outstanding opportunities for solitude and for a primitive, unconfined kind of recreation—there should be no doubt that areas where the human imprint is only slightly noticeable, with capability for restoration, are fully acceptable. Certainly they would have been to Arno Cammerer. Had they not, there would be no such areas as the Great Smoky Mountains National Park today.

Public enthusiasts have had to pick up the burden. Citizen study teams have made significant contributions by determining the adequacy of agency proposals. These teams have included local experts in conservation matters or professionals trained in biology, archeology, botany, and related fields. There have also been strong representations in support of wilderness proposals from specialized national groups. The Ecological Society of America, for example, provided important information on the probable ecological impact of the transmountain road proposal in the Great Smokies. Recommendations of the National Speleological Society for the protection of cave wilderness in Mammoth Cave National Park in Kentucky resulted in restudy and revision of master plans. Agency personnel may be fully qualified for the wilderness studies they are paid to undertake, but their freedom of judgment is circumscribed, whereas the external experts are able to apply their talents with independence and enthusiasm. In a number of cases citizens have agreed with boundary proposals of the agencies. In some, the citizen proposals have been larger; they have never been smaller.

Now is the time to act. If wild lands under federal administration are not placed in the wilderness system and protected by statute, the odds are they will disappear. The only parts of today's living wilderness that will remain alive are those designated specifically as such, and under the Wilderness Act these designations can be made. The process challenges the public will.

Chapter Twelve

Beyond the Wilderness Act

The decade of the 1960s marked an environmental awakening, a reaction of humanism against the high tide of materialism and supertechnology. Public concern so abundantly expressed in the 1964 passage of the Wilderness Act hardly stopped there. One federal law led to another. The idea spread among the states, and among nongovernmental agencies as well, for actions on their part, often with advancement or improvement on the national legislation. The momentum to save the wild places as a testament of man's faith has been growing steadily into the mid-1970s.

Following the Wilderness Act, the Rare and Endangered Species Act was adopted in 1966, reflecting a sense of concern and urgency that no portion of the nation's wildlife heritage should be lost. This new law, declaring it a national policy to protect species of native fish and wildlife threatened with extinction and to protect their habitat as well, has made federal agencies more conscious of their responsibilities and opportunities. The role of endangered species has become a strong basis of emphasis in wilderness proposals.

For example, protection of a wild species—the Puerto Rican parrot—is partly the reason the Forest Service has suggested designating a wilderness in the Caribbean National Forest in Puerto Rico, a rare true tropical forest under the American flag. One century ago the spectacular parrots, whose plumage was a mixture of red, green, and blue, flew in huge flocks, but over the years adult birds have been shot for food, nestlings taken for caged pets, and the natural forest destroyed. Now there may be no more than sixty parrots remaining in the Luquillo Mountains, and even they have been threatened by military projects, road construction, and recreational developments. Wilderness can save them.

The Rare and Endangered Species Act, in turn, stimulated the conscience of people the world over, as evidenced in March 1973, when eighty nations signed a convention to regulate international trade in endangered species. Written in the most enlightened language, the agreement places esthetic, scientific, cultural, and recreational reasons for preservation before economic motives. An endangered species is defined as "any species, subspecies, or geographically separate population," ensuring that an endangered population *segment* will be protected, that a species must not await the specter of worldwide extirpation before it can be protected—a concept that should be applied in the United States to coyotes, bears, eagles, and falcons. There may be some of these animals still around, but are they in their native range? The convention seeks especially to protect marine mammals and sea turtles that have been looked upon as everybody's property, yet subject to no one's jurisdiction. Like any international agreement, success depends upon acceptance and adherence, but it marks a truly enlightened step toward stewardship of the biosphere.*

In 1968 Congress adopted two additional significant laws with wilderness potential: the Wild and Scenic Rivers Act and the National Trails System Act. The Rivers Act defined a na-

* To illustrate the extent of damage to wildlife of other lands, between 1968 and 1970 almost 350,000 ocelot skins were exported from South and Central America to the United States alone; over 1 million ocelot skins were utilized during those years by the fur trade throughout the world. In addition to exploitation of wild animals for their products (hides, meat, or, as in the case of whales, oil), vast numbers of mammals, birds, reptiles, amphibians, and fish are shipped for use as pets and for biomedical research. Many creatures are protected in nations of origin, but laws are circumvented by smuggling animals into countries lacking such laws, from which they are then exported to lucrative markets. The Convention on International Trade in Endangered Species of Wild Fauna and Flora either outlaws or controls the trade of 650 species of plants and animals.

tional policy that "certain selected rivers of the Nation, which, with their immediate environments, possess outstandingly remarkable scenic, recreational, geologic, fish and wildlife, historic, cultural, or other similar values, shall be preserved in free-flowing condition, and that they and their immediate environments shall be protected for the benefit and enjoyment of present and future generations." This law charted a whole new philosophy and course of action. Until 1968 the nation had undertaken to protect forests and parks, to establish refuges for wildlife and reservoirs presumably to conserve water. The rivers, however, had been continually sacrificed to pollution and progress, rendered unfit for fishing and canoeing, unsafe for swimming, their beauty destroyed. Now, at last, the wild rivers were to be identified as a valued national resource, a heritage belonging to all Americans, to be kept free of dam-building projects and commercial encroachment.

A classification system of "wild," "scenic," and "recreational" —depending on degree of natural quality—was established with the Act. Eight rivers were designated by the law as qualifying under the wild category, all of them already in public ownership. Twenty-seven others were named to be studied by federal-state teams for possible later inclusion. Reports on these are scheduled for submission to Congress and the President by October 1978; in the meantime they were granted interim protection from dams, power lines, channelization, and other federally financed developments.

On any of these rivers that remain untamed, unspoiled, rich with living organisms, the traveler who takes it on its own terms can sense the natural conditions in which man first found it and enjoy the musical sounds of water running free and wild. Not only are the rivers saved, but also the banks and bordering meadows, forests, and valleys: the mosses, rocks, insects, algae, wild flowers and ferns, the rocky canyons, caves and waterfalls, and wildlife invariably found along the bottomlands.

The Trails Act established another system, of scenic and recreational trails, in order to provide hikers relief from concrete, motorized traffic, and gasoline fumes. Two scenic trails were designated by the law—the Appalachian Trail, covering

2,044 miles from Maine to Georgia, and the Pacific Crest Trail, 2,350 miles from the Canadian border to Mexico down the Cascades, Sierra, and joining ranges. Fourteen other trails were identified for study as potential additions, with reports to be made by 1976. Forty more were named as recreation trails to be administered by local, state, or federal agencies.

The Appalachian Trail, now to be known as the Appalachian National Scenic Trail, is inspiration for all who hike distant routes in back country. It was conceived and built on cooperative effort of trail clubs; it created a new kind of recreational area running through fourteen states, with a protected zone extending one mile on either side through federal lands (eight national forests and two national parks) and a quarter of a mile on either side through state lands. Alas for the hiker, the trail also crosses 866 miles of private land, or 43 per cent of its entire route; where thirty years ago he walked alone, he is now accompanied by a procession of ski slopes, summer homesites, condominium developments, and trailer camps. The challenge in fulfilling the Trails Act is to acquire enough buffer zone to preserve the essence of the "footpath in the wilderness."

Conservationists have been spurred by federal legislation to seek essential complementary laws in the states. As a result, more than half of the fifty states have established their own wild and scenic river systems and have identified hundreds of streams either as components or potential additions. In some ways the states have gone beyond federal concepts. For instance, Michigan's Natural Rivers Act of 1970 provides for protecting rivers through zoning of adjacent land. After designating a river for inclusion in its system, preparing long-range plans, and conducting public hearings, the Michigan Natural Resources Commission may announce that adjacent river lands will be zoned in order to ensure their preservation or control their development. The first option to do so falls to the county or township, but if the local jurisdiction fails to respond, the commission is authorized to fill the gap.

Michigan has been a leader on other fronts. In 1970 the Natural Resources Commission adopted a resolution calling for a study of Porcupine Mountains State Park in order to determine the true value of wilderness and to develop an effective management plan. The Porcupines, covering 58,000 acres along Lake Superior on the Upper Peninsula, had long been the jewel of the state park system but in recent years were plainly suffering from overuse and conflicting use. With about 300,000 visitors annually, the park had reached the point where control was essential to save its wild setting.

No sooner was the study resolution adopted than citizen groups volunteered to furnish specialized inputs of knowledge on geology, wildlife, birdlife, botany, hiking trails, history, and other values. Following completion and review of the studies in 1972, the park was renamed Porcupine Mountains Wilderness State Park and zoned into four sections (wilderness, wilderness study, scenic sites, intensive use) in order to protect its fragile qualities. In the same year the legislature voted to establish Michigan's own wilderness and natural areas system, consisting of wilderness areas of 3,000 acres or larger or an island of any size, wild areas under 3,000 acres, and natural areas, where the emphasis will be on scientific research and education.

New York offers a pre-eminent model in its program for the Adirondack Park. As early as 1885 the Adirondack Forest Preserve of 2.25 million acres had been established as a publicly owned area. Seven years later, in 1892, came designation of the Adirondack Park, more than twice the size of the preserve, almost 5.7 million acres, embracing both private and public lands, the largest area of its kind in the world. But the real touchstone of the wilderness concept came in 1894, with enactment of the epochal state constitutional amendment declaring that the preserve "shall be forever kept as wild forest lands." Pressures have been unrelenting since then to modify or eliminate the "forever wild" proviso, a triumph of preservation far ahead of its time and still unequaled in the United States.*

In many places and in many ways the vistas of the Adirondacks have scarcely changed from one century to the next. A man

---

* As a point of comparison, the combined area of Yellowstone, Yosemite, Grand Canyon, Glacier, and Olympic national parks totals approximately 5.15 million acres—more than half a million acres less than the Adirondack Park.

can stand on a rocky perch in order to observe weathered granite peaks just above the low-lying mists and feel himself in a past he might never have known otherwise—in a striking world of clear air, pure water, and natural beauty.

For many years private landowners had kept their holdings inside the park boundaries in an unspoiled natural condition. Enormous estates were owned by such families as the Morgans, Vanderbilts, and Whitneys. Then, in the years following World War II, subdivisions began to sprout, with planless growth inflicting problems of water supply and waste disposal on the local communities. Without restraints, private owners, many of them now absentee investment firms, could dictate the future of the area and destroy its quality. For instance, one end of Saranac Lake has been divided into numerous small homesites, spoiling the shoreline; in addition, their septic tanks seep into the lake, seriously affecting aquatic life. In another case, a developer had planned to subdivide a small key property north of Warrensburg on the periphery of a virgin stand of white pine utilized by the State College of Forestry. Fortunately, the Nature Conservancy entered the scene and purchased the land.

To meet the issues a Study Commission on the Future of the Adirondacks, appointed by Governor Nelson Rockefeller, issued a report in 1970 recommending a plan restricting uses of private lands in order to protect scenic, recreational, wilderness, and watershed values. But it went much further, proposing that almost 1 million acres in fifteen separate tracts, ranging in size from 230,000 acres down to 14,600 acres, be designated as wilderness and administered in accordance with principles patterned after the National Wilderness Preservation System. The commission also proposed a wild, scenic, and recreational rivers system, propagation of rare indigenous species of wildlife, such as marten, lynx, loon, and raven, and the re-introduction of extirpated native species, which may well include the wolf along with the moose. No federal program has gone this far.

"The Adirondacks are preserved forever," declared Governor Nelson Rockefeller on May 22, 1973, as he signed the legislation placing 3.7 million acres of private property within the bounds of the Adirondack Park under land-use restrictions. Together with

2.3 million acres already owned and protected by the state, this entire composition of valleys, lakes, rivers, and mountain peaks is the largest area in the country to come under comprehensive land-use control, including wilderness designation.

Tennessee has also taken progressive action to establish systems of trails and scenic rivers and, in addition, a system of natural areas. The objectives of the Natural Areas Act of 1971 are especially significant: (1) to preserve examples of all natural land types in Tennessee, (2) preserve natural areas in all sections of the state, (3) preserve all unique and outstanding natural areas, and (4) preserve habitats for rare or endangered plants or animals.

Acquisition priorities to carry out the objectives were placed first on privately held areas under immediate threat of destruction, second on unique areas that could not be duplicated if lost, and third on unique areas already in public ownership that should be further saved from intensive development. Under this program the first major acquisition was made in 1973: 11,410 acres of the Savage Gulf, northwest of Chattanooga on the Cumberland Plateau, embracing nearly 2,000 acres of virgin timber—giant beeches, tulip poplar, basswood, and maple—a treasure in trees that may be unmatched in the East.

Such sources of "new" wilderness were hardly envisioned during the campaign for the Wilderness Act, but no one then could possibly have anticipated the urgency to protect more of the resource from the onrush of development and growth that threaten the quality of life. Fortunately, even beyond the framework of the Act, additional supplies of wilderness are being safeguarded.*

Many colleges have their own natural study areas. One can

---

* More than 300 research natural areas have been set aside on federal lands for education and scientific study. They represent examples of forest, range, and aquatic life communities, examples of fish and animal habitats, of land forms, soil types, and mineral deposits in natural or near-natural conditions. They are part of a larger system including state and private lands as well and part of a worldwide system functioning under the International Biological Program as base lines for comparative study. The Smithsonian Institution in June 1972 established a Center for Natural Areas. Among its goals was to compile and computerize a comprehensive inventory of approximately 15,000 natural areas of varying size in the United States.

hardly imagine a school of botany or biology functioning without one, to say nothing of the enhancement of the college environment in general. A symposium on "College Natural Areas as Research and Training Facilities," sponsored in 1963 by the Nature Conservancy under the direction of Bruce Dowling, showed that nearly 100 tracts (ranging in size from 1.3 acres to 23,000 acres) were then owned by colleges and universities across the country.

An area of any size has some special value. In 1967 the University of Michigan accepted a gift of twenty-two acres of land adjacent to the university acreage known as Horner Woods. The director of the botanic gardens, Professor Warren H. Wagner, expressed his delight over the acquisition of "a different sort of area, full of natural flora different from the flora anywhere in the Botanical Gardens." Professor Alexander H. Smith, of the botany department, concurred. The acquisition of the twenty-two acres more than doubles the value of the total area for educational purposes, he said, since it includes a succession progressing from "old field" habitats, to brush encroachment, to hardwood forest, and lastly the climax forest of the original Horner Woods itself. He also noted that the drainage and soil types add to the diversity and will add values for studies of local environments. From an educational standpoint the acquisition of this land has been extremely advantageous to the botanists on the campus.

The University of California undertook in 1965 to establish a Natural Land and Water Reserves System, incorporating some land it already owned and seeking to acquire or share other land. One of the university's research sites, the Philip L. Boyd Desert Research Center, comprising several thousand acres near Palm Springs, is considered similar in many respects to other deserts around the world. Another unit, the Francis Simes Hastings Natural History Reservation, in the Santa Lucia Mountains south of Carmel, is used to study plants and animals in native habitat. The reservation was established in 1937; since then observers have spent long hours with telescopes and field glasses watching the behavior of mule deer, raccoons, woodrats, skunks, badgers, bobcats, as well as birds, reptiles, and amphibians—the idea being that members of the wild community contain secrets helpful to mankind if we preserve the chance to discover them.

The Nature Conservancy has conducted a monumental wilderness-saving campaign on its own. This private group began in 1917 as a national committee (on the preservation of natural conditions) of the Ecological Society of America; it was organized as an independent institution in 1946 and adopted its present name in 1950. By the end of 1973 the conservancy had engaged in more than 1,000 projects, involving the preservation of 400,000 acres. Many large and important tracts have been acquired for federal and state agencies, tracts that might have been lost because of the slowness of the government appropriations process. Most acquisitions are from gifts. Some tracts are large, others small, even ten acres or less. For example, the late Charles A. Borden, writer and conservationist, and his wife bequeathed four acres of high, rugged bluff overlooking the Pacific just north of San Francisco to be forever wild. "It is our desire," wrote Borden, "that a tradition will grow around Spindrift Point as a meeting of land, sea and sky held in trust for countless future individuals to retreat in peace, solitude and quiet hours of contemplation." When such areas are turned over to local groups or to universities, the conservancy attaches reverter clauses, requiring return of ownership if use of the land is in any way significantly altered.

In 1970, a parcel of 6,725 acres of woodland lakes, waterfalls, and forest glens in New York's Shawangunk Mountains was about to be sold at auction when the conservancy moved in with interim financing to hold it for later acquisition by the state; thus the area was safeguarded to become part of Minnewaska State Park, preserved as a wilderness for hikers and campers. In another case the conservancy was instrumental in arranging the gift of 50,000 acres in the Great Dismal Swamp of southern Virginia—a legendary land of untamed wild beauty, a meeting ground of southern swamp, coastal sand dune, and northern forest—by the Union Camp Corporation for ultimate protection as a national wildlife refuge. The gift marked the largest donation of land ever made by a private corporation to a conservation group, a breakthrough in the role landowning industry can play in preserving vast natural areas.

The land trust idea is part of a growing movement of science and citizens. In 1972 the Western Pennsylvania Conservancy joined forces with the Carnegie Museum of Pittsburgh to identify and preserve significant natural areas in their region. Within six months they identified over 300 areas worthy of attention in western Pennsylvania: forests, bogs, swamps, meadows, caves, eskers, streams, mountains, watergaps, and barrens. Then, in 1973, through a grant from the Allegheny Foundation, the conservancy conveyed a 9,300-acre tract of wild mountain land to the state. This area, bordering Laurel Ridge State Park fifty miles from Pittsburgh, had been logged in its day but was now generally undisturbed, containing the entire watershed of three clear mountain streams, accounting for its name, Mountain Streams. This brought to nearly 50,000 acres the total volume acquired by this regional conservancy for state parks, nature reserves, and other conservation uses. In the meantime it has also been working with the Bureau of Forestry in the Pennsylvania Department of Environmental Resources to set aside wild areas within the 2 million acres of state forest land.

Then there are significant private ventures in preservation. In the Southwest, the Research Ranch, sixty-five miles southeast of Tucson near the Mexican border, is a haven for migratory birds, golden eagles, ravens, and hawks, as well as a variety of mammals. It is also an outdoor laboratory for studies of a grassland environment, used by hundreds of Arizona students and professionals from many parts of the country. The study area comprises 8,000 acres, 3,200 of which are owned by Frank and Ariel Appleton; they have grazing rights to the remainder, composed of federal and state lands. One of their goals has been to seek practical legal means of ensuring protection on the entire 8,000 acres, based on the need for conservation and research in permanently natural settings.

The Mohonk Trust, protecting 6,000 acres of beautiful mountain land only ninety miles north of New York City, presents another illustration of note. For a full century this property has been treated with love and respect as part of the surroundings of the Mohonk Mountain House, a rambling brick-and-stone resort owned by the Smiley family throughout its entire existence. The hotel itself is not exactly for everyone. There's not a room in the house with a television set or even a telephone. Smoking is just not done in the main parlor and dining room. But everyone goes outdoors—some to admire the old-fashioned flower garden, others to the tower at Sky Top for the view over the unbroken Shawangunks. There are guided nature walks, bird talks, and 100 miles of trail to follow in all seasons.

The Mountain House is more than a resort; it is a distinctive refuge all its own governed by the Quaker philosophy of the owners—of man in peace with man and all men in harmony with their environment. With this goal in mind the Mohonk Trust was organized by the Smiley family in order to ensure preservation of this block of the Shawangunk Mountains for recreational, educational, scientific, and inspirational uses that are compatible with keeping the area unspoiled.

Since 1966 the transfer of land into the trust has been under way, supported by gifts of the Smiley family, hotel guests, individuals, groups, and an informal organization called Friends of the Shawangunks. The trust lands are extensively used, mostly by rock climbers (drawn to the widely known Trapps, the "rock-climbing cliffs") but also by hikers, naturalists, cross-country skiers, and students. The great variety of terrain, embracing streams, abandoned farmland, forest, and rock ledge, provides endless possibility for study of life sciences by visiting school groups and professionals.

As the wilderness concept spreads, endless new uses for it are being discovered and developed. The Outward Bound program, as an example, originated during World War II to give British youth an extra touch of strength, courage, and will. Adapted to this country, it was designed to help the individual gain a better understanding of his own resources, his outer limits, entirely on the basis of wilderness encounters. Participants in small groups are placed in circumstances that demand more of one than each can expect of himself, where they must all co-operate in order to survive. They learn to accomplish skills they never dreamed they could master—climbing rocky pinnacles, wading waist-deep rapids by forming a human chain, and living on natural foods—and to take care of themselves and each other.

Outward Bound has proved valid to the point where schools and colleges send groups of students to its six wilderness camps for credit courses. Other schools have modified the Outward Bound curriculum, or adopted parts of it, to meet their own goals. The University of Oregon conducts a program (which some other colleges have picked up) called Cooperative Wilderness Adventure, with activities in river-running, backpacking, rock-climbing, and snow-climbing. In this case the idea is not to force people to pit themselves against nature, though they do engage in more rigorous physical activities than ever before, but rather to attain individual independence, group coopera-tion, ecological awareness, and return to an environmentally oriented simpler life. In 1973 Dr. Jonathan Fairbanks, of the English department at the State University of New York, Pots-dam, a veteran wilderness traveler and ex-Outward Bound instructor, offered still another type of program: a five-week Wil-derness Workshop, consisting of readings in literature, history, anthropology, and ecology, followed by ten days of wilderness experience in the Adirondacks.

Then there are various programs conducted by psychothera-pists to treat disturbed patients or victims of drug abuse by placing them under situations of stress and challenge, most for the first time in their lives. In one program dealing with young people the object has been to get them away from environments in which they have not succeeded, whether school, home, or the drug scene, and give them a new outlook on life. As part of the training they take long hikes in rough country, limited in food and water, finding their own ways through canyons and hills, in solitude. In another program, involving mental patients who haven't been out of hospital walls in years, the goal is to shake them out of their protective habits of defeat, dependence, helplessness, and passive compliance by showing that each one can achieve minor personal success each day through wilderness adventure.*

These developments demonstrate that the Wilderness Act represents a beginning rather than a conclusion in itself, that an entire series of new questions, concerning understanding, interpretation, and utilization of wild places, as well as their preservation, are now pressing for attention. Yet no federal agency is responsible for a coordinated approach or involvement in the wilderness issue beyond the scope of federal land, though people everywhere crave to save the remaining primeval fragments.

As strongly indicated earlier in this book, no federal agency is directing itself with passion to fulfillment of the Wilderness Act. Therefore, since we pay officials in government to serve mining, grazing, timber, and other special economic interests, why not underwrite a corps of men for a new agency to be known as the U.S. Wilderness Service, men committed to the people's wilderness cause?

The Wilderness Service would undertake many missions now unmet.

It would prepare and publish a periodic inventory of the wilderness now reserved and survey opportunities to protect additional units by all levels of government. Certainly, the purview of the Wilderness Act needs to be extended to cover the Bureau of Land Management, which administers 175 million acres (an area greater in size than California and Nevada combined), plus 282 million acres in Alaska, all open to exploitation by miners, loggers, stockmen, oil and gas interests, and land speculators. Yet these lands embrace cactus and creosote desert, grassland of the plains, Douglas fir forests of the Northwest, and the tundra and icecaps of the North. They are the home-

---

* The Oregon State Hospital Adventure Camp was organized in 1972 by Dr. Luther Jerstad, Everest climber and guide, and Dr. Dean Brooks, superintendent of the Oregon State Hospital. A total of fifty-one chronically disturbed patients volunteered to undergo sixteen days of stress and challenge. No one drew a direct cause-and-effect conclusion, but within eight months following the camp, twenty-eight of the fifty-one patients had been discharged, including one who had been in the hospital for twenty-four years. Hospital personnel and guides helped the patients through the field trip.

grounds of caribou and mountain goats in Alaska, antelope in Wyoming, bighorn sheep in Nevada, peccary, wild turkeys, and mountain lions in Arizona, and doubtless a large number of endangered species that have never been inventoried.

The Wilderness Service would delineate the diverse values of wilderness of specific ecological types, show they can be saved, and report on threats to them. It could spotlight attention on such events as that in 1957, when Middlesex County, Massachusetts, decided to develop a beach on the shore of Thoreau's Walden Pond, the source spot of wilderness inspiration the world over. No advance announcement was made. The crew simply arrived one morning, sawed through 200 full-grown oaks and pines, and bulldozed tons of forest humus and topsoil into the water to improve the beach. The deed was done in the name of recreation, though such a crude blunder could never occur in a land where consciousness of wilderness values prevails.

Given areas may be protected by federal or state law, but subtle assaults on ecologically important land proceed quietly nearby. In a short span of ten or fifteen years a prized area is apt to deteriorate to the point where it may be declared scarcely worth saving. The Tinicum Marsh, a tideland marsh in the Delaware River Basin of southwestern Philadelphia, provides a classic example, a vivid display of environmental catastrophe. One of the largest city-operated wildlife sanctuaries, Tinicum served for generations as feeding and nesting ground for mallards, black ducks, and blue-winged teals, and a resting place for migratory species of waterfowl, shore birds, and land birds. It was richly endowed in fish, shellfish, reptiles, and amphibians, as well as mink, muskrats, river otters, and foxes.

Alas, over the years the marsh suffered nibbling encroachment and destruction—at the hands of everyone from the first settlers to the developers of Philadelphia International Airport. Then came the most devastating blow, the construction of Interstate Highway 95. Like a giant military pincer movement, the freeway was pressed from both directions to the edge of the marsh. Despite the outcry from concerned citizens, the commitment was made to link the two sections and inflict irreparable damage on the marsh.

Tragedies of this nature have become common fare. Still, it's not yet too late to preserve the shreds of naturalness within metropolitan areas, where the grace and beauty of nature are most needed. The Wilderness Act has furnished the technique for preservation of large tracts in national parks, national forests, and national wildlife refuges. The states have developed their own initiatives from that foundation. Now there is need to identify and to provide firm statutory protection for smaller tracts in urban areas still in a relatively untouched state. Determining how this can best be done would be another function of the Wilderness Service.

This agency would be deeply involved in research covering ecology, economics, utilization, and human impact. The federal resource agencies have conducted some studies in these fields, but they can't yield an ultimate understanding because their approach is too narrowly directed and the efforts of their few wilderness-oriented personnel are circumscribed. The ecological approach, after all, is not limited to things, processes, and conditions, as though they exist in isolation, but is directed at the interrelationships among them.

One subject demanding study and interpretation involves natural fire, the wild force of nature. Before the coming of the white man, fire as part of the cycle of life both destroyed and created. Fire became evil when man provided the means for it to become so. For instance, lumbermen in their wasteful orgies left huge quantities of fuel, called slash piles, in otherwise naturally cleared forest floors. When fire then affected the lumbermen's commercial interest, they demanded and received government subsidies for total suppression of fire.

The exclusion of fire in many wilderness areas has since led to the encroachment of trees into meadows and brushfields, causing a decline of deer and elk and serious effects on birds, small mammals, and other organisms. How much fire should be allowed back into the ecosystem? How much *can* be allowed back without causing danger to lives and adjacent areas? These are key questions in a valid preservation system. With better knowledge of wilderness fuels, fire danger rating, natural fire barriers, and with new control methods and improved weather forecasting, wilderness managers might allow some natural fires to burn freely.

The Wilderness Service would also try to determine how much human use an area can absorb without being destroyed. The population explosion has come to the wilderness almost overnight. The concept of human impact upon wilderness values has developed so rapidly it's hard to fully comprehend or to figure how the trends in deterioration can be reversed. The Sierra Club has underwritten a series of valuable studies that can serve as the basis of a broad federal research project into such problems as the impact of hiking and camping upon alpine flora; effects of pack animals on meadows, trails, and campsites; garbage disposal and its effects on the ecosystem; and disposal of human waste.

Determining carrying capacity may be the simplest aspect of use. How to impart to the visitor the sense of what wilderness is all about is a deeper issue. How to use it as an educational document, as well as a recreational resource, so that oncoming generations appreciate and respect the natural world around them may be the most fundamental issue to consider for the future beyond the Wilderness Act.

Epilogue

Where the Battle Begins

On the day in 1968 when Martin Luther King was shot and killed, I was at Yale University to speak on some phase or other of conservation policy. It would be highly unlikely that I didn't touch, or even dwell at length, on wilderness. After the program was through and I was finally alone for the night, however, I tried to equate my actions and personal goals with the tragedy in Memphis and with what Dr. King had been working for. Is wilderness valid, after all, in the face of poverty, inequality, the social issues of man's relationships with man, his brother?

To the dweller in the slum, ghetto, or inner city, whatever trim euphemism it may be called, national parks and wilderness are beyond reach, beyond concept. Slum children do have a certain association with wildlife, not with bears, deer, squirrels, or snakes, but rather with Norway rats—the more squalid the slum, the fatter the rats.

The ghetto is the symbol of modern environmental disaster. On one hand, the affluent, in order to escape crowds and concrete, move to the suburbs. When sprawl of shopping centers and subdivisions catch up with them, they are apt to move again, to the house with full conveniences, surrounded by wooded land. They breathe cleaner air in a cleaner environment. On the other hand, the poor can't make it, either because they lack the down payment or because of racial discrimination. Disenfranchised from the bounties of our time, they inherit the dying inner city.

The lower the income, the higher the air pollution (and the diseases from it). Highway builders have seen to it in their own way. They have destroyed whole neighborhoods, ruined or buried parks and waterfronts, displaced entire communities—always those occupied by the poorest people, who are then driven to another slum at the edge of the freeways.

Parks and open space belong where people live as part of their environment. An established park represents an integral and sacred part of the American city. It makes the city habitable. When the choice must be made between such urban open space and a highway, it makes more sense to locate the highway elsewhere or maybe even not to build it at all.

I learned this lesson in Memphis, the very city where Martin Luther King was slain. I had been there before his death and had written about the conservation efforts of a group called the Citizens to Preserve Overton Park. On the face of it, they had nothing in common with the humble black garbage workers whose cause Dr. King had come to Memphis to defend. Or perhaps they did, considering they were fighting exactly the same economic and political forces.

Overton has been a park for almost seventy years. Though less than half the size of Central Park in New York, the woodlands of Overton, with seventy-five varieties of trees, are probably richer. It is, in fact, one of the few urban forests left in the world today. As fine an asset as any city could hold or hope for, Overton embraces playgrounds, baseball fields, a golf course, an art gallery and academy, a nationally known shell for music and drama, facilities that serve all the people of the city and not just the commercial interests.

However, when downtown merchants and developers became convinced that a freeway through the park would jingle coins in their pockets, that distinctive urban forest became expendable. For ten years the two Memphis daily newspapers led the battle in their behalf, suppressing news, slanting and distorting news, ridiculing park defenders, browbeating and belittling any politician who dared stand up in behalf of the park. A former mayor of the city, Watkins Overton, great-grandson of the man for whom the park was named, courageously spoke of the park as hallowed ground—a priceless possession of the people beyond commercial value. Nevertheless, he and Memphis learned painfully that democracy can be "a government of bullies." As Overton said, "Entrenched bureaucracy disdains the voice of the people but eventually the people will be heard."

Gifford Pinchot expressed the same idea. He saw conservation as a social crusade. Repeatedly, he defined equality of opportunity for every citizen as the real object of laws and institutions. The rightful use and purpose of our natural resources, as he saw them, are to make all the people strong and well, able and wise, well taught, well fed, well clothed, full of knowledge and initiative, with equal opportunity for all and special privilege for none. In 1910, when forestry was still in the forefront of the crusade, Pinchot wrote:

We have allowed the great corporations to occupy with their own men the strategic points in business, in social and in political life. It is our fault more than theirs. We have allowed it when we could have stopped it. Too often we have seemed to forget that a man in public life can no more serve both the special interests and the people than he can serve God and Mammon. There is no reason why the American people should not take into their hands again the full political power which is theirs by right, and which they exercised before the special interests began to nullify the will of the majority.

A conservationist's concern is with forests, water, soil, fish and game, coal and oil and other minerals, and the diverse uses of natural resources. But how can the problems of human rights, war and peace, pyramiding population of the earth, and use of resources be dealt with separately, if the majority is to assert its will through the process of political power?

Presidents and Congresses, one after the other, have opposed anything but the most niggardly appropriations to educate and house the poor, to provide for the old, to rehabilitate the imprisoned or the mentally ill—in the very same fashion that they cannot find funds to protect the soil, safeguard the wilderness, or enhance wildlife. The United States has spent vast sums for "security" from other nations, while for a fraction of the amount it could have given the world humanitarian aid and eliminated the threat of war.

These official actions reflect a system that places low priorities on both human values and natural values—a system in trouble, not simply because the rules are dictated by a minority of vested interests for a majority of common men, but because it allows one generation to dictate the future of the next through the overuse of resources.

The system is based on the theory that industrial productivity must continually be increased, and the larger the consuming population grows the better. That industrial concentrations breed garbage, waste, pollution, congestion, and crime is overlooked. So is the fact that however substantive a resource may be, once the population is doubled, the per capita share must be halved. For resources in limited supply, halving them makes them unequal to the demand and more and more expensive. Mines bear no second crop. The known reserves of many valuables are running low or running out. Yet business and government pursue policies based on the inexhaustibility of space and raw materials, not only petroleum, but bismuth, iron, manganese, aluminum, copper, tin, and silver. The idea is to develop and exploit every last inch of the United States, to "reclaim" marshes and wetlands, to establish new communities, while the old ones are left to die and pollution is written off as profit— all in the name of expanding industry, placing more land on the tax rolls, encouraging capital investment, creating jobs, and providing for a growing population, without reference to a resource policy of any kind or the saving of anything for the future.

This is justified in the name of aiding the common man. America is told that the last glorious forests of redwood and Douglas fir, for example, must be cut in order to furnish housing for the poor. Yet forest management destroys the environment of all, with the worst kind of herbicides and pesticides implicit tools. Erosion of hillsides and streams from logging roads is widespread. But much of the wood cut is left in the forest; much of the remainder is discarded in processing. Air is then polluted by the burning of logging slash and of sawmill wastes. Water is fouled when mills dump their residues into streams. And still the housing needs of the poor are not met. Sawlogs go into the luxury and second-home market; pulpwood, into the quick-profit paper market. The poor have been double-crossed again.

If this course continues, every wilderness will be taken. The process is now under way in all corners of America. In the northern plains of Montana, Wyoming, and the Dakotas, one of our last large natural frontiers, industries and federal agencies are promoting strip-mining of coal on a massive scale, as well as a gigantic network of power plants that would irrevocably disrupt the character of the land and change the cleanest air in the country to the dirtiest. Strip-mining is new to eastern Montana, but the scene there has been rapidly transformed into a rerun of Appalachia, with the same technological overkill produced by the same mechanized shovels of immense proportions.

The power companies and government agencies speak optimistically of reclamation, but semi-arid conditions on the plains make regrowth a costly, if not impossible, process. Even so, reclamation is only one part of it. Water will be required in immense quantities for electric-power generation and related activities. Rivers all over the state—the famous Powder, Bighorn, Little Bighorn, Tongue, Yellowstone, Missouri, and probably many of their tributaries—will have to be dammed, diverted, and channelized, their natural quality destroyed forever.

The future of the northern Plains can be envisioned by the massive, coal-fired, steam and electricity generation and transmission system operating in the Four Corners region of the Southwest. In 1966 the Department of the Interior announced an agreement with a syndicate of public and private utilities to build the supercomplex in the desert, where clean air has been a primary asset for many years. On April 12 of that year Interior Secretary Stewart L. Udall pledged the project would be an absolute model of pollution control, showing how resources could actually be developed without damage to the environment.

The Hopi and Navajo Indians of the region, he said, would especially benefit from exploitation of "their under-utilized coal resources."

On June 2, 1971, however, two identical suits were filed by conservationists and Indians asking a halt to any further development, alleging that federal approval had violated a number of statutes, including the Historic Preservation Act, Fish and Wildlife Coordination Act, Outdoor Recreation Act, and National Environmental Policy Act. The first unit of the supercomplex, the Fruitland plant, was then emitting more particulate matter than all stationary sources in New York City and Los Angeles combined. A color photo made during the Apollo 9 space mission showed a clearly identifiable smoke plume extending from the plant into the San Luis Valley of Colorado, 250 miles eastward. Although the utilities were pledged to substantially clean up this plant and to reduce emissions from the next five plants either already under construction or planned, when all six enter operation they will still emit enough fly ash, sulfur oxide, and nitrogen oxide to render the Four Corners smoggier and smokier than any city in the United States.

An environmental calamity of this nature would hardly be allowed in, or close to, a metropolitan area. This doubtless was one of the reasons for setting up the complex in the Four Corners, although the electric power is meant to be used in the booming population centers of Southern California, Nevada, and Arizona. The impacts will be felt locally in the Southwest, however, on six national parks, three national recreation areas, twenty-eight national monuments, and additional national historic sites.

More than half of all American Indians now living on reservations would be subject to the air pollution. But this is only part of the impact that the Indians, notably the Hopi and Navajo, will feel should the project be completed. Hundreds of Navajo are being displaced from the high plateau known as Black Mesa to make way for strip-mining of those "under-utilized coal resources." The Hopi, however, the last acculturative Indian group in the United States, who have lived in harmony with their environment for seven centuries, will be hit the hardest and gain the least. Few in number, they stand in the way of the demands of supercities.

And now Alaska, the greatest wilderness left to us, is endangered, vanishing, fragmented under the impact of technology responding to the same syndrome of growth. Picture the deep silent valleys of the Brooks Range on the Arctic slope, immense in their solitude, filling with the sound of migrating caribou, then falling silent again. When I saw the valleys in August 1969 the first frosts had already turned the grasses, willow and birch, lichen and sedge into a pattern of russet and gold. The Arctic struck me as a pleasing land for those willing to understand and appreciate it on its own terms, though belonging by right of occupancy to natives, human and otherwise.

Soon after I left there would be flocks of snow geese by the thousands resting briefly on the northern Arctic plain during fall migrations, feeding on tundra berries before their long flights south. The oil companies operating in the Arctic would say they want only a small part of the region, that millions of acres would remain. But some animals and birds are crowded into small parts of the Arctic so that even localized changes can cause havoc. Others require vast areas, with each habitat essential at some time of year and all parts needed. The presence of men and machinery must cause some species to avoid areas that could provide food and shelter but are simply too close to people.

Before the oil strikes at Prudhoe Bay in 1968, and the availability of greatly improved surface access, the Arctic still represented a land isolated from aggression, the last remaining wilderness on North America so little altered by mechanical change, a field laboratory for study of natural plant and animal communities and their relationships, offering comparison to regions out of balance. As a source of petroleum the Arctic will serve America for a brief period only. As a wilderness it can serve the world forever.

Oil is not a new story to Alaska. Major deposits were discovered and made available for exploitation in 1957 beneath the waters of Cook Inlet and in the Kenai National Moose Range on the Kenai Peninsula. Could there be development without serious disruption? Where the Interior Department backed instructions with daily surveillance, moose habitat was not seriously damaged. But beyond the borders of the Moose Range, oil spills and pipeline leaks scarred waterfowl marshes, killed sea ducks, and caused serious economic loss to crab and salmon fishermen. Flares of gases—a resource wasted—sent streamers of smoke into the hitherto clear air of middle Cook Inlet, fulfilling the truth that petrochemical exploitation leads inevitably to pollution and environmental degradation.

It is better to leave the last wild areas untouched, adhering to social discipline in respect of natural law. Do we have so much earth that we can afford to destroy forever any one part of it? The idea of draining the resources in wilderness in order "to meet the needs of a growing population" is unworkable. The United States would do far better to accept a policy of limitations on a population of 200 million now, permitting the people to obtain the broadest possible benefits of civilization as individuals, with the hope this will make a desperate and crowded population of 300 million less likely in years to come. With no such restrictions, there will only be a larger and larger number experiencing less and less of life.

How much wilderness does it take to fulfill the needs of civilization? That really isn't the key question. What counts more is whether each succeeding generation must settle for an increasingly degraded world and know the experience of the past from books and pictures only. Must the future be satisfied with mediocrity because nothing better will be known?

There is tragedy in the grayed skies and clouded rivers that characterize modern America, but the greater tragedy is that such blight is so widely taken for granted—as though nothing serious has been lost so long as the environment can still yield material sustenance. The greatest tragedy of all is the failure to recognize that as the nature of places is altered so too are we. It's not simply nostalgia for a romantic rural past that causes grief over the loss of natural open space.

Too many people are degrading their way of life by competing for too little of what we all need. Elbow room is the essence of life, whether in primitive or modern society. As the old mountain hunter reckoned after watching the miracles of the twentieth century crowd his style, "The longer I live the less I get interested in shooting animals, and the more I get a hankering for shooting people."

Promoters of the "green revolution," tiered freeways, and super-high-rise cities above the clouds claim that we can solve problems of subsistence irrespective of numbers, without stringent effort to achieve balance with living space and resources. Possibly so, but living standards are based on space as well as subsistence, if man is to be more than an organic machine functioning in a simplified, rigidly controlled biological factory. Adequate space, free of water pollution and air pollution, should be the key to determining the optimum density of man. America is already overpopulated, but there is no reason to accept continued growth as inevitable or to feel that reversal of the trend is beyond us.

It is time to reintroduce wilderness into civilization. Every city should have its inner woodlands and greenbelts, convenient to all and extending to surrounding forests and swamps. The environment surrounding people as they follow their daily rounds to work, shop, school, and play profoundly affects the quality of their existence. In the restoration of a habitable environment for all people, I venture, is where the battle for wilderness begins.

In a private home the father is motivated by a desire to leave a worthy estate for his heirs. What form can it take? A house, perhaps. A parcel of land, material goods of one sort or another, an insurance policy, or cash in the bank. In a broader sense the earth is the home we all share. As our common estate we can leave a scientifically valuable, aesthetically attractive natural endowment, in which options remain open. In saving the living wilderness, one generation makes an investment that will appreciate in value to the benefit of ages still to come.

Text of the Wilderness Act

An Act To establish a National Wilderness Preservation System for the permanent good of the whole people, and for other purposes.

Public Law 88-577, 88th Congress, S. 4, September 3, 1964

Be it enacted by the Senate and House of Representatives of the United States of America in Congress assembled,

SHORT TITLE

SECTION 1. This Act may be cited as the "Wilderness Act."

WILDERNESS SYSTEM ESTABLISHED—STATEMENT OF POLICY

SECTION 2. (a) In order to assure that an increasing population, accompanied by expanding settlement and growing mechanization, does not occupy and modify all areas within the United States and its possessions, leaving no lands designated for preservation and protection in their natural condition, it is hereby declared to be the policy of the Congress to secure for the American people of present and future generations the benefits of an enduring resource of wilderness. For this purpose there is hereby established a National Wilderness Preservation System to be composed of federally owned areas designated by Congress as "wilderness areas", and these shall be administered for the use and enjoyment of the American people in such manner as will leave them unimpaired for future use and enjoyment as wilderness, and so as to provide for the protection of these areas, the preservation of their wilderness character, and for the gathering and dissemination of information regarding their use and enjoyment as wilderness; and no Federal lands shall be designated as "wilderness areas" except as provided for in this Act or by a subsequent Act.

(b) The inclusion of an area in the National Wilderness Preservation System notwithstanding, the area shall continue to be managed by the Department and agency having jurisdiction thereover immediately before its inclusion in the National Wilderness Preservation System unless otherwise provided by Act of Congress. No appropriation shall be available for the payment of expenses or salaries for the administration of the National Wilderness Preservation System as a separate unit nor shall any appropriations be available for additional personnel stated as being required solely for the purpose of managing or administering areas solely because they are included within the National Wilderness Preservation System.

DEFINITION OF WILDERNESS

(c) A wilderness, in contrast with those areas where man and his own works dominate the landscape, is hereby recognized as an area where the earth and its community of life are untrammeled by man, where man himself is a visitor who does not remain. An area of wilderness is further defined to mean in this Act an area of undeveloped Federal land retaining its primeval character and influence, without permanent improvements or human habitation, which is protected and managed so as to preserve its natural conditions and which (1) generally appears to have been affected primarily by the forces of nature, with the imprint of man's work substantially unnoticeable; (2) has outstanding opportunities for solitude or a primitive and unconfined type of recreation; (3) has at least five thousand acres of land or is of sufficient size as to make practicable its preservation and use in an unimpaired condition; and (4) may also contain ecological, geological, or other features of scientific, educational, scenic, or historical value.

SECTION 3. (a) All areas within the national forests classified at least 30 days before the effective date of this Act by the Secretary of Agriculture or the Chief of the Forest Service as "wilderness," "wild," or "canoe" are hereby designated as wilderness areas. The Secretary of Agriculture shall—

(1) Within one year after the effective date of this Act, file a map and legal description of each wilderness area with the Interior and Insular Affairs Committees of the United States Senate and the House of Representatives, and such descriptions shall have the same force and effect as if included in this Act: *Provided, however,* That correction of clerical and typographical errors in such legal descriptions and maps may be made.

(2) Maintain, available to the public, records pertaining to said wilderness areas, including maps and legal descriptions, copies of regulations governing them, copies of public notices of, and reports submitted to Congress regarding pending additions, eliminations, or modifications. Maps, legal descriptions, and regulations pertaining to wilderness areas within their respective jurisdictions also shall be available to the public in the offices of regional foresters, national forest supervisors, and forest rangers.

Classification. (b) The Secretary of Agriculture shall, within ten years after the enactment of this Act, review, as to its suitability or nonsuitability for preservation as wilderness, each area in the national forests classified on the effective date of this Act by the Secretary of Agriculture or the Chief of the Forest Service as "primitive" and report his findings to the President.

Presidential recommendation to Congress. The President shall advise the United States Senate and House of Representatives of his recommendations with respect to the designation as "wilderness" or other reclassification of each area on which review has been completed, together with maps and a definition of boundaries. Such advice shall be given with respect to not less than one-third of all the areas now classified as "primitive" within three years after the enactment of this Act, not less than two-thirds within seven years after the enactment of this Act, and the remaining areas within ten years after the enactment of this Act.

Congressional approval. Each recommendation of the President for designation as "wilderness" shall become effective only if so provided by an Act of Congress. Areas classified as "primitive" on the effective date of this Act shall continue to be administered under the rules and regulations affecting such areas on the effective date of this Act until Congress has determined otherwise. Any such area may be increased in size by the President at the time he submits his recommendations to the Congress by not more than five thousand acres with no more than one thousand two hundred and eighty acres of such increase in any one compact unit; if it is proposed to increase the size of any such area by more than five thousand acres or by more than one thousand two hundred and eighty acres in any one compact unit the increase in size shall not become effective until acted upon by Congress. Nothing herein contained shall limit the President in proposing, as part of his recommendations to Congress, the alteration of existing boundaries of primitive areas or recommending the addition of any contiguous area of national forest lands predominantly of wilderness value. Notwithstanding any other provisions of this Act, the Secretary of Agriculture may complete his review and delete such area as may be necessary, but not to exceed seven thousand acres, from the southern tip of the Gore Range-Eagles Nest Primitive Area, Colorado, if the Secretary determines that such action is in the public interest.

Report to President. (c) Within ten years after the effective date of this Act the Secretary of the Interior shall review every roadless area of five thousand contiguous acres or more in the national parks, monuments and other units of the national park system and every such area of, and every roadless island within, the national wildlife refuges and game ranges, under his jurisdiction on the effective date of this Act and shall report to the

President his recommendation as to the suitability or non-suitability of each such area or island for preservation as wilderness.

Presidential recommendation to Congress. The President shall advise the President of the Senate and the Speaker of the House of Representatives of his recommendation with respect to the designation as wilderness of each such area or island on which review has been completed, together with a map thereof and a definition of its boundaries. Such advice shall be given with respect to not less than one-third of the areas and islands to be reviewed under this subsection within three years after enactment of this Act, not less than two-thirds within seven years of enactment of this Act, and the remainder within ten years of enactment of this Act.

Congressional approval. A recommendation of the President for designation as wilderness shall become effective only if so provided by an Act of Congress. Nothing contained herein shall, by implication or otherwise, be construed to lessen the present statutory authority of the Secretary of the Interior with respect to the maintenance of roadless areas within units of the national park system.

Suitability. (d) (1) The Secretary of Agriculture and the Secretary of the Interior shall, prior to submitting any recommendations to the President with respect to the suitability of any area for preservation as wilderness—

Publication in Federal Register. (A) give such public notice of the proposed action as they deem appropriate, including publication in the Federal Register and in a newspaper having general circulation in the area or areas in the vicinity of the affected land;

Hearings. (B) hold a public hearing or hearings at a location or locations convenient to the area affected. The hearings shall be announced through such means as the respective Secretaries involved deem appropriate, including notices in the Federal Register and in newspapers of general circulation in the area: *Provided.* That if the lands involved are located in more than one State, at least one hearing shall be held in each State in which a portion of the land lies;

(C) at least thirty days before the date of a hearing advise the Governor of each State and the governing board of each county, or in Alaska the borough, in which the lands are located, and Federal departments and agencies concerned, and invite such officials and Federal agencies to submit their views on the proposed action at the hearings or by no later than thirty days following the date of the hearing.

(2) Any views submitted to the appropriate Secretary under the provisions of (1) of this subsection with respect to any area shall be included with any recommendations to the President and to Congress with respect to such area.

Proposed modification. (e) Any modification or adjustment of boundaries of any wilderness area shall be recommended by the appropriate Secretary after public notice of such proposal and public hearing or hearings as provided in subsection (d) of this section. The proposed modification or adjustment shall then be recommended with map and description thereof to the President. The President shall advise the United States Senate and the House of Representatives of his recommendations with respect to such modification or adjustment and such recommendations shall become effective only in the same manner as provided for in subsections (b) and (c) of this section.

USE OF WILDERNESS AREAS

SECTION 4. (a) The purposes of this Act are hereby declared to be within and supplemental to the purposes for which national forests and units of the national park and wildlife refuge systems are established and administered and—

(1) Nothing in this Act shall be deemed to be in interference with the purpose for which national forests are established as set forth in the Act of June 4, 1897 (30 Stat. 11), and the Multiple-Use Sustained-Yield Act of June 12, 1960 (74 Stat. 215).

(2) Nothing in this Act shall modify the restrictions and provisions of the Shipstead-Nolan Act (Public Law 539, Seventy-first Congress, July 10, 1930; 46 Stat. 1020), the Thye-Blatnik Act (Public Law 733, Eightieth Congress, June 22,

1948; 62 Stat. 568), and the Humphrey-Thye-Blatnik-Andresen Act (Public Law 607, Eighty-fourth Congress, June 22, 1956; 70 Stat. 326), as applying to the Superior National Forest or the regulations of the Secretary of Agriculture.

(3) Nothing in this Act shall modify the statutory authority under which units of the national park system are created. Further, the designation of any area of any park, monument, or other unit of the national park system as a wilderness area pursuant to this Act shall in no manner lower the standards evolved for the use and preservation of such park, monument, or other unit of the national park system in accordance with the Act of August 25, 1916, the statutory authority under which the area was created, or any other Act of Congress which might pertain to or affect such area, including, but not limited to, the Act of June 8, 1906 (34 Stat. 225; 16 U.S.C. 432 et seq.); section 3(2) of the Federal Power Act (16 U.S.C. 796 (2)); and the Act of August 21, 1935 (49 Stat. 666; 16 U.S.C. 461 et seq.).

(b) Except as otherwise provided in this Act, each agency administering any area designated as wilderness shall be responsible for preserving the wilderness character of the area and shall so administer such area for such other purposes for which it may have been established as also to preserve its wilderness character. Except as otherwise provided in this Act, wilderness areas shall be devoted to the public purposes of recreational, scenic, scientific, educational, conservation, and historical use.

PROHIBITION OF CERTAIN USES

(c) Except as specifically provided for in this Act, and subject to existing private rights, there shall be no commercial enterprise and no permanent road within any wilderness area designated by this Act and, except as necessary to meet minimum requirements for the administration of the area for the purpose of this Act (including measures required in emergencies involving the health and safety of persons within the area), there shall be no temporary road, no use of motor vehicles, motorized equipment or motorboats, no landing of aircraft, no other form of mechanical transport, and no structure or installation within any such area.

(d) The following special provisions are hereby made:

(1) Within wilderness areas designated by this Act the use of aircraft or motorboats, where these uses have already become established, may be permitted to continue subject to such restrictions as the Secretary of Agriculture deems desirable. In addition, such measures may be taken as may be necessary in the control of fire, insects, and disease, subject to such conditions as the Secretary deems desirable.

(2) Nothing in this Act shall prevent within national forest wilderness areas any activity, including prospecting, for the purpose of gathering information about mineral or other resources, if such activity is carried on in a manner compatible with the preservation of the wilderness environment. Furthermore, in accordance with such program as the Secretary of the Interior shall develop and conduct in consultation with the Secretary of Agriculture, such areas shall be surveyed on a planned, recurring basis consistent with the concept of wilderness preservation by the Geological Survey and the Bureau of Mines to determine the mineral values, if any, that may be present; and the results of such surveys shall be made available to the public and submitted to the President and Congress.

Mineral leases, claims, etc. (3) Notwithstanding any other provisions of this Act, until midnight December 31, 1983, the United States mining laws and all laws pertaining to mineral leasing shall, to the same extent as applicable prior to the effective date of this Act, extend to those national forest lands designated by this Act as "wilderness areas"; subject, however, to such reasonable regulations governing ingress and egress as may be prescribed by the Secretary of Agriculture consistent with the use of the land for mineral location and development and exploration, drilling, and production, and use of land for transmission lines, waterlines, telephone lines, or facilities necessary in exploring, drilling, producing, mining, and processing operations, including where essential the use of mechanized ground or air equipment and restoration as near as practicable of the surface of the land disturbed in performing prospecting, location, and, in oil and gas leasing, discovery work, exploration, drilling, and production, as soon as they have served their purpose. Mining locations lying within the boundaries of said wilderness areas shall be held and used solely for mining or processing operations and uses reasonably incident thereto; and hereafter, subject to valid existing rights, all patents issued under the mining laws of the United States affecting national forest lands designated by this Act as wilderness areas shall convey title to the mineral deposits within the claim, together with the right to cut and use so much of the mature timber therefrom as may be needed in the extraction, removal, and beneficiation of the mineral deposits, if the timber is not otherwise reasonably available, and if the timber is cut under sound principles of forest management as defined by the national forest rules and regulations, but each such patent shall reserve to the United States all title in or to the surface of the lands and products thereof, and no use of the surface of the claim or the resources therefrom not reasonably required for carrying on mining or prospecting shall be allowed except as otherwise expressly provided in this Act: *Provided,* That, unless hereafter specifically authorized, no patent within wilderness areas designated by this Act shall issue after December 31, 1983, except for the valid claims existing on or before December 31, 1983. Mining claims located after the effective date of this Act within the boundaries of wilderness areas designated by this Act shall create no rights in excess of those rights which may be patented under the provisions of this subsection. Mineral leases, permits, and licenses covering lands within national forest wilderness areas designated by this Act shall contain such reasonable stipulations as may be prescribed by the Secretary of Agriculture for the protection of the wilderness character of the land consistent with the use of the land for the purpose for which they are leased, permitted, or licensed. Subject to valid rights then existing, effective January 1, 1984, the minerals in lands designated by this Act as wilderness areas are withdrawn from all forms of appropriation under the mining laws and from disposition under all laws pertaining to mineral leasing and all amendments thereto.

Water resources. (4) Within wilderness areas in the national forests designated by this Act, (1) the President may, within a specific area and in accordance with such regulations as he may deem desirable, authorize prospecting for water resources, the establishment and maintenance of reservoirs, water-conservation works, power projects, transmission lines, and other facilities needed in the public interest, including the road construction and maintenance essential to development and use thereof, upon his determination that such use or uses in the specific area will better serve the interests of the United States and the people thereof than will its denial; and (2) the grazing of livestock, where established prior to the effective date of this Act, shall be permitted to continue subject to such reasonable regulations as are deemed necessary by the Secretary of Agriculture.

(5) Other provisions of this Act to the contrary notwithstanding, the management of the Boundary Waters Canoe Area, formerly designated as the Superior, Little Indian Sioux, and Caribou Roadless Areas, in the Superior National Forest, Minnesota, shall be in accordance with regulations established by the Secretary of Agriculture in accordance with the general purpose of maintaining, without unnecessary restrictions on other uses, including that of timber, the primitive character of the area, particularly in the vicinity of lakes, streams, and portages: *Provided,* That nothing in this Act shall preclude the continuance within the area of any already established use of motorboats.

(6) Commercial services may be performed within the wilderness areas designated by this Act to the extent necessary for activities which are proper for realizing the recreational or other wilderness purposes of the areas.

(7) Nothing in this Act shall constitute an express or im-

plied claim or denial on the part of the Federal Government as to exemption from State water laws.

(8) Nothing in this Act shall be construed as affecting the jurisdiction or responsibilities of the several States with respect to wildlife and fish in the national forests.

STATE AND PRIVATE LANDS WITHIN WILDERNESS AREAS

SECTION 5. (a) In any case where State-owned or privately owned land is completely surrounded by national forest lands within areas designated by this Act as wilderness, such State or private owner shall be given such rights as may be necessary to assure adequate access to such State-owned or privately owned land by such State or private owner and their successors in interest, or the State-owned land or privately owned land shall be exchanged for federally owned land in the same State of approximately equal value under authorities available to the Secretary of Agriculture:

Transfers, restriction. Provided, however, That the United States shall not transfer to a State or private owner any mineral interests unless the State or private owner relinquishes or causes to be relinquished to the United States the mineral interest in the surrounded land.

(b) In any case where valid mining claims or other valid occupancies are wholly within a designated national forest wilderness area, the Secretary of Agriculture shall, by reasonable regulations consistent with the preservation of the area as wilderness, permit ingress and egress to such surrounded areas by means which have been or are being customarily enjoyed with respect to other such areas similarly situated.

Acquisition. (c) Subject to the appropriation of funds by Congress, the Secretary of Agriculture is authorized to acquire privately owned land within the perimeter of any area designated by this Act as wilderness if (1) the owner concurs in such acquisition or (2) the acquisition is specifically authorized by Congress.

GIFTS, BEQUESTS, AND CONTRIBUTIONS

SECTION 6. (a) The Secretary of Agriculture may accept gifts or bequests of land within wilderness areas designated by this Act for preservation as wilderness. The Secretary may also accept gifts or bequests of land adjacent to wilderness areas designated by this Act for preservation as wilderness if he has given sixty days advance notice thereof to the President of the Senate and the Speaker of the House of Representatives. Land accepted by the Secretary of Agriculture under this section shall become part of the wilderness area involved. Regulations with regard to any such land may be in accordance with such agreements, consistent with the policy of this Act, as are made at the time of such gift, or such conditions, consistent with such policy, as may be included in, and accepted with, such bequest.

(b) The Secretary of Agriculture or the Secretary of the Interior is authorized to accept private contributions and gifts to be used to further the purposes of this Act.

ANNUAL REPORTS

SECTION 7. At the opening of each session of Congress, the Secretaries of Agriculture and Interior shall jointly report to the President for transmission to Congress on the status of the wilderness system, including a list and descriptions of the areas in the system, regulations in effect, and other pertinent information, together with any recommendations they may care to make. Approved September 3, 1964.

LEGISLATIVE HISTORY:

HOUSE REPORTS:
No. 1538 accompanying H. R. 9070 (Committee on Interior & Insular Affairs) and No. 1829 (Committee of Conference).

SENATE REPORT:
No. 109 (Committee on Interior & Insular Affairs).

CONGRESSIONAL RECORD:

Vol. 109 (1963): April 4, 8, considered in Senate.

April 9, considered and passed Senate.

Vol. 110 (1964): July 28, considered in House.

July 30, considered and passed House, amended, in lieu of H. R. 9070.

August 20, House and Senate agreed to conference report.

Appendix B
Landmarks in Wilderness Preservation

BEFORE THE WILDERNESS ACT

1864 To protect Yosemite Valley and the Mariposa Grove of Big Trees from exploitation, Congress cedes these areas to California as a state park (later to be returned as the nucleus of Yosemite National Park).

1872 Yellowstone is established as the country's first national park.

1891 The Forest Reserve Act authorizes the President to withdraw portions of the public domain and designate them as "forest reserves," marking the beginning of a national system of wildland protection.

1892 John Muir organizes the Sierra Club to advance his belief that "wildness is a necessity." Initially the Club conducts "outings" in wilderness, emerging in time as a strong citizen voice for preservation.

1894 New York adopts a constitutional amendment providing that 2.7 million acres of state lands "shall be kept forever wild," reinforcing protection of the Adirondack Forest Preserve (established in 1885)

1903 President Theodore Roosevelt proclaims the first national wildlife refuge, Pelican Island in the Florida Keys, to insure protection of nesting birds.

1916 Congress establishes the National Park Service, with a mixed mandate to (a) preserve the parks inviolate for (b) public use and enjoyment.

1919–1923 Arthur Carhart, working for the Forest Service, recommends that the Trapper Lake area in the White River National Forest, Colorado, remain wild and undeveloped. Then, in Minnesota, he declares that the heart of the Superior National Forest could be "as priceless as Yellowstone, Yosemite or the Grand Canyon—if it remained a water-trail wilderness."

1921   Benton MacKaye conceives the Appalachian Trail as the backbone of a connected network of wild reservations and parks extending from Maine to Georgia, in due course to become "a footpath for those who seek fellowship with the wilderness."

1924   On Aldo Leopold's recommendation, the Forest Service administratively designates the first area to be known officially as "wilderness," 574,000 acres on the Gila National Forest, New Mexico, one manifestation of Leopold's lifelong call for a "land ethic" and "ecological conscience."

1930   Percival Baxter, on leaving office as governor of Maine, purchases 5,000 acres, including most of Mount Katahdin, which he deeds to the state. He continues to buy land, increasing the size of Baxter State Park over the years to 200,000 acres, to be "forever left in the natural wild state."

1935   Based largely on Robert Marshall's idea for uniting "all friends of wilderness," the Wilderness Society is organized by Marshall, Harold Anderson, Harvey Broome, Bernard Frank, Benton MacKaye, Ernest Oberholtzer, and Robert Sterling Yard.

1939   Through Robert Marshall's influence, the Forest Service adopts the historic U regulations, directing that primitive areas in national forests be reviewed and reclassified as "wilderness," "wild," or "roadless," depending on size.

1950-56 Conservationists defeat a proposed dam at Echo Park in Dinosaur National Monument, leading Howard Zahniser to identify the need for statutory protection of wilderness and to write the first draft of the wilderness bill.

1956 Senator Hubert Humphrey and Senate co-sponsors and Representative John Saylor introduce the first wilderness bills in Congress, largely as drafted by Howard Zahniser.

1964   After eighteen congressional hearings in Washington and in the field, Congress passes the Wilderness Act, and President Lyndon B. Johnson on September 3 signs it into law.

SINCE PASSAGE OF THE WILDERNESS ACT

1966   In the first wilderness review in the national parks, conducted in the Great Smoky Mountains of North Carolina-Tennessee, the National Park Service advances a bizarre plan for a major trans-mountain road, plus other roads and large campgrounds, stirring wide protest. The agency withdraws its proposal.

1967   More than a thousand people throng the wilderness hearing on the Great Swamp National Wildlife Refuge, conducted at Morristown, New Jersey. Congress responds by enacting a Great Swamp Wilderness substantially larger than that proposed by the Fish and Wildlife Service.

1968   In the same year, Congress supplements the Wilderness Act by adopting the Wild and Scenic Rivers Act and the National Trails System Act.

1971   The Forest Service conducts the first inventory of roadless areas (later to be known as RARE I) to determine suitability for wilderness designation. The agency decides that areas must be removed from "sights and sounds" of civilization to qualify, and that none qualify in the eastern forests.

1975   The Eastern Wilderness Act designates sixteen national forest wilderness areas in thirteen eastern states.

1976   The Federal Land Policy and Management Act (FLPMA)–the long awaited "BLM Organic Act"–broadens the wilderness system by directing the Bureau of Land Management to evaluate roadless land it administers in the forty-eight lower states to determine suitability for wilderness.

   The National Forest Management Act of 1976 (NFMA) establishes a process for forest planning, including evaluation of roadless areas for recommendation as potential wilderness.

1978   Congress adopts the Endangered American Wilderness Act, protecting significant wilderness in the West, and making clear that candidate areas cannot be disqualified because cities or towns can be seen or heard from them.

1978   Congress designates the first BLM wilderness areas: Santa Lucia in California and Rogue River in Oregon.
   The Forest Service completes its second roadless inventory (RARE II), of 62 million acres of roadless forest lands, the starting point for designating wilderness state-by-state during the 1980s.

1980   Alaska National Interest Lands Conservation Act (ANILCA) triples the size of the wilderness system, adding 56.5 million acres of wilderness in the national parks; it adds 54 million acres to the National Wildlife Refuge System, including 18.5 million acres as wilderness.

1984   Congress designates 8.3 million acres of national forest wilderness in twenty statewide bills. Ronald Reagan without fanfare signs legislation for more additions to the wilderness system than any president except Carter (because of the Alaska Lands Act).

1989   The Wilderness Society commemorates the twenty-fifth anniversary of passage of the Wilderness Act with a program in Washington, D.C. Congress adds 733,400 acres in Nevada to the wilderness system.

1990   The Arizona Desert Wilderness Act, the first statewide wilderness legislation enacted for the Bureau of Land Management, includes more than 1 million acres of BLM land—representing Sonoran, Mohave and Chihuanan deserts—plus 1.3 million acres of national forest and 1.3 million acres of national wildlife refuges.

1992   Dave Foreman and associates initiate The Wildlands Project, designed to connect wilderness, parks, and reserves with natural undisturbed corridors.

1994   The California Desert Protection Act elevates Death Valley and Joshua Tree national monuments to national parks, establishes the Mohave National Preserve and designates 69 new wilderness areas covering eight million acres. Death Valley National Park

Wilderness, with 3,158,038 acres, becomes the largest wilderness unit in the lower 48 states.

1995   Congress passes, and President Clinton signs, the "salvage rider," a small-print proviso attached to the Oklahoma City disaster relief bill, allowing the Forest Service to market timber without regard for wilderness potential, environmental laws, or rules of public scrutiny. It remained in effect until December 1996.

1998   The Sixth World Wilderness Congress is scheduled to meet in October in Bangalore, India, the first time in Asia, with sessions considering global biodiversity values and protection of cultural and ancestral values in wilderness.

Appendix C
National Wilderness Preservation System
An Overview

Wilderness Area Name	Administrative Unit	Size in Acres	Date of Designation
ALABAMA			
Forest Service			
Cheaha	Talladega NF	7,245	01/03/83
Cheaha	Talladega NF		10/28/88
Sipsey	William B. Bankhead NF	25,906	01/03/75
Sipsey	William B. Bankhead NF		10/28/88
TOTAL NFS ACRES IN ALABAMA:		33,151	

Total Alabama Wilderness: 33,151

Wilderness Area Name	Administrative Unit	Size in Acres	Date of Designation
ALASKA			
Fish and Wildlife Service			
Aleutian Islands	Alaska Maritime NWR	1,300,000	12/20/80
Andreafsky	Yukon Delta NWR	1,300,000	12/20/80
Arctic	Arctic NWR	8,000,000	12/20/80
Becharof	Becharof NWR	400,000	12/20/80
Bering Sea	Alaska Maritime NWR	81,340	10/23/70
Bogoslof	Alaska Maritime NWR	175	10/23/70
Chamisso	Alaska Maritime NWR	455	01/03/75
Forrester Island	Alaska Maritime NWR	2,832	10/23/70
Hazy Island	Alaska Maritime NWR	32	10/23/70
Innoko	Innoko NWR	1,240,000	12/20/80
Izembek	Izembek NWR	300,000	12/20/80
Kenai	Kenai NWR	1,350,000	12/20/80
Koyukuk	Koyukuk NWR	400,000	12/20/80
Nunivak	Yukon Delta NWR	600,000	12/20/80
Saint Lazaria	Alaska Maritime NWR	65	10/23/70
Selawik	Selawik NWR	240,000	12/20/80
Semidi	Alaska Maritime NWR	250,000	12/20/80
Simeonof	Alaska Maritime NWR	25,855	10/19/76
Togiak	Togiak NWR	2,270,000	12/20/80
Tuxedni	Alaska Maritime NWR	5,566	10/23/70
Unimak	Alaska Maritime NWR	910,000	12/20/80
TOTAL FWS ACRES IN ALASKA:		18,676,320	

WILDERNESS AREA NAME	ADMINISTRATIVE UNIT	SIZE IN ACRES	DATE OF DESIGNATION
Forest Service			
Chuck River	Tongass NF	74,298	11/28/90
Coronation Island	Tongass NF	19,232	12/20/80
Endicott River	Tongass NF	98,729	12/20/80
Karta River	Tongass NF	39,889	11/28/90
Kootznoowoo —Admiralty Island	Tongass NF	955,694	12/20/80
Kootznoowoo —Young Lake Addition	Tongass NF		11/28/90
Kuiu	Tongass NF	60,581	11/28/90
Maurelle Islands	Tongass NF	4,937	12/20/80
Misty Fjords	Tongass NF	2,142,307	12/20/80
Petersburg Creek-Duncan Salt Chuck	Tongass NF	46,849	12/20/80
Pleasant/Lemusurier/ Inian Islands	Tongass NF	23,096	11/28/90
Russell Fjord	Tongass NF	348,701	12/20/80
South Baranof	Tongass NF	319,568	12/20/80
South Etolin	Tongass NF	83,371	11/28/90
South Prince of Wales	Tongass NF	90,996	12/20/80
Stikine-LeConte	Tongass NF	448,841	12/20/80
Tebenkof Bay	Tongass NF	66,812	12/20/80
Tracy Arms-Fords Terror	Tongass NF	653,179	12/20/80
Warren Island	Tongass NF	11,181	12/20/80
West Chichagof-Yakobi	Tongass NF	264,491	12/20/80
TOTAL NFS ACRES IN ALASKA:		5,752,752	
Park Service			
Denali	Denali NP	2,124,783	12/20/80
Gates of the Arctic	Gates of the Arctic NP	7,167,192	12/20/80
Glacier Bay	Glacier Bay NP & Preserve	2,664,840	12/20/80
Katmai	Katmai NP & Preserve	3,384,358	12/29/80
Kobuk Valley	Kobuk Valley NP	174,545	12/20/80
Lake Clark	Lake Clark NP	2,619,550	12/20/80
Noatak	Noatak Natl Preserve	5,765,427	12/20/80
Wrangell-St. Elias	Wrangell-St. Elias NP & Preserve	9,078,675	12/20/80
TOTAL NPS ACRES IN ALASKA:		32,979,370	

Total Alaska Wilderness: 57,408,442

ARIZONA

Bureau of Land Management

Wilderness Area Name	Administrative Unit	Size in Acres	Date of Designation
Aravaipa Canyon	Safford District	19,700	08/28/84
Aravaipa Canyon	Safford District		11/28/90
Arrastra Mountain	Phoenix District	129,800	11/28/90
Aubrey Peak	Phoenix District	15,400	11/28/90
Baboquivari Peak	Safford District	2,040	11/28/90
Beaver Dam Mountains	Arizona Strip District	15,000	08/28/84
Big Horn Mountains	Phoenix District	21,000	11/28/90
Cottonwood Point	Arizona Strip District	6,860	08/28/84
Coyote Mountains	Safford District	5,100	11/28/90
Dos Cabezas Mountains	Safford District	11,700	11/28/90
Eagletail Mountains	Yuma District	100,600	11/28/90
East Cactus Plain	Yuma District	14,630	11/28/90
Fishhooks	Safford District	10,500	11/28/90
Gibraltar Mountain	Yuma district	18,790	11/28/90
Grand Wash Cliffs	Arizona Strip District	37,030	08/28/84
Harcuvar Mountains	Yuma District	25,050	11/28/90
Harquahala Mountains	Phoenix District	22,880	11/28/90
Hassayampa River Canyon	Phoenix District	12,300	11/28/90
Hells Canyon	Phoenix District	10,600	11/28/90
Hummingbird Springs	Phoenix District	31,200	11/28/90
Kanab Creek	Arizona Strip District	6,700	08/28/84
Mount Logan	Arizona Strip District	14,650	08/28/84
Mount Nutt	Phoenix District	27,660	11/28/90
Mount Tipton	Phoenix District	32,760	11/28/90
Mount Trumbull	Arizona Strip District	7,880	08/28/84
Mount Wilson	Phoenix District	23,900	11/28/90
Muggins Mountains	Yuma District	7,640	11/28/90
Needle's Eye	Phoenix District	8,760	11/28/90
New Water Mountains	Yuma District	24,600	11/28/90
North Maricopa Mountains	Phoenix District	63,200	11/28/90
North Santa Teresa	Safford District	5,800	11/28/90
Paiute	Arizona Strip District	87,900	08/28/84
Paria Canyon-Vermilion Cliffs	Arizona Strip District	89,400	08/28/84
Peloncillo Mountains	Safford District	19,440	11/28/90
Rawhide Mountains	Yuma District	38,470	11/28/90
Redfield Canyon	Safford District	9,930	11/28/90
Sierra Estrella	Phoenix District	14,400	11/28/90

WILDERNESS AREA NAME	ADMINISTRATIVE UNIT	SIZE IN ACRES	DATE OF DESIGNATION
Signal Mountain	Phoenix District	13,350	11/28/90
South Maricopa Mountains	Phoenix District	60,100	11/28/90
Swansea	Yuma District	16,400	11/28/90
Table Top	Phoenix District	34,400	11/28/90
Tres Alamos	Phoenix District	8,300	11/28/90
Trigo Mountains	Yuma District	30,300	11.28/90
Upper Burro Creek	Phoenix District	27,440	11/28/90
Wabayuma Peak	Phoenix District	40,000	11/28/90
Warm Springs	Phoenix District	112,400	11/28/90
White Canyon	Phoenix District	5,790	11/28/90
Woolsey Peak	Phoenix District	64,000	11/28/90
TOTAL BLM ACRES IN ARIZONA:		1,405,750	
Fish and Wildlife Service			
Cabeza Prieta	Cabeza Prieta NWR	803,418	11/28/90
Havasu	Havasu NWR	14,606	11/28/90
Imperial	Imperial NWR	9,220	11/28/90
Kofa	Kofa NWR	516,200	11/28/90
TOTAL FWS ACRES IN ARIZONA:		1,343,444	
Forest Service			
Apache Creek	Prescott NF	5,666	08/28/84
Bear Wallow	Apache NF	11,080	08/28/84
Castle Creek	Prescott NF	25,215	08/28/84
Cedar Bench	Prescott NF	14,950	08/28/84
Chiricahua	Coronado NF	87,700	09/03/64
Chiracahua	Coronado NF		08/28/84
Escudilla	Apache NF	5,200	08/28/84
Fossil Springs	Coconino NF	22,149	08/28/84
Four Peaks	Tonto NF	61,074	08/28/84
Galiuro	Coronado NF	76,317	09/03/64
Galiuro	Coronado NF		08/28/84
Granite Mountain	Prescott NF	9,762	08/28/84
Hellsgate	Tonto NF	37,440	08/28/84
Juniper Mesa	Prescott NF	7,406	08/28/84
Kachina Peaks	Coconino NF	18,616	08/28/84
Kanab Creek	Kaibab NF	63,760	08/28/84
Kendrick Mountain	Coconino NF	1,510	08/28/84
Kendrick Mountain	Kaibab NF	5,000	08/28/84
Mazatzal	Coconino NF	4,275	08/28/84
Mazatzal	Tonto NF	248,115	09/03/64
Mazatzal	Tonto NF		08/28/84
Miller Peak	Coronado NF	20,228	08/28/84

Wilderness Area Name	Administrative Unit	Size in Acres	Date of Designation
Mount Baldy	Apache NF	7,079	10/23/70
Mount Wrightson	Coronado NF	25,260	08/28/84
Munds Mountain	Coconino NF	24,411	08/28/84
Pajarita	Coronado NF	7,553	08/28/84
Pine Mountain	Prescott NF	8,609	02/15/72
Pine Mountain	Tonto NF	11,452	02/15/72
Pusch Ridge	Coronado NF	56,933	02/24/78
Red Rock-Secret Mountain	Coconino NF	47,194	08/28/84
Rincon Mountain	Coronado NF	38,590	08/28/84
Saddle Mountain	Kaibab NF	40,539	08/28/84
Salome	Tonto NF	18,531	08/28/84
Salt River Canyon	Tonto NF	32,101	08/28/84
Santa Teresa	Coronado NF	26,780	08/28/84
Sierra Ancha	Tonto NF	20,850	09/03/64
Strawberry Crater	Coconino NF	10,743	08/28/84
Superstition	Tonto NF	159,757	09/03/64
Superstition	Tonto NF		08/28/84
Sycamore Canyon	Coconino NF	23,325	03/06/72
Sycamore Canyon	Coconino NF		08/28/84
Sycamore Canyon	Kaibab NF	7,125	03/06/72
Sycamore Canyon	Prescott NF	25,487	03/06/72
Sycamore Canyon	Prescott NF		08/28/84
West Clear Creek	Coconino NF	15,238	08/28/84
Wet Beaver	Coconino NF	6,155	08/28/84
Woodchute	Prescott NF	5,833	08/28/84
TOTAL NFS ACRES IN ARIZONA:		1,345,008	

Park Service

Chiricahua	Chiricahua NM	9,440	10/20/76
Organ Pipe Cactus	Organ Pipe Cactus NM	312,600	11/10/78
Petrified Forest	Petrified Forest NP	50,260	10/23/70
Saguaro	Saguaro NM	71,400	10/20/76
TOTAL NPS ACRES IN ARIZONA:		443,700	

Total Arizona Wilderness: 4,537,902

ARKANSAS

Fish and Wildlife Service

Big Lake	Big Lake NWR	2,144	10/19/76
TOTAL FWS ACRES IN ARKANSAS:		2,144	

WILDERNESS AREA NAME	ADMINISTRATIVE UNIT	SIZE IN ACRES	DATE OF DESIGNATION
Forest Service			
Black Fork Mountain	Ouachita NF	8,350	10/19/84
Caney Creek	Ouachita NF	14,460	01/03/75
Dry Creek	Ouachita NF	6,310	10/19/84
East Fork	Ozark NF	10,688	10/19/84
Flatside	Ouachita NF	9,507	10/19/84
Hurricane Creek	Ozark NF	15,307	10/19/84
Leatherwood	Ozark NF	16,838	10/19/84
Poteau Mountain	Ouachita NF	11,299	10/19/84
Richland Creek	Ozark NF	11,801	10/19/84
Upper Buffalo	Ozark NF	12,000	01/03/75
TOTAL NFS ACRES IN ARKANSAS:		116,560	
Park Service			
Buffalo National River	Buffalo National River	10,529	11/10/78
TOTAL NPS ACRES IN ARKANSAS:		10,529	

Total Arkansas Wilderness: 129,233

CALIFORNIA

Bureau of Land Management			
Argus Range	Calif. Desert District	74,890	10/22/94
Big Maria Mountains	Calif. Desert District	47,570	10/22/94
Bigelow Cholla Garden	Calif. Desert District	10,380	10/22/94
Bighorn Mountain	Calif. Desert District	26,685	10/22/94
Black Mountain	Calif. Desert District	13,940	10/22/94
Bright Star	Calif. Desert District	9,520	10/22/94
Bristol Mountains	Calif. Desert District	68,515	10/22/94
Cadiz Dunes	Calif. Desert District	39,740	10/22/94
Carrizo Gorge	Calif. Desert District	15,700	10/22/94
Chemehuevi Mountains	Calif. Desert District	64,320	10/22/94
Chimney Peak	Calif. Desert District	13,700	10/22/94
Chuckwalla Mountains	Calif. Desert District	80,770	10/22/94
Cleghorn Lakes	Calif. Desert District	33,980	10/22/94
Clipper Mountain	Calif. Desert District	26,000	10/22/94
Coso Range	Calif. Desert District	50,520	10/22/94
Coyote Mountains	Calif. Desert District	17,000	10/22/94
Darwin Falls	Calif. Desert District	8,600	10/22/94
Dead Mountains	Calif. Desert District	48,850	10/22/94
Domeland	Calif. Desert District	36,300	10/22/94
El Paso Mountains	Calif. Desert District	23,780	10/22/94
Fish Creek Mountains	Calif. Desert District	25,940	10/22/94
Funeral Mountains	Calif. Desert District	28,110	10/22/94

(CALIFORNIA CONTINUED)				
Golden Valley	Calif. Desert District	37,700	10/22/94	
Grass Valley	Calif. Desert District	31,695	10/22/94	
Hollow Hills	Calif. Desert District	22,240	10/22/94	
Ibex	Calif. Desert District	26,460	10/22/94	
Indian Pass	Calif. Desert District	33,855	10/22/94	
Inyo Mountains	Calif. Desert District	172,020	10/22/94	
Ishi	Ukiah District	240	09/28/84	
Jacumba	Calif. Desert District	33,670	10/22/94	
Kelso Dunes	Calif. Desert District	129,580	10/22/94	
Kiavah	Calif. Desert District	40,290	10/22/94	
Kingston Range	Calif. Desert District	209,608	10/22/94	
Little Chuckwalla Mountains	Calif. Desert District	29,880	10/22/94	
Little Picacho	Calif. Desert District	33,600	10/22/94	
Machesna Mountain	Bakersfield District	120	09/28/84	
Malpais Mesa	Calif. Desert District	32,360	10/22/94	
Manly Peak	Calif. Desert District	16,105	10/22/94	
Mecca Hills	Calif. Desert District	24,200	10/22/94	
Mesquite	Calif. Desert District	47,330	10/22/94	
Newberry Mountains	Calif. Desert District	22,900	10/22/94	
Nopah Range	Calif. Desert District	110,860	10/22/94	
North Algodones Dunes	Calif. Desert District	32,240	10/22/94	
North Mesquite Mountains	Calif. Desert District	25,540	10/22/94	
Old Woman Mountains	Calif. Desert District	146,020	10/22/94	
Orocopia Mountains	Calif. Desert District	40,735	10/22/94	
Owens Peak	Calif. Desert District	74,060	10/22/94	
Pahrump Valley	Calif. Desert District	74,800	10/22/94	
Palen/McCoy	Calif. Desert District	270,629	10/22/94	
Palo Verde Mountains	Calif. Desert District	32,310	10/22/94	
Picacho Peak	Calif. Desert District	7,700	10/22/94	
Piper Mountain	Calif. Desert District	72,575	10/22/94	
Piute Mountains	Calif. Desert District	36,840	10/22/94	
Resting Spring Range	Calif. Desert District	78,868	10/22/94	
Rice Valley	Calif. Desert District	40,820	10/22/94	
Riverside Mountains	Calif. Desert District	22,380	10/22/94	
Rodman Mountains	Calif. Desert District	27,690	10/22/94	
Sacatar Trail	Calif. Desert District	51,900	10/22/94	
Saddle Peak Hills	Calif. Desert District	1,440	10/22/94	
San Gorgonio	Calif. Desert District	37,980	10/22/94	
Santa Lucia	Bakersfield District	1,733	02/24/78	
Santa Rosa	Calif. Desert District	64,340	10/22/94	
Sawtooth Mountains	Calif. Desert District	35,080	10/22/94	

WILDERNESS AREA NAME	ADMINISTRATIVE UNIT	SIZE IN ACRES	DATE OF DESIGNATION
Sheephole Valley	Calif. Desert District	174,800	10/22/94
South Nopah Range	Calif. Desert District	16,780	10/22/94
Stateline	Calif. Desert District	7,050	10/22/94
Stepladder Mountains	Calif. Desert District	81,600	10/22/94
Surprise Canyon	Calif. Desert District	29,180	10/22/94
Sylvania Mountains	Calif. Desert District	17,820	10/22/94
Trilobite	Calif. Desert District	31,160	10/22/94
Trinity Alps	Ukiah District	4,623	09/28/84
Turtle Mountains	Calif. Desert District	144,500	10/22/94
Whipple Mountains	Calif. Desert District	77,520	10/22/94
Yolla Bolly-Middle Eel	Ukiah District	7,145	09/28/84
TOTAL BLM ACRES IN CALIFORNIA:		3,587,381	

Fish and Wildlife Service

Farallon	Farallon NWR	141	12/26/74
Havasu	Havasu NWR	3,195	10/22/94
Imperial	Imperial NWR	5,836	10/22/94
TOTAL FWS ACRES IN CALIFORNIA:		9,172	

Forest Service

Agua Tibia	Cleveland NF	15,933	01/03/75
Ansel Adams	Inyo NF	78,775	09/03/64
Ansel Adams	Sierra NF	151,483	09/03/64
Ansel Adams	Sierra NF		09/28/84
Bighorn Mountain	Inyo NF	11,800	10/22/94
Bucks Lake	Plumas NF	23,958	09/28/84
Caribou	Lassen NF	20,546	09/03/64
Caribou	Lassen NF		09/28/84
Carson-Iceberg	Stanislaus NF	77,993	09/28/84
Carson-Iceberg	Toiyabe NF	83,188	09/28/84
Castle Crags	Shasta NF	8,627	09/28/84
Chanchelulla	Trinity NF	8,200	09/28/84
Chumash	Los Padres NF	38,150	06/19/92
Cucamonga	Angeles NF	4,200	09/28/84
Cucamonga	San Bernardino NF	8,581	09/03/64
Desolation	Eldorado NF	63,475	10/10/69
Dick Smith	Los Padres NF	67,800	09/28/84
Dinkey Lakes	Sierra NF	30,000	09/28/84
Dome Land	Sequoia NF	93,781	09/03/64
Dome Land	Sequoia NF		09/28/84
Emigrant	Stanislaus NF	112,277	01/03/75
Emigrant	Stanislaus NF		09/28/84
Garcia	Los Padras NF	14,100	06/19/92
Golden Trout	Inyo NF	192,765	02/24/78

WILDERNESS AREA NAME	ADMINISTRATIVE UNIT	SIZE IN ACRES	DATE OF DESIGNATION
(CALIFORNIA CONTINUED)			
Golden Trout	Sequoia NF	110,746	02/24/78
Granite Chief	Tahoe NF	19,048	09/28/84
Hauser	Cleveland NF	7,547	09/28/84
Hoover	Inyo NF	9,507	09/03/64
Hoover	Toiyabe NF	39,094	09/03/64
Inyo Mountains	Inyo NF	73,300	10/22/94
Ishi	Lassen NF	41,099	09/28/84
Jennie Lakes	Sequoia NF	10,289	09/28/84
John Muir	Inyo NF	228,366	09/03/64
John Muir	Sierra NF	351,957	09/03/64
John Muir	Sierra NF		09/28/84
Kaiser	Sierra NF	22,700	10/19/76
Kiavah	Inyo NF	42,115	10/22/94
Machesna Mountain	Los Padres NF	19,760	09/28/84
Marble Mountain	Klamath NF	241,744	09/03/64
Marble Mountain	Klamath NF		09/28/84
Matilija	Los Padres NF	29,600	06/19/92
Mokelumne	Eldorado NF	60,154	09/03/64
Mokelumne	Eldorado NF		09/28/84
Mokelumne	Stanislaus NF	22,267	09/03/64
Mokelumne	Stanislaus NF		09/28/84
Mokelumne	Toiyabe NF	16,740	09/28/84
Monarch	Sequoia NF	24,152	09/28/84
Monarch	Sierra NF	20,744	09/28/84
Mount Shasta	Shasta NF	33,845	09/28/84
North Fork	Six Rivers NF	7,999	09/28/84
Pine Creek	Cleveland NF	13,480	09/28/84
Red Buttes	Rogue River NF	16,150	09/28/84
Russian	Klamath NF	12,000	09/28/84
San Gabriel	Angeles NF	36,118	05/24/68
San Gorgonio	San Bernardino NF	56,722	09/03/64
San Gorgonio	San Bernardino NF		09/28/84
San Jacinto	San Bernardino NF	32,248	09/03/64
San Jacinto	San Bernardino NF		09/28/84
San Mateo Canyon	Cleveland NF	38,484	09/28/84
San Rafael	Los Padres NF	150,980	03/21/68
San Rafael	Los Padres NF		09/28/84
San Rafael	Los Padres NF	46,400	06/19/92
Santa Lucia	Los Padres NF	18,679	02/24/78
Santa Rosa	San Bernardino NF	13,787	09/28/84
Sespe	Angeles NF		06/19/92
Sespe	Los Padres NF	219,700	06/19/92
Sheep Mountain	Angeles NF	39,482	09/28/84

WILDERNESS AREA NAME	ADMINISTRATIVE UNIT	SIZE IN ACRES	DATE OF DESIGNATION
Sheep Mountain	San Bernardino NF	2,401	09/28/84
Silver Peak	Los Padres NF	14,500	06/19/92
Siskiyou	Klamath NF	75,680	09/28/84
Siskiyou	Siskiyou NF	5,300	09/28/84
Siskiyou	Six Rivers NF	71,700	09/28/84
Snow Mountain	Mendocino NF	36,370	09/28/84
South Sierra	Inyo NF	31,865	09/28/84
South Sierra	Sequoia NF	28,219	09/28/84
South Warner	Modoc NF	70,614	09/03/64
South Warner	Modoc NF		09/28/84
Thousand Lakes	Lassen NF	16,335	09/03/64
Trinity Alps	Klamath NF	77,860	09/28/84
Trinity Alps	Shasta NF	102,821	09/28/84
Trinity Alps	Six Rivers NF	25,400	09/28/84
Trinity Alps	Trinity NF	292,060	09/28/84
Ventana	Los Padres NF	164,178	08/16/69
Ventana	Los Padres NF		02/24/78
Ventana	Los Padres NF		09/28/84
Ventana	Los Padres NF	38,000	06/19/92
Yolla Bolly-Middle Eel	Mendocino NF	98,323	09/03/64
Yolla Bolly-Middle Eel	Mendocino NF		09/28/84
Yolla Bolly-Middle Eel	Six Rivers NF	10,813	09/28/84
Yolla Bolly-Middle Eel	Trinity NF	37,560	09/03/64
TOTAL NFS ACRES IN CALIFORNIA:		4,432,634	

Park Service

Death Valley	Death Valley NP	3,158,038	10/22/94
Joshua Tree	Joshua Tree	793,955	10/20/76
Joshua Tree	Joshua Tree		10/22/94
Lassen Volcanic	Lassen Volcanic NP	78,982	10/19/72
Lava Beds	Lava Beds NM	28,460	10/13/72
Mojave	Mojave	1,419,800	10/22/94
Philip Burton	Point Reyes NSS		10/18/76
Philip Burton	Point Reyes NSS	25,370	10/20/76
Philip Burton	Point Reyes NSS		07/19/85
Pinnacles	Pinnacles NM	12,952	10/20/76
Sequoia-Kings Canyon	Sequoia-Kings Canyon NP	736,980	09/28/84
Yosemite	Yosemite NP	677,600	09/28/84
TOTAL NPS ACRES IN CALIFORNIA:		6,932,137	

Total California Wilderness: 14,961,324

COLORADO

Bureau of Land Management

Powderhorn	Montrose District	48,115	08/13/93
Uncompahgre	Montrose District	3,390	08/13/93
TOTAL BLM ACRES IN COLORADO:		51,505	

Fish and Wildlife Service

Mount Massive	Leadville NFH	2,560	12/22/80
TOTAL FWS ACRES IN COLORADO:		2,560	

Forest Service

Buffalo Peaks	Pike NF	22,810	08/13/93
Buffalo Peaks	San Isabel NF	20,600	08/13/93
Byers Peak	Arapaho NF	8,095	08/13/93
Cache La Poudre	Roosevelt NF	9,238	12/22/80
Collegiate Peaks	Gunnison NF	48,986	12/22/80
Collegiate Peaks	San Isabel NF	82,470	12/22/80
Collegiate Peaks	White River NF	35,482	12/22/80
Comanche Peak	Roosevelt NF	66,791	12/22/80
Eagles Nest	Arapaho NF	82,324	07/12/76
Eagles Nest	White River NF	50,582	07/12/76
Flat Tops	Routt NF	38,870	12/12/75
Flat Tops	White River NF	196,165	12/12/75
Fossil Ridge	Gunnison NF	32,838	08/13/93
Greenhorn Mountain	San Isabel NF	22,040	08/13/93
Holy Cross	San Isabel NF	9,489	12/22/80
Holy Cross	White River NF	113,308	12/22/80
Hunter-Fryingpan	White River NF	81,866	02/24/78
Hunter-Fryingpan −Spruce Creek Additions	White River NF	8,330	08/13/93
Indian Peaks	Arapaho NF	40,109	10/11/78
Indian Peaks	Arapaho NF		12/22/80
Indian Peaks	Roosevelt NF	30,265	10/11/78
Indian Peaks	Roosevelt NF		12/22/80
La Garita	Gunnison NF	79,822	09/03/64
La Garita	Gunnison NF		12/22/80
La Garita	Rio Grande NF	24,164	09/03/64
La Garita	Rio Grande NF		12/22/80
La Garita −Wheeler Additions	Rio Grande NF	25,640	08/13/93
Lizard Head	San Juan NF	20,802	12/22/80
Lizard Head	Uncompahgre NF	20,391	12/22/80
Lost Creek	Pike NF	105,090	12/22/80

WILDERNESS AREA NAME	ADMINISTRATIVE UNIT	SIZE IN ACRES	DATE OF DESIGNATION
(COLORADO CONTINUED)			
Lost Creek	Pike NF	14,700	08/13/93
Maroon Bells-Snowmass	Gunnison NF	19,194	12/22/80
Maroon Bells-Snowmass	White River NF	161,923	09/03/64
Maroon Bells-Snowmass	White River NF		12/22/80
Mount Evans	Arapaho NF	40,274	12/22/80
Mount Evans	Pike NF	34,127	12/22/80
Mount Massive	San Isabel NF	27,980	12/22/80
Mount Sneffels	Uncompahgre NF	16,565	12/22/80
Mount Zirkel	Routt NF	139,818	09/03/64
Mount Zirkel	Routt NF		12/22/80
Mount Zirkel	Routt NF	20,750	08/13/93
Neota	Roosevelt NF	9,657	12/22/80
Neota	Routt NF	267	12/22/80
Never Summer	Arapaho NF	7,098	12/22/80
Never Summer −Bowen Gulch Additions	Arapaho NF	6,990	08/13/93
Never Summer	Routt NF	6,659	12/22/80
Platte River	Routt NF	743	10/30/84
Powderhorn	Gunnison NF	13,599	08/13/93
Ptarmigan Peak	Arapaho NF	13,175	08/13/93
Raggeds	Gunnison NF	64,928	12/22/80
Raggeds	White River NF		12/22/80
Rawah	Roosevelt NF	71,606	09/03/64
Rawah	Roosevelt NF		12/22/80
Rawah	Routt NF	1,462	12/22/80
Sangre de Cristo	Rio Grande NF	133,780	08/13/93
Sangre de Cristo	San Isabel NF	92,640	08/13/93
Sarvis Creek	Routt NF	47,140	08/13/93
South San Juan	Rio Grande NF	87,847	12/22/80
South San Juan	San Juan NF	39,843	12/22/80
South San Juan	San Juan NF	31,100	08/13/93
Uncompahgre	Uncompahgre NF	98,516	12/22/80
Uncompahgre	Uncompahgre NF	815	08/13/93
Vasquez Peak	Arapaho NF	12,300	08/13/93
Weminuche	Rio Grande NF	164,715	01/03/75
Weminuche	Rio Grande NF		12/22/80
Weminuche	San Juan NF	322,989	01/03/75
Weminuche	San Juan NF		12/22/80
Weminuche	San Juan NF		08/13/93
West Elk	Gunnison NF	176,172	09/03/64
West Elk	Gunnison NF		12/22/80
TOTAL NFS ACRES IN COLORADO:		3,155,939	

WILDERNESS AREA NAME	ADMINISTRATIVE UNIT	SIZE IN ACRES	DATE OF DESIGNATION
Park Service			
Black Canyon of the Gunnison	Black Canyon of the Gunnison NM	11,180	10/20/76
Great Sand Dunes	Great Sand Dunes NM	33,450	10/20/76
Indian Peaks	Rocky Mountain NP	2,917	12/12/75
Mesa Verde	Mesa Verde NP	8,100	10/20/76
TOTAL NPS ACRES IN COLORADO:		55,647	

Total Colorado Wilderness: 3,265,651

FLORIDA

Fish and Wildlife Service			
Cedar Keys	Cedar Keys NWR	379	08/07/72
Chassahowitzka	Chassahowitzka NWR	23,580	10/19/76
Florida Keys	Great White Heron NWR	1,900	01/03/75
Florida Keys	Key West NWR	2,019	01/03/75
Florida Keys	National Key Deer Reef	2,278	01/03/75
Island Bay	Island Bay NWR	20	10/23/70
J. N. "Ding" Darling	J. N. "Ding" Darling NWR	2,619	10/19/76
Lake Woodruff	Lake Woodruff NWR	1,066	10/19/76
Passage Key	Passage Key NWR	36	10/23/70
Pelican Island	Pelican Island NWR	6	10/23/70
St. Marks	St. Marks NWR	17,350	01/03/75
TOTAL FWS ACRES IN FLORIDA:		51,253	
Forest Service			
Alexander Springs	Ocala NF	7,941	09/28/84
Big Gum Swamp	Osceola NF	13,660	09/28/84
Billies Bay	Ocala NF	3,092	09/28/84
Bradwell Bay	Apalachicola NF	24,602	01/03/75
Bradwell Bay	Apalachicola NF		09/28/84
Juniper Prairie	Ocala NF	14,277	09/28/84
Little Lake George	Ocala NF	2,833	09/28/84
Mud Swamp/New River	Apalachicola NF	8,090	09/28/84
TOTAL NFS ACRES IN FLORIDA:		74,495	
Park Service			
Everglades	Everglades NP	1,296,500	11/10/78
TOTAL NPS ACRES IN FLORIDA:		1,296,500	

Total Florida Wilderness: 1,422,248

WILDERNESS AREA NAME	ADMINISTRATIVE UNIT	SIZE IN ACRES	DATE OF DESIGNATION

GEORGIA

Fish and Wildlife Service

Blackbeard Island	Blackbeard Island NWR	3,000	01/03/75
Okefenokee	Okefenokee NWR	353,981	10/01/74
Wolf Island	Wolf Island NWR	5,126	01/03/75
TOTAL FWS ACRES IN GEORGIA:		362,107	

Forest Service

Big Frog	Chattahoochee NF	89	10/30/84
Blood Mountain	Chattahoochee NF	7,800	12/11/91
Brasstown	Chattahoochee NF	11,178	10/27/86
Brasstown	Chattahoochee NF	1,160	12/11/91
Cohutta	Chattahoochee NF	35,265	01/03/75
Cohutta	Chattahoochee NF		10/27/86
Ellicott Rock	Chattahoochee NF	2,021	01/03/75
Ellicott Rock	Chattahoochee NF		10/19/84
Mark Trail	Chattahoochee NF	16,400	12/11/91
Raven Cliffs	Chattahoochee NF	8,562	10/27/86
Rich Mountain	Chattahoochee NF	9,476	10/27/86
Southern Nantahala	Chattahoochee NF	11,770	10/19/84
Tray Mountain	Chattahoochee NF	9,702	10/27/86
TOTAL NFS ACRES IN GEORGIA:		113,423	

Park Service

Cumberland Island	Cumberland Island NSS	8,840	09/08/82
TOTAL NPS ACRES IN GEORGIA:		8,840	

Total Georgia Wilderness: 484,370

HAWAII

Park Service

Haleakala	Haleakala NP	19,270	10/20/76
Hawaii Volcanoes	Hawaii Volcanoes NP	123,100	11/10/78
TOTAL NPS ACRES IN HAWAII:		142,370	

Total Hawaii Wilderness: 142,370

IDAHO

Bureau of Land Management

Frank Church-River of No Return	Coeur d'Alene District	802	07/23/80

Wilderness Area Name	Administrative Unit	Size in Acres	Date of Designation
Frank Church-River of No Return	Coeur d'Alene District		03/14/84
TOTAL BLM ACRES IN IDAHO:		802	

Forest Service

Frank Church-River of No Return	Bitterroot NF	193,703	07/23/80
Frank Church-River of No Return	Bitterroot NF		03/14/84
Frank Church-River of No Return	Boise NF	332,891	07/23/80
Frank Church-River of No Return	Boise NF		03/14/84
Frank Church-River of No Return	Challis NF	515,421	07/23/80
Frank Church-River of No Return	Challis NF		03/14/84
Frank Church-River of No Return	Nez Perce NF	110,698	07/23/80
Frank Church-River of No Return	Nez Perce NF		03/14/84
Frank Church-River of No Return	Payette NF	791,675	07/23/80
Frank Church-River of No Return	Payette NF		03/14/84
Frank Church-River of No Return	Salmon NF	421,433	07/23/80
Frank Church-River of No Return	Salmon NF		03/14/84
Gospel Hump	Nez Perce NF	205,764	02/24/78
Hells Canyon	Nez Perce NF	59,900	12/31/75
Hells Canyon	Payette NF	23,911	12/31/75
Sawtooth	Boise NF	150,071	08/22/72
Sawtooth	Challis NF	12,020	08/22/72
Sawtooth	Sawtooth NF	54,997	08/22/72
Selway-Bitterroot	Bitterroot NF	270,321	09/03/64
Selway-Bitterroot	Bitterroot NF		07/23/80
Selway-Bitterroot	Clearwater NF	259,165	09/03/64
Selway-Bitterroot	Nez Perce NF	559,531	09/03/64
TOTAL NFS ACRES IN IDAHO:		3,961,501	

Park Service

Craters of the Moon	Crates of the Moon NM	43,243	10/23/70
TOTAL NPS ACRES IN IDAHO:		43,243	

WILDERNESS AREA NAME	ADMINISTRATIVE UNIT	SIZE IN ACRES	DATE OF DESIGNATION
Total Idaho Wilderness:	4,005,546		

ILLINOIS

Fish and Wildlife Service
| Crab Orchard | Crab Orchard NWR | 4,050 | 10/19/76 |
| TOTAL FWS ACRES IN ILLINOIS: | | 4,050 | |

Forest Service
Bald Knob	Shawnee NF	5,863	11/28/90
Bay Creek	Shawnee NF	2,866	11/28/90
Burden Falls	Shawnee NF	3,671	11/28/90
Clear Springs	Shawnee NF	4,730	11/28/90
Garden of the Gods	Shawnee NF	3,268	11/28/90
Lusk Creek	Shawnee NF	4,466	11/28/90
Panther Den	Shawnee NF	774	11/28/90
TOTAL NFS ACRES IN ILLINOIS:		25,638	

| Total Illinois Wilderness: | 29,688 | | |

INDIANA

Forest Service
| Charles C. Deam | Hoosier NF | 12,935 | 12/22/82 |
| TOTAL NFS ACRES IN INDIANA: | | 12,935 | |

| Total Indiana Wilderness: | 12,935 | | |

KENTUCKY

Forest Service
Beaver Creek	Daniel Boone NF	4,753	01/03/75
Clifty	Daniel Boone NF	11,662	12/23/85
TOTAL NFS ACRES IN KENTUCKY:		16,415	

| Total Kentucky Wilderness: | 16,415 | | |

LOUISIANA

Fish and Wildlife Service
Breton	Breton NWR	5,000	01/03/75
Lacassine	Lacassine NWR	3,346	10/19/76
TOTAL FWS ACRES IN LOUISIANA:		8,346	

WILDERNESS AREA NAME	ADMINISTRATIVE UNIT	SIZE IN ACRES	DATE OF DESIGNATION
Forest Service			
Kisatchie Hills	Kisatchie NF	8,679	12/22/80
TOTAL NFS ACRES IN LOUISIANA:		8,679	

Total Louisiana Wilderness: 17,025

MAINE

Fish and Wildlife Service			
Baring Unit	Moosehorn NWR	4,680	01/03/75
Birch Islands Unit	Moosehorn NWR	6	10/23/70
Edmunds Unit	Moosehorn NWR	2,706	10/23/70
TOTAL FWS ACRES IN MAINE:		7,392	
Forest Service			
Caribou-Speckled Mountain	White Mountain NF	12,000	09/28/90
TOTAL NFS ACRES IN MAINE:		12,000	

Total Maine Wilderness: 19,392

MASSACHUSETTS

Fish and Wildlife Service			
Monomoy	Monomoy NWR	2,420	10/23/70
TOTAL FWS ACRES IN MASSACHUSETTS:		2,420	

Total Massachusetts Wilderness: 2,420

MICHIGAN

Fish and Wildlife Service			
Huron Islands	Huron NWR	147	10/23/70
Michigan Islands	Michigan Islands NWR	12	10/23/70
Seney	Seney NWR	25,150	10/23/70
TOTAL FWS ACRES IN MICHIGAN:		25,309	
Forest Service			
Big Island Lake	Hiawatha NF	5,856	12/08/87
Delirium	Hiawatha NF	11,870	12/08/87
Horseshoe Bay	Hiawatha NF	3,790	12/08/87
Mackinac	Hiawatha NF	12,230	12/08/87
McCormick	Ottawa NF	16,850	12/08/87
Nordhouse Dunes	Manistee NF	3,450	12/08/87

WILDERNESS AREA NAME	ADMINISTRATIVE UNIT	SIZE IN ACRES	DATE OF DESIGNATION
Rock River Canyon	Hiawatha NF	4,640	12/08/87
Round Island	Hiawatha NF	378	12/08/87
Sturgeon River Gorge	Ottawa NF	14,500	12/08/87
Sylvania	Ottawa NF	18,327	12/08/87
TOTAL NFS ACRES IN MICHIGAN:		91,891	
Park Service			
Isle Royale	Isle Royale NP	132,018	10/20/76
TOTAL NPS ACRES IN MICHIGAN:		132,018	

Total Michigan Wilderness: 249,218

MINNESOTA

Fish and Wildlife Service			
Agassiz	Agassiz NWR	4,000	10/19/76
Tamarac	Tamarac NWR	2,180	10/19/76
TOTAL FWS ACRES IN MINNESOTA:		6,180	
Forest Service			
Boundary Waters Canoe Area	Superior NF	807,451	09/03/64
Boundary Waters Canoe Area	Superior NF		10/21/78
TOTAL NFS ACRES IN MINNESOTA:		807,451	

Total Minnesota Wilderness: 813,631

MISSISSIPPI

Forest Service			
Black Creek	Desoto NF	5,052	10/19/84
Leaf	Desoto NF	994	10/19/84
TOTAL NFS ACRES IN MISSISSIPPI:		6,046	
Park Service			
Gulf Islands	Gulf Islands NSS	5,514	11/10/78
TOTAL NPS ACRES IN MISSISSIPPI:		5,514	

Total Mississippi Wilderness: 11,560

MISSOURI

Fish and Wildlife Service

Mingo	Mingo NWR	7,730	10/19/76
TOTAL FWS ACRES IN MISSOURI:		7,730	

Forest Service

Bell Mountain	Mark Twain NF	8,977	12/22/80
Devils Backbone	Mark Twain NF	6,595	12/22/80
Hercules-Glades	Mark Twain NF	12,314	10/19/76
Irish	Mark Twain NF	16,117	05/21/84
Paddy Creek	Mark Twain NF	7,019	01/03/83
Piney Creek	Mark Twain NF	8,087	12/22/80
Rockpile Mountain	Mark Twain NF	4,089	12/22/80
TOTAL NFS ACRES IN MISSOURI:		63,198	

Total Missouri Wilderness: 70,928

MONTANA

Bureau of Land Management

Lee Metcalf —Bear Trap Canyon Unit	Butte District	6,000	10/31/83
TOTAL BLM ACRES IN MONTANA:		6,000	

Fish and Wildlife Service

Medicine Lake	Medicine Lake NWR	11,366	10/19/76
Red Rock Lakes	Red Rock Lakes NWR	32,350	10/19/76
UL Bend	UL Bend NWR	20,819	10/19/76
TOTAL FWS ACRES IN MONTANA:		64,535	

Forest Service

Absaroka-Beartooth	Custer NF	345,589	03/27/78
Absaroka-Beartooth	Gallatin NF	574,738	03/27/78
Absaroka-Beartooth	Gallatin NF		10/31/83
Anaconda-Pintlar	Beaverhead NF	72,677	09/03/64
Anadonda-Pintlar	Bitterroot NF	41,162	09/03/64
Anaconda-Pintlar	Deerlodge NF	44,175	09/03/64
Bob Marshall	Flathead NF	709,356	09/03/64
Bob Marshall	Lewis & Clark NF	300,000	09/03/64
Bob Marshall	Lewis & Clark NF		10/28/78
Cabinet Mountains	Kaniksu NF	44,320	09/03/64
Cabinet Mountains	Kootenai NF	49,952	09/03/64
Gates of the Mountains	Helena NF	28,562	09/03/64

WILDERNESS AREA NAME	ADMINISTRATIVE UNIT	SIZE IN ACRES	DATE OF DESIGNATION
Great Bear	Flathead NF	286,700	10/28/78
Lee Metcalf	Beaverhead NF	108,350	10/31/83
Lee Metcalf	Gallatin NF	140,594	10/31/83
Mission Mountains	Flathead NF	73,877	01/03/75
Rattlesnake	Lolo NF	32,844	10/19/80
Scapegoat	Helena NF	80,697	08/20/72
Scapegoat	Lewis & Clark NF	84,407	08/20/72
Scapegoat	Lolo NF	74,192	08/20/72
Selway-Bitterroot	Bitterroot NF	241,676	09/03/64
Selway-Bitterroot	Lolo NF	9,767	09/03/64
Welcome Creek	Lolo NF	28,135	02/24/78
TOTAL NFS ACRES IN MONTANA:		3,371,770	

Total Montana Wilderness: 3,442,305

NEBRASKA

Fish and Wildlife Service

Fort Niobrara	Fort Niobrara NWR	4,635	10/19/76
TOTAL FWS ACRES IN NEBRASKA:		4,635	

Forest Service

Soldier Creek	Nebraska NF	7,794	10/20/86
TOTAL NFS ACRES IN NEBRASKA:		7,794	

Total Nebraska Wilderness: 12,429

NEVADA

Bureau of Land Management

Mount Moriah	Ely District	6,435	12/05/89
TOTAL BLM ACRES IN NEVADA:		6,435	

Forest Service

Alta Toquima	Toiyabe NF	38,000	12/05/89
Arc Dome	Toiyabe NF	115,000	12/05/89
Boundary Peak	Inyo NF	10,000	12/05/89
Currant Mountain	Humboldt NF	36,000	12/05/89
East Humboldts	Humboldt NF	36,900	12/05/89
Grant Range	Humboldt NF	50,000	12/05/89
Jarbidge	Humboldt NF	113,167	09/03/64
Jarbidge	Humboldt NF		12/05/89
Mount Charleston	Toiyabe NF	43,000	12/05/89
Mount Moriah	Humboldt NF	70,000	12/05/89
Mount Rose	Toiyabe NF	28,121	12/05/89

Quinn Canyon	Humboldt NF	27,000	12/05/89
Ruby Mountains	Humboldt NF	90,000	12/05/89
Santa Rosa-Paradise Peak	Humboldt NF	31,000	12/05/89
Table Mountain	Toiyabe NF	98,000	12/05/89
TOTAL NFS ACRES IN NEVADA:		786,188	

Total Nevada Wilderness: 792,623

NEW HAMPSHIRE

Forest Service

Great Gulf	White Mountain NF	5,552	09/03/64
Pemigewasset	White Mountain NF	45,000	06/19/84
Presidential Range-Dry River	White Mountain NF	27,380	01/03/75
Presidential Range-Dry River	White Mountain NF		06/19/84
Sandwich Range	White Mountain NF	25,000	06/19/84
TOTAL NFS ACRES IN NEW HAMPSHIRE:		102,932	

Total New Hampshire Wilderness: 102,932

NEW JERSEY

Fish and Wildlife Service

Brigantine	Edwin B. Forsythe NWR	6,681	01/03/75
Great Swamp	Great Swamp NWR	3,660	09/28/68
TOTAL FWS ACRES IN NEW JERSEY:		10,341	

Total New Jersey Wilderness: 10,341

NEW MEXICO

Bureau of Land Management

Bisti/De-na-zin	Albuquerque District	42,925	10/30/84
Bisti/De-na-zin	Albuquerque District		11/12/96
Cebolla	Albuquerque District	62,800	12/31/87
West Malpais	Albuquerque District	39,700	12/31/87
TOTAL BLM ACRES IN NEW MEXICO:		145,425	

Fish and Wildlife Service

Chupadera Unit	Bosque del Apache NWR	5,289	01/03/75
Indian Well Unit	Bosque del Apache NWR	5,139	01/03/75
Little San Pascual Unit	Bosque del Apache NWR	19,859	01/03/75

WILDERNESS AREA NAME	ADMINISTRATIVE UNIT	SIZE IN ACRES	DATE OF DESIGNATION
Salt Creek	Bitter Lake NWR	9,621	10/23/70
TOTAL FWS ACRES IN NEW MEXICO:		39,908	
Forest Service			
Aldo Leopold	Gila NF	202,016	12/19/80
Apache Kid	Cibola NF	44,626	12/19/80
Blue Range	Apache NF	28,104	12/19/80
Blue Range	Gila NF	1,200	12/19/80
Capitan Mountains	Lincoln NF	34,658	12/19/80
Chama River Canyon	Carson NF	2,900	02/24/78
Chama River Canyon	Sante Fe NF	47,400	02/24/78
Cruces Basin	Carson NF	18,000	12/19/80
Dome	Sante Fe NF	5,200	12/19/80
Gila	Gila NF	558,014	09/03/64
Gila	Gila NF		12/19/80
Latir Peak	Carson NF	20,000	12/19/80
Manzano Mountain	Cibola NF	36,875	02/24/78
Pecos	Carson NF	24,736	09/03/64
Pecos	Santa Fe NF	198,597	09/03/64
Pecos	Santa Fe NF		12/19/80
San Pedro Parks	Santa Fe NF	41,132	09/03/64
Sandia Mountain	Cibola NF	37,877	02/24/78
Sandia Mountain	Cibola NF		05/23/80
Sandia Mountain	Cibola NF		10/30/84
Wheeler Peak	Carson NF	19,661	09/03/64
Wheeler Peak	Carson NF		12/19/80
White Mountain	Lincoln NF	48,208	09/03/64
White Mountain	Lincoln NF		12/19/80
Withington	Cibola NF	19,000	12/19/80
TOTAL NFS ACRES IN NEW MEXICO:		1,388,204	
Park Service			
Bandelier	Bandelier NM	23,267	10/20/76
Carlsbad Caverns	Carlsbad Caverns NP	33,125	11/10/78
TOTAL NPS ACRES IN NEW MEXICO:		56,392	

Total New Mexico Wilderness: 1,629,929

NEW YORK

Park Service			
Fire Island	Fire Island NSS	1,363	12/23/80
TOTAL NPS ACRES IN NEW YORK:		1,363	

Total New York Wilderness: 1,363

NORTH CAROLINA

Fish and Wildlife Service

Swanquarter	Swanquarter NWR	8,785	10/19/76
TOTAL FWS ACRES IN NORTH CAROLINA:		8,785	

Forest Service

Birkhead Mountains	Uwharrie NF	5,025	06/19/84
Catfish Lake South	Croatan NF	8,530	06/19/84
Ellicott Rock	Nantahala NF	3,394	01/03/75
Ellicatt Rock	Nantahala NF		06/19/84
Joyce Kilmer-Slickrock	Nantahala NF	13,562	01/03/75
Joyce Kilmer-Slickrock	Nantahala NF		06/19/84
Linville Gorge	Pisgah NF	11,786	09/03/64
Linville Gorge	Pisgah NF		06/19/84
Middle Prong	Pisgah NF	7,460	06/19/84
Pocosin	Croatan NF	11,709	06/19/84
Pond Pine	Croatan NF	1,685	06/19/84
Sheep Ridge	Croatan NF	9,297	06/19/84
Shining Rock	Pisgah NF	18,483	09/03/64
Shining Rock	Pisgah NF		06/19/84
Southern Nantahala	Nantahala NF	11,703	06/19/84
TOTAL NFS ACRES IN NORTH CAROLINA:		102,634	

Total North Carolina Wilderness: 111,419

NORTH DAKOTA

Fish and Wildlife Service

Chase Lake	Chase Lake NWR	4,155	01/03/75
Lostwood	Lostwood NWR	5,577	01/03/75
TOTAL FWS ACRES IN NORTH DAKOTA:		9,732	

Park Service

Theodore Roosevelt	Theodore Roosevelt NP	29,920	11/10/78
TOTAL NPS ACRES IN NORTH DAKOTA:		29,920	

Total North Dakota Wilderness: 39,652

OHIO

Fish and Wildlife Service

West Sister Island	West Sister Island NWR	77	01/03/75
TOTAL FWS ACRES IN OHIO:		77	

WILDERNESS AREA NAME	ADMINISTRATIVE UNIT	SIZE IN ACRES	DATE OF DESIGNATION
Total Ohio Wilderness:	77		

OKLAHOMA

Fish and Wildlife Service
Charons Garden Unit	Wichita Mountains NWR	5,723	10/23/70
North Mountain Unit	Wichita Mountains NWR	2,847	10/23/70
TOTAL FWS ACRES IN OKLAHOMA:		8,570	

Forest Service
Black Fork Mountain	Ouachita NF	4,629	10/18/88
Upper Kiamichi River	Ouachita NF	9,802	10/18/88
TOTAL NFS ACRES IN OKLAHOMA:		14,431	

| Total Oklahoma Wilderness: | 23,001 | | |

OREGON

Bureau of Land Management
Hells Canyon	Vale District	1,038	06/26/84
Table Rock	Salem District	5,750	06/26/84
TOTAL BLM ACRES IN OREGON:		6,788	

Fish and Wildlife Service
Oregon Islands	Oregon Islands NWR	21	10/23/70
Oregon Islands	Oregon Islands NWR	459	10/11/78
Three Arch Rocks	Three Arch Rocks NWR	15	10/23/70
TOTAL FWS ACRES IN OREGON:		495	

Forest Service
Badger Creek	Mount Hood NF	24,000	06/26/84
Black Canyon	Ochoco NF	13,400	06/26/84
Boulder Creek	Umpqua NF	19,100	06/26/84
Bridge Creek	Ochoco NF	5,400	06/26/84
Bull of the Woods	Mount Hood NF	27,427	06/26/84
Bull of the Woods	Willamette NF	7,473	06/26/84
Cummins Creek	Siuslaw NF	9,173	06/26/84
Diamond Peak	Deschutes NF	34,413	09/03/64
Diamond Peak	Deschutes NF		06/26/84
Diamond Peak	Willamette NF	19,772	09/03/64
Diamond Peak	Willamette NF		06/26/84
Drift Creek	Siuslaw NF	5,798	06/26/84
Eagle Cap	Wallowa NF	212,699	09/03/64
Eagle Cap	Wallowa NF		10/21/72

Wilderness Area Name	Administrative Unit	Size in Acres	Date of Designation
(OREGON CONTINUED)			
Eagle Cap	Wallowa NF		06/26/84
Eagle Cap	Whitman NF	145,762	09/03/64
Eagle Cap	Whitman NF		10/21/72
Eagle Cap	Whitman NF		06/26/84
Gearhart Mountain	Fremont NF	22,809	09/03/64
Gearhart Mountain	Fremont NF		06/26/84
Grassy Knob	Siskiyou NF	17,200	06/26/84
Hells Canyon	Wallowa NF	118,247	12/31/75
Hells Canyon	Wallowa NF		06/26/84
Hells Canyon	Whitman NF	11,848	12/31/75
Hells Canyon	Whitman NF		06/26/84
Kalmiopsis	Siskiyou NF	179,655	09/03/64
Kalmiopsis	Siskiyou NF		02/24/78
Mark O. Hatfield	Mount Hood NF	39,000	06/26/84
Menagerie	Willamette NF	4,800	06/26/84
Middle Santiam	Willamette NF	7,500	06/26/84
Mill Creek	Ochoco NF	17,400	06/26/84
Monument Rock	Malheur NF	12,620	06/26/84
Monument Rock	Whitman NF	7,030	06/26/84
Mount Hood	Mount Hood NF	47,160	09/03/64
Mount Hood	Mount Hood NF		02/24/78
Mount Jefferson	Deschutes NF	32,734	10/02/68
Mount Jefferson	Mount Hood NF	5,021	10/02/68
Mount Jefferson	Willamette NF	69,253	10/02/68
Mount Jefferson	Willamette NF		06/26/84
Mount Thielsen	Deschutes NF	7,107	06/26/84
Mount Thielsen	Umpqua NF	21,593	06/26/84
Mount Thielsen	Winema NF	25,567	06/26/84
Mount Washington	Deschutes NF	14,116	09/03/64
Mount Washington	Deschutes NF		06/26/84
Mount Washington	Willamette NF	38,622	09/03/64
Mount Washington	Willamette NF		06/26/84
Mountain Lakes	Winema NF	23,071	09/03/64
North Fork John Day	Umatilla NF	107,058	06/26/84
North Fork John Day	Whitman NF	14,294	06/26/84
North Fork Umatilla	Umatilla NF	20,435	06/26/84
Red Buttes	Rogue River NF	350	09/28/84
Red Buttes	Siskiyou NF	3,400	06/26/84
Rock Creek	Siuslaw NF	7,486	06/26/84
Rogue-Umpqua Divide	Rogue River NF	6,850	06/26/84
Rogue-Umpqua Divide	Umpqua NF	26,350	06/26/84
Salmon-Huckleberry	Mount Hood NF	44,560	06/26/84
Sky Lakes	Rogue River NF	75,695	06/26/84

WILDERNESS AREA NAME	ADMINISTRATIVE UNIT	SIZE IN ACRES	DATE OF DESIGNATION
Sky Lakes	Winema NF	40,605	06/26/84
Strawberry Mountain	Malheur NF	68,700	09/03/64
Strawberry Mountain	Malheur NF		06/26/84
Three Sisters	Deschutes NF	94,370	09/03/64
Three Sisters	Deschutes NF		06/26/84
Three Sisters	Willamette NF	192,338	09/03/64
Three Sisters	Willamette NF		02/24/78
Three Sisters	Willamette NF		06/26/84
Waldo Lake	Willamette NF	39,200	06/26/84
Wenaha-Tucannon	Umatilla NF	66,375	02/24/78
Wild Rogue	Siskiyou NF	25,658	02/24/78
TOTAL NFS ACRES IN OREGON:		2,080,594	

Total Oregon Wilderness: 2,087,877

PENNSYLVANIA

Forest Service

Allegheny Islands	Allegheny NF	368	10/30/84
Hickory Creek	Allegheny NF	8,570	10/30/84
TOTAL NFS ACRES IN PENNSYLVANIA:		8,938	

Total Pennsylvania Wilderness: 8,938

SOUTH CAROLINA

Fish and Wildlife Service

Cape Romain	Cape Romain NWR	29,000	01/03/75
TOTAL FWS ACRES IN SOUTH CAROLINA:		29,000	

Forest Service

Ellicott Rock	Sumter NF	2,859	01/03/75
Hell Hole Bay	Francis Marion NF	2,125	12/22/80
Little Wambaw Swamp	Francis Marion NF	5,047	12/22/80
Wambaw Creek	Francis Marion NF	1,825	12/22/80
Wambaw Swamp	Francis Marion NF	4,815	12/22/80
TOTAL NFS ACRES IN SOUTH CAROLINA:		16,671	

Park Service

Congaree Swamp	Congaree Swamp NM	15,010	10/24/88
TOTAL NPS ACRES IN SOUTH CAROLINA:		15,010	

Total South Carolina Wilderness: 60,681

WILDERNESS AREA NAME	ADMINISTRATIVE UNIT	SIZE IN ACRES	DATE OF DESIGNATION
SOUTH DAKOTA			
Forest Service			
Black Elk	Black Hills NF	9,826	12/22/80
TOTAL NFS ACRES IN SOUTH DAKOTA:		9,826	
Park Service			
Badlands	Badlands NM	64,250	10/20/76
TOTAL NPS ACRES IN SOUTH DAKOTA:		64,250	
Total South Dakota Wilderness:	74,076		
TENNESSEE			
Forest Service			
Bald River Gorge	Cherokee NF	3,721	10/30/84
Big Frog	Cherokee NF	7,193	10/30/84
Big Frog	Cherokee NF		10/16/86
Big Laurel Branch	Cherokee NF	6,251	10/16/86
Citico Creek	Cherokee NF	16,226	10/30/84
Cohutta	Cherokee NF	1,709	01/03/75
Gee Creek	Cherokee NF	2,493	01/03/75
Joyce Kilmer-Slickrock	Cherokee NF	3,832	01/03/75
Little Frog Mountain	Cherokee NF	4,666	10/16/86
Pond Mountain	Cherokee NF	6,626	10/16/86
Sampson Mountain	Cherokee NF	7,991	10/16/86
Unaka Mountain	Cherokee NF	4,700	10/16/86
TOTAL NFS ACRES IN TENNESSEE:		65,408	
Total Tennessee Wilderness:	65,408		
TEXAS			
Forest Service			
Big Slough	Davy Crockett NF	3,455	10/30/84
Indian Mounds	Sabine NF	10,917	10/30/84
Indian Mounds	Sabine NF		10/29/86
Little Lake Creek	Sam Houston NF	3,855	10/30/84
Little Lake Creek	Sam Houston NF		10/29/86
Turkey Hill	Angelina NF	5,473	10/30/84
Turkey Hill	Angelina NF		10/29/86
Upland Island	Angelina NF	13,330	10/30/84
Upland Island	Angelina NF		10/29/86
TOTAL NFS ACRES IN TEXAS:		37,030	

WILDERNESS AREA NAME	ADMINISTRATIVE UNIT	SIZE IN ACRES	DATE OF DESIGNATION
Park Service			
Guadalupe Mountains	Guadalupe Mountains NP	46,850	11/10/78
TOTAL NPS ACRES IN TEXAS:		46,850	

Total Texas Wilderness: 83,880

UTAH

Bureau of Land Management			
Beaver Dam Mountains	Cedar City District	3,630	08/28/84
Paria Canyon-Vermilion Cliffs	Cedar City District	23,000	08/28/84
TOTAL BLM ACRES IN UTAH:		26,630	
Forest Service			
Ashdown Gorge	Dixie NF	7,043	09/18/84
Box-Death Hollow	Dixie NF	25,751	09/18/84
Dark Canyon	Manti-La Sal NF	47,116	09/18/84
Deseret Peak	Wasatch NF	25,212	09/18/84
High Uintas	Ashley NF	276,175	09/18/84
High Uintas	Wasatch NF	180,530	09/18/84
Lone Peak	Uinta NF	21,166	02/24/78
Lone Peak	Wasatch NF	8,922	02/24/78
Mount Naomi	Cache NF	44,523	09/18/84
Mount Nebo	Uinta NF	27,010	09/18/84
Mount Olympus	Wasatch NF	15,300	09/18/84
Mount Timpanogos	Uinta NF	10,518	09/18/84
Pine Valley Mountain	Dixie NF	50,232	09/18/84
Twin Peaks	Wasatch NF	11,334	09/18/84
Wellsville Mountain	Cache NF	22,986	09/18/84
TOTAL NFS ACRES IN UTAH:		773,818	

Total Utah Wilderness: 800,448

VERMONT

Forest Service			
Big Branch	Green Mountain NF	6,720	06/19/84
Breadloaf	Green Mountain NF	21,480	06/19/84
Bristol Cliffs	Green Mountain NF	3,738	01/03/75
Bristol Cliffs	Green Mountain NF		04/16/76
George D. Aiken	Green Mountain NF	5,060	06/19/84
Lye Brook	Green Mountain NF	15,503	01/03/75
Lye Brook	Green Mountain NF		06/19/84

WILDERNESS AREA NAME	ADMINISTRATIVE UNIT	SIZE IN ACRES	DATE OF DESIGNATION
Peru Peak	Green Mountain NF	6,920	06/19/84
TOTAL NFS ACRES IN VERMONT:		59,421	

Total Vermont Wilderness: 59,421

VIRGINIA

Forest Service

Barbours Creek	George Washington NF	5	06/07/88
Barbours Creek	Jefferson NF	5,695	06/07/88
Beartown	Jefferson NF	5,609	10/30/84
James River Face	Jefferson NF	8,886	01/03/75
James River Face	Jefferson NF		10/30/84
Kimberling Creek	Jefferson NF	5,542	10/30/84
Lewis Fork	Jefferson NF	5,618	10/30/84
Little Dry Run	Jefferson NF	2,858	10/30/84
Little Wilson Creek	Jefferson NF	3,613	10/30/84
Mountain Lake	Jefferson NF	8,187	10/30/84
Peters Mountain	Jefferson NF	3,328	10/30/84
Ramseys Draft	George Washington NF	6,518	10/30/84
Rich Hole	George Washington NF	6,450	06/07/88
Rough Mountain	George Washington NF	9,300	06/07/88
Saint Mary's	George Washington NF	9,835	10/30/84
Shawvers Run	George Washington NF	101	06/07/88
Shawvers Run	Jefferson NF	3,366	06/07/88
Thunder Ridge	Jefferson NF	2,344	10/30/84
TOTAL NFS ACRES IN VIRGINIA:		87,255	

Park Service

Shenandoah	Shenandoah NP	79,579	10/20/76
TOTAL NPS ACRES IN VIRGINIA:		79,579	

Total Virginia Wilderness: 166,834

WASHINGTON

Bureau of Land Management

Juniper Dunes	Spokane District	6,900	07/03/84
TOTAL BLM ACRES IN WASHINGTON:		6,900	

Fish and Wildlife Service

San Juan Islands	San Juan Islands NWR	353	10/19/76
Washington Islands	Copalis NWR	60	10/23/70
Washington Islands	Flattery Rocks NWR	125	10/23/70

WILDERNESS AREA NAME	ADMINISTRATIVE UNIT	SIZE IN ACRES	DATE OF DESIGNATION
Washington Islands	Quillayute Needles NWR	300	10/23/70
TOTAL FWS ACRES IN WASHINGTON:		838	

Forest Service

Alpine Lakes	Snoqualmie NF	117,825	07/12/76
Alpine Lakes	Wenatchee NF	244,845	07/12/76
Boulder River	Mount Baker NF	48,674	07/03/84
Buckhorn	Olympic NF	44,258	07/03/84
Buckhorn	Olympic NF		11/07/86
Clearwater	Snoqualmie NF	14,374	07/03/84
Colonel Bob	Olympic NF	11,961	07/03/84
Glacier Peak	Mount Baker NF	283,252	09/03/64
Glacier Peak	Mount Baker NF		10/02/68
Glacier Peak	Mount Baker NF		07/03/84
Glacier Peak	Wenatchee NF	289,086	09/03/64
Glacier Peak	Wenatchee NF		10/02/68
Glacier Peak	Wenatchee NF		07/03/84
Glacier View	Gifford Pinchot NF	3,123	07/03/84
Goat Rocks	Gifford Pinchot NF	71,203	09/03/64
Goat Rocks	Gifford Pinchot NF		07/03/84
Goat Rocks	Snoqualmie NF	37,076	09/03/64
Goat Rocks	Snoqualmie NF		07/03/84
Henry M. Jackson	Mount Baker NF	27,417	07/03/84
Henry M. Jackson	Snoqualmie NF	47,504	07/03/84
Henry M. Jackson	Wenatchee NF	25,416	07/03/84
Indian Heaven	Gifford Pinchot NF	20,960	07/03/84
Lake Chelan-Sawtooth	Okanogan NF	95,021	07/03/84
Lake Chelan-Sawtooth	Wenatchee NF	56,414	07/03/84
Mount Adams	Gifford Pinchot NF	46,626	09/03/64
Mount Adams	Gifford Pinchot NF		07/03/84
Mount Baker	Mount Baker NF	117,528	07/03/84
Mount Skokomish	Olympic NF	13,015	07/03/84
Mount Skokomish	Olympic NF		11/07/86
Noisy-Diobsud	Mount Baker NF	14,133	07/03/84
Norse Peak	Snoqualmie NF	52,180	07/03/84
Pasayten	Mount Baker NF	107,039	10/02/68
Pasayten	Okanogan NF	422,992	10/02/68
Pasayten	Okanogan NF		07/03/84
Salmo-Priest	Colville NF	29,386	07/03/84
Salmo-Priest	Kaniksu NF	11,949	07/03/84
Tatoosh	Gifford Pinchot NF	15,750	07/03/84
The Brothers	Olympic NF	16,682	07/03/84
The Brothers	Olympic NF		11/07/86
Trapper Creek	Gifford Pinchot NF	5,970	07/03/84

Wilderness Area Name	Administrative Unit	Size in Acres	Date of Designation
Wenaha-Tucannon	Umatilla NF	111,048	02/24/78
William O. Douglas	Gifford Pinchot NF	15,469	07/03/84
William O. Douglas	Snoqualmie NF	152,688	07/03/84
Wonder Mountain	Olympic NF	2,349	07/03/84
TOTAL NFS ACRES IN WASHINGTON:		2,573,213	

Park Service

Mount Rainier	Mount Rainier	228,488	11/16/88
Olympic	Olympic NP	876,669	11/16/88
Stephen Mather	North Cascades NP	634,614	11/16/88
TOTAL NPS ACRES IN WASHINGTON:		1,739,771	

Total Washington Wilderness: 4,320,722

WEST VIRGINIA

Forest Service

Cranberry	Monongahela NF	35,864	01/13/83
Cranberry	Monongahela NF		11/05/90
Dolly Sods	Monongahela NF	10,215	01/03/75
Laurel Fork North	Monongahela NF	6,055	01/13/83
Laurel Fork South	Monongahela NF	5,997	01/13/83
Mountain Lake	Jefferson NF	2,721	06/07/88
Otter Creek	Monongahela NF	20,000	01/03/75
TOTAL NFS ACRES IN WEST VIRGINIA:		80,852	

Total West Virginia Wilderness: 80,852

WISCONSIN

Fish and Wildlife Service

Wisconsin Islands	Gravel Island NWR	27	10/23/70
Wisconsin Islands	Green Bay NWR	2	10/23/70
TOTAL FWS ACRES IN WISCONSIN:		29	

Forest Service

Blackjack Springs	Nicolet NF	5,886	10/21/78
Headwaters	Nicolet NF	18,188	06/19/84
Porcupine Lake	Chequamegon NF	4,292	06/19/84
Rainbow Lake	Chequamegon NF	6,583	01/03/75
Whisker Lake	Nicolet NF	7,345	10/21/78
TOTAL NFS ACRES IN WISCONSIN:		42,294	

Total Wisconsin Wilderness: 42,323

WILDERNESS AREA NAME	ADMINISTRATIVE UNIT	SIZE IN ACRES	DATE OF DESIGNATION
WYOMING			
Forest Service			
Absaroka-Beartooth	Shoshone NF	23,283	10/30/84
Bridger	Bridger NF	428,087	09/03/64
Bridger	Bridger NF		10/30/84
Cloud Peak	Bighorn NF	189,039	10/30/84
Encampment River	Medicine Bow NF	10,124	10/30/84
Fitzpatrick	Shoshone NF	198,525	10/19/76
Fitzpatrick	Shoshone NF		10/20/76
Fitzpatrick	Shoshone NF		10/30/84
Gros Ventre	Teton NF	317,874	10/30/84
Huston Park	Medicine Bow NF	30,588	10/30/84
Jedediah Smith	Targhee NF	123,451	10/30/84
North Absaroka	Shoshone NF	350,488	09/03/64
Platte River	Medicine Bow NF	22,749	10/30/84
Popo Agie	Shoshone NF	101,870	10/30/84
Savage Run	Medicine Bow NF	14,927	02/24/78
Teton	Teton NF	585,238	09/03/64
Teton	Teton NF		10/30/84
Washakie	Shoshone NF	704,274	09/03/64
Washakie	Shoshone NF		10/09/72
Washakie	Shoshone NF		10/30/84
Winegar Hole	Targhee NF	10,715	10/30/84
TOTAL NFS ACRES IN WYOMING:		3,111,232	

Total Wyoming Wilderness: 3,111,232

NATIONAL WILDERNESS PRESERVATION SYSTEM: Summary Data

Agency	Units	Acres
Bureau of Land Management, USDI:	134	5,243,616
Fish and Wildlife Service, USDI:	75	20,685,372
Forest Service, USDA:	412	34,750,221
National Park Service, USDI:	44	44,083,003
GRAND TOTAL	665	104,762,212

National Wilderness Preservation System (excluding Alaska)

Agency	Units	Acres
Bureau of Land Management, USDI:	134	5,243,616
Fish and Wildlife Service, USDI:	54	2,009,052
Forest Service, USDA:	393	28,997469

WILDERNESS AREA NAME	ADMINISTRATIVE UNIT	SIZE IN ACRES	DATE OF DESIGNATION
National Park Service, USDI:		36	11,103,633
TOTAL		617	47,353,770

National Wilderness Preservation System (Alaska)

Agency	Units	Acres
Fish and Wildlife Service, USDI:	21	18,676,320
Forest Service, USDA:	19	5,752,752
National Park Service, USDI:	8	32,979,370
TOTAL	48	57,408,442

A Reading List

TWENTY-FIVE BOOKS THAT HELP TO UNDERSTAND AND APPRECIATE WILDERNESS

Abbey, Edward. *Desert Solitaire: A Season in the Wilderness.* Ballantine, 1968.

Broome, Harvey. *Faces of the Wilderness.* Mountain Press, 1972.

Brown, David E. and Neil B. Carmony. *Aldo Leopold's Wilderness.* Stackpole, 1990.

Douglas, William O. *A Wilderness Bill of Rights.* Little Brown, 1965.

Foreman, Dave, and Howie Wolke. *The Big Outside: A Descriptive Inventory of the Big Wilderness Areas of the United States.* Ned Ludd, 1989.

Frome, Michael. *Promised Land: Adventures and Encounters in Wild America.* Tennessee, 1994.

Frome, Michael, ed. *Issues in Wilderness Management,* based on proceedings of the National Wilderness Management Workshop at Moscow, Idaho, October 1985.Westview, 1986.

Glover, James M. *A Wilderness Original: The Life of Bob Marshall.* The Mountaineers, 1986.

Grumbine, R. Edward. *Ghost Bears—Exploring the Biodiversity Crisis.* Island, 1992.

Hampton, Bruce, and David Cole. *Soft Paths—How to Enjoy the Wilderness without Harming It.* Stackpole, 1995.

Hendee, John C., George H. Stankey, and Robert C. Lucas. *Wilderness Management,* 2d Ed. Fulcrum, 1994.

Leopold, Aldo. *A Sand County Almanac.* Ballantine, 1970.

Lime, David W., ed., *Managing America's Enduring Wilderness*, proceedings of the conference September 11-17, 1989, in Minneapolis. University of Minnesota, 1990.

Mills, Stephanie. *In Service of the Wild*. Beacon, 1995.

Nash, Roderick. *Wilderness and the American Mind*, 3d Ed. Yale, 1982.

Odum, Eugene. *Ecology and Our Endangered Life-Support Systems—A Citizen's Guide*. Sinauer, 1989.

Oelschlager, Max. *The Idea of Wilderness: From Prehistory to the Age of Ecology*. Yale, 1991.

Peacock, Douglas. *Grizzly Years*. Holt, 1990.

Power, Thomas M. *Extraction and the Environment: The Economic Battle to Control Our Natural Landscape*. Island, 1996.

Rudzitis, Gundars. *Wilderness and the Changing American West*. Wiley, 1996.

Schaefer, Paul. *Defending the Wilderness—The Adirondack Writings of Paul Schaefer*. Syracuse, 1989.

Tilton, Buck. *America's Wilderness: The Complete Guide to More Than 600 National Wilderness Areas*. Foghorn, 1997.

Wilson, Edward O. *The Diversity of Life*. Harvard, 1992.

Wolfe, Linnie Marsh. *Son of the Wilderness: The Life of John Muir*. Wisconsin, 1973.

Wolke, Howie. *Wilderness on the Rocks*. Ned Ludd, 1991.

Notes

CHAPTER 2: "AN AMERICAN HAPPENING"

1. Henry David Thoreau, *The Maine Woods* (Princeton, N.J.: Princeton University Press, 1972), p. 156.
2. Henry David Thoreau, *The Writings of Thoreau* (Boston: Riverside Press, 1906), Walden Edition, 18: 387.
3. John Muir, *Our National Parks* (Boston: Houghton Mifflin, 1901), Sierra Edition, p. 5.
4. Albert Szent-Gyorgi, quoted in Helena Curtis, "A Nobel Scientist's Gloomy Outlook," *Smithsonian Magazine* 2, no. 4 (July 1971): 35.

CHAPTER 3: "THE CULTURAL HERITAGE IN WILDERNESS"

1. *Notes on the State of Virginia,* the only full-length volume Jefferson ever wrote, was first issued by the English bookseller John Stockdale in 1787. It was roundly attacked by Jefferson's American critics and largely forgotten until the 1955 edition, edited by William Peden and published by the University of North Carolina Press. *The Travels of William Bartram* and *Notes on the State of Virginia* are like companion pieces, both ranking among the nation's first permanent literary and intellectual landmarks, and both are American classics.
2. George Catlin, *Letters and Notes on the Manners, Customs, and Conditions of the North American Indians* (New York: Dover, 1973), pp. 260, 261–62.
3. Van Wyck Brooks, *The Times of Melville and Whitman* (New York: E. P. Dutton, 1947), p. 125.

269

4. Ralph Waldo Emerson, *Essays* (New York: Thomas Y. Crowell, 1926), p. 381.

5. E. B. White, *The Points of My Compass* (New York: Harper & Row, 1954), p. 16.

6. Henry David Thoreau, *The Writings of Thoreau* (Boston: Riverside Press, 1906), Walden Edition, 4: 457.

7. *Ibid.,* 6: 9.

8. Henry David Thoreau, *Thoreau's Writings* (Boston: Riverside Press, 1906), 14, Journal 8: 221.

9. Henry David Thoreau, *The Maine Woods* (Princeton, N.J.: Princeton University Press, 1972), p. 81.

10. Charles M. Russell, quoted in J. Frank Dobie, "Conservatism of Charles M. Russell," *Montana: The Magazine of Western History*, Special Edition (Fall 1958): 59.

11. John Muir, *John of the Mountains* (Boston: Houghton Mifflin, 1938), p. 315.

12. John Muir, *Ibid.,* p. 131.

13. John Muir, *The Mountains of California* (New York: Century, 1911), p. 256.

14. *Not Man Apart* is the title of a book published in 1965 by the Sierra Club, featuring lines from the poetry of Robinson Jeffers and photography of the Big Sur coast by eminent nature photographers. *Not Man Apart* is also the monthly journal issued by Friends of the Earth.

15. Ansel Adams, *Portfolio Three: Yosemite Valley* (San Francisco: Sierra Club, 1961), Introduction, unnumbered.

CHAPTER 4: "A SCIENTIFIC RESOURCE"

1. Hugh Iltis, "We Need Many More Scientific Areas," *Wisconsin Conservation Bulletin* 24, no. 9 (September 1959): 3–8.

2. Eugene P. Odum, "The Strategy of Ecosystems," *Science* 164 (April 1969): 265.

CHAPTER 5: "A PLACE FOR WILD ANIMALS, WILD PLANTS"

1. Thomas L. Kimball, "Marine Mammals," Hearings Before the Subcommittee on Merchant Marine and Fisheries, U.S. House of Representatives, Serial No. 92-10 (Washington, D.C.: Government Printing Office), p. 65.

2. Joseph Wood Krutch, "Conservation," *Wildlife Review* 6, no. 2 (December 1971): 3.

CHAPTER 6: "RECREATION FOR EVERYONE . . ."

1. Henry David Thoreau, *The Maine Woods* (Princeton, N.J.: Princeton University Press, 1972), p. 81.
2. George Graham Vest, cited in Robert Shankland, *Steve Mather of the National Parks* (New York: Alfred A. Knopf, 1951), p. 4.
3. Stewart L. Udall, *The National Parks of America* (New York: G. P. Putnam's, 1966), p. 14.
4. Adolph Murie, *A Naturalist in Alaska* (Garden City, N.Y.: Doubleday, 1963), Natural History Library ed., p. 54.
5. Robert Marshall, "The Universe of the Wilderness Is Vanishing," *Nature Magazine* (April 1937), reprinted in *The Living Wilderness* 35, no. 114 (Summer 1971): 11.

CHAPTER 8: "SAVING WILDERNESS BY LAW—THE ANCIENT CREED"

1. Frederick Law Olmsted, quoted in Elizabeth Barlow and William Alex, *Frederick Law Olmsted's New York* (New York: Praeger, 1972), p. 72.
2. Hiram M. Chittenden, *Yellowstone National Park* (Stanford, Calif.: Stanford University Press, 1949), p. 69.
3. Gustavus C. Doane, *The Report of Lieutenant Gustavus C. Doane upon the So-called Yellowstone Expedition of 1870,* Senate Executive Document 51, 41st Cong., 3d Sess. (March 3, 1871).
4. Carl Schurz, "The Need of a Rational Forest Policy," *Report of Secretary of the Interior to Congress,* 46th Cong., 2d Sess., 1879.
5. John Wesley Powell's *Report on the Lands of the Arid Region of the United States,* published in 1878, has been praised as the "blueprint for a dryland democracy." It resulted in establishment of the Irrigation Division of the U.S. Geological Survey in 1888 and passage in 1903 of the Reclamation Act, which provided funds for irrigation purposes. On publication, however, Powell's idea of restricting settlement in the arid lands stirred protest.
6. Sherman Adams, *A New Hampshire Everlasting and Unfallen* (Concord, N.H.: 1969), pp. 88–89.
7. Arthur Carhart, "Preliminary Report, Recreation Reconnaissance, Superior National Forest, Minnesota, 1919," in *Carhart Papers,* p. 76.
8. Aldo Leopold, "Origins and Ideals of Wilderness," *The Living Wilderness* 5, no. 5 (July 1940): 7.

CHAPTER 9: "SAVING WILDERNESS BY LAW—THE ULTIMATE SHOWDOWN"

1. U.S. Senate, Hearings on S.1176, National Wilderness Preservation Act, June 19–20, 1957, p. 11.

CHAPTER 10: "HEARING THE PEOPLE'S CASE"

1. Brock Evans, "The Alpine Lakes, Stepchild of the North Cascades," *The Living Wilderness* 32, no. 101 (Spring 1968): 21–31.
2. Morton R. Brigham, "Proposed St. Joe Wilderness," *The Living Wilderness* 33, no. 106 (Summer 1969): 15–18.

Index

273